ArtScroll Series®

Rabbi Nosson Scherman / Rabbi Meir Zlotowitz

General Editors

PARTNERS WITH HASHEM

Published by

Mesorah Publications, ltd

*Effective guidelines
for successful parenting*

DR. MEIR WIKLER

FIRST EDITION
First Impression … January 2000

Published and Distributed by
MESORAH PUBLICATIONS, LTD.
4401 Second Avenue / Brooklyn, N.Y 11232

Distributed in Europe by
J. LEHMANN HEBREW BOOKSELLERS
20 Cambridge Terrace
Gateshead, Tyne and Wear
England NE8 1RP

Distributed in Israel by
SIFRIATI / A. GITLER
10 Hashomer Street
Bnei Brak 51361

Distributed in Australia and New Zealand by
GOLDS BOOK & GIFT SHOP
36 William Street
Balaclava 3183, Vic., Australia

Distributed in South Africa by
KOLLEL BOOKSHOP
Shop 8A Norwood Hypermarket
Norwood 2196, Johannesburg, South Africa

Typography by CompuScribe at ArtScroll Studios, Ltd.
Printed in the United States of America by Noble Book Press Corp.
Bound by Sefercraft, Quality Bookbinders, Ltd., Brooklyn N.Y. 11232

This book is dedicated

in fond memory to

my late sister-in-law,

Chaya Liebe Beyman, A"H

חי׳ ליבא בת החבר ר׳ שלמה פערבער, ע"ה

mother of seven children,

who demonstrated through her life

that there is no role

or occupation

which represents a calling

higher than being a parent.

She taught by her shining example

how to mold without breaking,

how to be firm without force,

and how to love without smothering.

נלב"ע: ד׳ סיון, תשמ"ט

כ״ק אדמו״ר מבוסטון שליט״א
עיה״ק ירושלים ת״ו
Grand Rabbi Levi. I Horowitz
The Bostoner Rebbe

I have known Dr. Meir Wikler for many years. He knows my approach both to matters of halacha and the more mundane day to day aspects of life. He is gifted with the quality of presenting his material by illustrating his points through parable or true-life stories that lucidly depict the idea being exemplified to the reader.

As we all know, throughout the Gemara, stories are brought down which reinforce and support a concept even if at times the allegory is followed by a question that occasionally appears to contradict the original idea. However, the fact that good ideas are backed up by easily understood parables is very important.

His new book "Partners With Hashem: Practical Guidelines for Successful Parenting," concisely seeks to awaken the reader to the issues parents face and the need to deal with those issues through a clear perspective of Torah hashkafa. Drawing on his own experience as a counselor, Reb Meir has produced an illuminating book that will contribute to helping parents deal with many of today's challenges.

May Reb Meir Wikler's writings help the Jewish community to act in accordance with the will of Hashem.

Grand Rabbi Levi Yitzchak Horowitz
THE BOSTONER REBBE

Rabbi CHAIM P. SHEINBERG
Rosh Hayeshiva "TORAH ORE"
and Morah Hora'ah of Kiryat Mattersdorf

הרב חיים פינחס שיינברג
ראש ישיבת "תורה אור"
ומורה הוראה דקרית מטרסדורף

Rosh Chodesh Sivan, 5759

The mitzvah of *chinuch habanim* is so important
that it is included in the *Sh'ma* which we recite
twice daily, as it is written, *"V'shinantam
l'vonecha* (and you shall teach them to your children)" (*Devarim* 6:7); and, *"V'limad'tem osam es
b'neichem* (and you shall teach them to your children)" (*Devarim* 11:19). In addition, the Torah also
reminds us, *"V'hodatam l'vonecha v'livnei vonecha*
(and you shall make them known to your children and
your children's children)" (*Devarim* 4:9).

Dr. Meir Wikler's newest *sefer,* **Partners With
Hashem: Practical Guidelines for Successful
Parenting,** offers much needed guidance to parents
of children of all ages. The book contains helpful
advice on many everyday challenges parents face in
raising children in a Torah home. It should be read
by all parents who seek to properly fulfill their
responsibilities of *chinuch habanim.*
Dr. Wikler is a true *ben Torah* and it is clear that
his *yiras Shomayim* has not been compromised by his
professionalism. May he see much *hatzlochoh* from
all of his work.

Rabbi Chaim P. Scheinberg

רחוב פנים מאירות 2, ירושלים, ת.ד. 6979, טל, 537-1513 (02), ישראל
2 Panim Meirot St., Jerusalem, P.O.B. 6979, Tel. (02) 537-1513, Israel

RABBI YAAKOV PERLOW
1569 - 47TH STREET
BROOKLYN, N.Y. 11219

יעקב פרלוב
ביהמ״ד עדת יעקב נאוואמינסק
ברוקלין, נ.י.

בס״ד: ב׳ תמוז תשנ״ט

Dr. Meir Wikler, whom I have known for many
years, has distinguished himself as a family
counselor, a guide and therapist to many people,
and above all a keen observer of the ongoing
social problems that occur in our community.
His rich experience comes with a perspective of
Torah insight that is important to the direction
of older and younger people struggling to cope
with life-situations in this difficult world.

Dr. Wikler's book on parenting will certainly
be an important contribution and a "helping hand"
to all families, and all parents seeking a better
understanding of their crucial roles.

Rabbi Yaakov Perlow

My good friend, Dr. Meir Wikler, has enriched the Jewish people with important books on topics such as marriage, hospitality, Divine intervention in daily events, etc. Orthodox Jewish magazines abound with his many informative and inspiring articles. Dr. Wikler has demonstrated, time and again, that he is sincerely devoted to the spiritual betterment of the Jewish people.

Presently, Dr. Wikler is publishing a book on the topic of Jewish parenting in our times. One cannot over-estimate the supreme importance of this topic. "Chinuch Habonim" has always been the duty and responsibility of Jewish parents. However, in our times, its importance has increased significantly. The world, outside of one's house, has lost morality and decency to an astounding degree. Children, as they step out of their homes, are immediately faced with the most corrupting influences, wherever they turn.

Thus, "Chinuch" in our times, is much more difficult and complex than ever before. Parents must literally dedicate their time, patience, brains, and energy towards instilling the pure, spiritual, and holy light of Torah into their children, in such a manner as to insulate and protect them from the numerous evil influences of the environment. This is almost a super-human task. It necessitates an abundant amount of divine assistance.

The task of "Chinuch" must be fulfilled by the parents. They dare not place this holy task upon the schools. At most, the schools may compliment that which the parents have accomplished.

Dr. Wikler's present publication, with it's wealth of advice, guidance and information for Jewish parents, is a timely book, indeed. Jewish parents facing the numerous complexities of "Chinuch" today, should greatly benefit from the wisdom, experience and professional expertise of the author.

Sincerely,

Shlomo Brevda

Shlomo Brevda

It is a great pleasure to hear that my ידיד, R' Meir
Wikler, author of *Bayis Ne'eman B'Yisroel; Practical Steps to
Success in marriage, AiSHel: Contemporary Stories on
Jewish Hospitality,* and *Eini Hashem: Contemporary Stories
of Divine Providence in Eretz Yisroel*, is publishing a new
work, **Partners with Hashem: Practical Guidelines For
Successful Parenting.**

Reb Meir, whom I have known for many years, is a
protege of the Bostoner Rebbe, **Grand Rebbi Levi Yitzchok
Horowitz שליט"א**, and the esteem in which he holds דעת
תורה is apparent in his writing and his clinical practice.
His house is open to people from all walks of life whom
he greets with a listening ear and a sympathetic heart. His
public lectures and his writings are always flavored with
warmth and humor.

R' Meir's keen insight into human nature coupled with
his literary expertise guarantee that this new book will be
agreat asset to the Jewish reading public, in general, and to
Jewish parents, in particular.

Eliezer Ginsburg

Table of Contents

Preface

CHAZAL HAVE STATED, "*SHIV'IM PANIM LATORAH*, THERE ARE seventy facets to the Torah." And although different opinions may, at times, even contradict each other, like the views of Hillel and Shamai, "*Eilu v'eilu divrei Elokim chayim —* these and those are both the words of the living G-d" (*Eruvin* 13b and *Gittin* 6b).

Just as this is so in interpreting the *Torah Shebichsav*, the Written Torah, this also applies to the *Toras Habayis*, the Torah guidelines for family relations. When it comes to parenting, therefore, there is simply no one right way to do things. Children can grow up in homes that are run very, very differently and still become Torah-true, satisfied, secure and successful adults.

If there is no right and wrong regarding parenting, then why write a book on the subject?

While there may not be a *single* correct approach to raising children, there can be many methods of parenting which are clearly helpful. And while there may be many useful strategies for the rearing of children, there are some techniques which are simply much more effective than others.

This book was not designed, therefore, to be used as the final word on any of the subjects covered. It was not meant to serve as a "Dr. Spock" for Jewish parents. Rather, it was conceived to provide some insights into childhood behavior, offer some practical suggestions for meeting the challenges of parenthood, and stimulate some thought about matters which should concern every Jewish parent today.

It is not my goal to have readers angrily confront their spouses, jabbing the print on these pages with their forefingers, and declare, "See, even Dr. Wikler says that parents should ... !"

What would gratify me, however, would be for readers to put this book down (gently) and turn to their spouses, remarking, "You know, the chapter I just read has caused me to stop and think. Maybe we need to reevaluate the way we've been handling the situation at home with..."

The thoughts presented in this book have been reworked, rewritten and revised for over a quarter of a century. Many of the chapters of this book began as speeches or articles in newspapers or magazines such as *The Jewish Observer*, and were published over a twenty-year period. Other chapters were written specifically for inclusion in this book and are being published here for the first time.

All of the previously published material in this book has been re-edited, updated and amended to take advantage of my current thoughts on each subject. As a retired seminary principal and prolific author once said, "I reserve the right to get smarter as I get older."

This book is intended for recently married couples standing on the threshold of parenthood as they expect their first child; young parents with small children who are groping to "get a handle" on what parenthood is all about; parents of school-aged children who are looking for new approaches to familiar child-rearing dilemmas; parents of adolescents who are finding new meaning in the phrase "end of the rope;" wounded parents who are trying to pick up the pieces of their lives after divorce or remarriage; more seasoned parents who are faced with the challenges of marrying off their children; and, finally, grandparents who wish to deal with their grandchildren differently from the way they raised their own children.

Parenting can be a lonely, thankless and frustrating proposition. But it can also be rewarding, uplifting and deeply gratifying. It is my fervent wish that this book help parents avoid the former experience and achieve the latter.

Ideally, this will not be a book which is read once and then relegated to the back row of a bookshelf. Rather, it is my hope that this book serve as a constant, supportive and encouraging companion and guide to parents as they traverse the winding, tortuous, but always noble, path of parenthood.

Meir Wikler, D.S.W
Brooklyn, New York

Acknowledgments

I WELCOME THIS OPPORTUNITY TO EXPRESS MY HEARTFELT appreciation to *Hashem* and to those people who contributed to this book and without whom its publication would not have been possible.

First and foremost, I would like to thank all of the children, adolescents and their parents with whom I have worked, who taught me more about the realities and dynamics of family life than I ever could have learned in a classroom or from textbooks. As Dovid *Hamelech* said, "*Mikol m'lamdai hiskalti*, I became wise from all of those whom I have taught." (*Tehilim* 119:99).

In addition, I am grateful to:

Grand Rabbi Levi I. Horowitz, the Bostoner Rebbe, *shlita,* for his lifelong inspiration, guiding hand, boundless *chesed,* and intimate concern for me and my family, and for his *haskamah;*

HaGa'on HaRav Chaim P. Scheinberg, *shlita,* for his perennially open door, and for his *haskamah;*

Harav Yaakov Perlow, the Novominsker Rebbe, *shlita,* for his *shiurim,* priceless guidance, longstanding personal interest, and for his *haskamah;*

HaRav Shlomo Brevda, *shlita,* for his *shiurim,* sage counsel, making my concerns his concerns, and for his *haskamah;*

HaRav Eliezer Ginsburg, *shlita,* for his *shiurim,* accessibility and for his haskamah;

Rabbi Yosef Wikler, editor and publisher of **Kashrus Magazine** and *menahel,* Yeshiva Birkas Reuven, for his thoughtful fraternal guidance in this and other projects;

Rabbi Nisson Wolpin, for his editorial assistance on those chapters which appeared in their original form in **The Jewish Observer;**

Rabbi Paysach Krohn, for his enduring friendship and his enthusiastic support of this and other ventures;

Rabbi Yaakov Salomon, C.S.W., a *yedid ne'eman,* for his creative contributions to this book, and for his uncompromising personal commitment to me, in times of both joy and challenge;

Dr. Gail Bessler, Dr. Larry Bryskin, Dr. Rashi Shapiro, Dr. Benzion Sorotzkin, and **Dr. Elin Weinstein,** the current members of the professional peer supervision group to which I have belonged for the past 15 years, for providing me a fertile forum in which to cultivate many of the concepts, insights and formulations included here and for their encouragement to compile and complete this book;

Rabbi Yisroel Ehrman, for his invitation to contribute to his forthcoming book, "Building Self-Esteem in Children: The Experts Speak," and for his permission to include that chapter in this book;

Rabbi Meir Zlotowitz and **Rabbi Nosson Scherman,** General Editors of Artscroll/Mesorah Publications, for their vote of confidence by including me in the Artscroll "family"; and to the following dedicated Artscroll staff: **Mrs. Devorah Schechter,** for her editing of the manuscript, her invaluable suggestions, and, most of all, for the regard and esteem she showed this project from the start; **Mr. Avrohom Biderman** and **Mrs. Rivkah Hamaoui,** for their faithful shepherding of the manuscript through the final stages of publication; **Mr. Eli Kroen,** for his creative design of the cover; and, **Mrs. Toby Goldzweig,** for her efficient typing of the manuscript and for her helpful comments;

Sarah, and **Yeshaya,** my children, for having turned me into a father, for enjoying listening to my bedtime stories when they were younger as much as I enjoyed telling them, for teaching me the true joys of parenthood by constantly making me proud of them, and, for giving up their time with me so that I could complete this book;

"Achronah, achronah, chavivah," my wife, **Malka,** for her painstaking review of each draft of the manuscript, and for her faithful support and patient indulgence throughout my career for which she deserves all of the credit for whatever I have accomplished, with the help of *HaShem.* Of her it may be said, "That which is mine and that which is yours — all belongs to her," (*Kesubos* 63a).

PART ONE:
Laying the Foundations for Successful Parenting

1

Becoming a Partner With Hashem:
An Introduction

S UPPOSE YOU ARE A SHOPKEEPER, A LAWYER OR A PLUMBER. And suppose the most successful, talented, and famous person in your field invites you to become his partner. *His partner!* Would you hesitate for a second? Would you prefer to remain in business for yourself? Would you pass up this golden opportunity to learn, grow, and advance your career? Of course not.

Moreover, once you agree to become his partner, would you conduct your work, "business as usual"? Would you go about your work as if you were still on your own? Or would you take your work more seriously than ever before?

Chazal tell us that when we become parents, we automatically become partners with none other than *Hashem Yisborach.*

> There are three partners in [the creation of] man: *Hakadosh Baruch Hu*, his father and his mother (*Kiddushin* 30b).

Thus, there is, perhaps, no greater role in Jewish life than that of parenthood, and the Torah emphasizes the importance of respecting that role by including the *mitzvah* of honoring parents among the *Asseres Hadibros*. If any further emphasis is needed, this *mitzvah* is one of only two in the entire Torah for which the reward of longevity is promised.

> Honor your father and your mother so that your days will be lengthened upon the land which *Hashem* your G-d gives you (*Shemos* 20:12).

If being a parent is given so much weight by the Torah, we would expect that *preparing* for that role should also be of paramount importance. Perhaps the best illustration of preparing for parenthood is the example set by *Yaakov Avinu*.

When Yaakov left Beer Sheva (*Bereishis* 28:10), he was satisfying the wishes of both his father and mother, thereby fulfilling the *mitzvah* of *kibud av v'eim*. His father, Yitzchak, wanted him to go to Padan Aram in order to find a wife (*Bereishis* 28:2), while his mother, Rivkah, wanted him to go to Padan Aram to save himself from Eisav (*Bereishis* 27:42-45).

In spite of the fact that his trip to Padan Aram was one which both parents wanted him to make, Yaakov stopped off along the way at a yeshivah, delaying the completion of his journey for 14 years! (See *Rashi, Bereishis* 28:11, 35:29.)

During one of his *derashos*, Rabbi Avigdor Miller posed the following question: How could someone of Yaakov's elevated stature tolerate such a long delay in his completion of the *mitzvah* of *kibud av v'eim*? Would we not expect greater alacrity on the part of one of the *Avos* (Patriarchs)? Would we not expect Yaakov to *rush* to fulfill his parents' wishes rather than tarry along the way?

Rabbi Miller went on to explain that Yaakov's 14-year stopover was not at all a postponement of the fulfillment of his parents' wishes. In fact, Rabbi Miller said, those 14 years represented the realization of Yaakov's parents' objectives. How could this be?

Yaakov recognized that the saving of his life and his starting a family were tasks of monumental and historic proportions. He was about to create a family that would produce *Klal Yisrael* — and the entire world was created only for the sake of *Klal Yisrael*. (See *Rashi, Bereishis* 1:1.)

Yaakov understood, therefore, that each and every step of the way toward building his family had to be taken carefully, thoughtfully, and with only the highest and purest intentions. A minor flaw at the outset could have catastrophic consequences for all future generations. "*Tov achris davar meireishiso*, the good at the end [of anything emanates only] from the [right] beginning." (See *Rashi, Koheles* 7:8.)

The first step Yaakov took in starting his family, then, was to immerse himself in Torah study at the Yeshivah of Shem and Ever. There he delved into the Torah guidelines for husbands and fathers. He studied what the Torah expects of a husband and father and how best to perform those responsibilities. And, as *Rashi* points out (*Bereishis* 28:11), Yaakov toiled so diligently at these studies that he did not lay down once for a proper sleep throughout the entire 14 years!

That was how Yaakov prepared for his becoming a parent. How does that compare with our preparation?

To obtain a driver's license, both written and road tests are required. Barely a few weeks' preparation are required to pass both. To get married, at least a license is required. To become a parent, however, one need not have any license or pass any test. Does that mean that we know more than Yaakov? Are we better equipped to discharge our responsibilities as parents than he was? Or are we simply taking the most important task of our lives too lightly?

In the secular society around us, parenthood is frequently taken for granted. In a world devoid of values, the birth of a child is all too often seen as a mistake, or even a misfortune. One need only glance at any newspaper today to see the devastating consequences of the prevailing "no big deal" attitude toward parenting.

But we are the chosen people. We are the *Am Hashem*, G-d's People. We are the descendants of the *Avos*. And, even more importantly, we are the forebears of *all* future generations of *Klal Yisrael*. The way we raise our children will have a profound impact on the rest of Jewish history. Dare we take this task lightly? Can we afford to adopt the "no big deal" attitude toward parenting demonstrated by the surrounding culture?

If we recognize the gravity of the responsibility *Hashem* has placed on our shoulders by including us as His partner in the creation of human life, then we should devote at least some time to the proper preparation for parenthood. As Harav Shlomo Wolbe observes: "Today, what is most lacking is the awareness that parenting is a skill that requires study."[1] And even if you are already a grandparent, it is still not too late to learn and improve your attitude, approach, and skills as a parent. We may not be able to devote the same uninterrupted 14 years that Yaakov did before he became a parent, but we can, at least, consider, reflect, and study how best to fulfill our responsibilities as parents.

Parenthood brings unending challenges. And there is more than one helpful way to meet those challenges. The ideas presented here are culled from Torah study, from consultations with *Gedolei Torah*, from discussions with colleagues, and from over a quarter of a century of full-time clinical work, counseling hundreds of parents and children.

Not everything you need to know as a parent is contained within these pages, but you will find much practical advice. Perhaps more important, however, are the thoughts, introspection, and discussion this book can provoke. If it stimulates any greater attention to this most vital and daunting of tasks — that of raising children — then it will have been more than worthwhile.

Do not take this book as the final word on any of the subjects covered. That was certainly not the intended goal. Rather use this

---

1. My own translation of *Zeriah Ubinyan Bechinuch* (Hebrew) by Harav Shlomo Wolbe (Yerushalayim: Feldheim Publishers, 1995), p.8.

book as a coach, consultant, and companion on the long and sometimes lonely road all parents must travel toward the goal of guiding their children successfully. Use this book as well, as a springboard for discussion, debate, and dialogue with your spouse, with your Rabbi, and most of all, with yourself. Use it to help you become all that you can be as a Jewish parent, thus linking the exhaustive preparation for parenting of Yaakov *Avinu* with all future generations until *Mashiach*.

2

Where to Make Your Home: An Out-of-Towner's Dilemma

"Women, slaves, and minors are not obligated [to fulfill the mitzvah *of sitting] in the* succah. *[However,] a minor who [is mature enough] not to need [to be constantly with] his mother is obligated [to sit] in the* succah. *It once happened that the daughter-in-law of Shammai the Elder gave birth [shortly before the Yom Tov of Succos] and he opened the roof and placed* s'chach *over the crib for the sake of the baby boy"* (Mishnah Succah 2:8).

The Gemara discusses the apparent contradiction between the ruling of this mishnah *and the accompanying anecdote regarding Shammai the Elder.*

This mishnah *is dealing with the* mitzvah *of* chinuch, *which requires parents to train their minor children in the performance of* mitzvos *even before they become adults so that they will know how to do so when they reach the age of maturity. Even though boys are not obligated by Torah law to sit in a* succah *until they are 13 years old, they are required to sit in a* succah *from a much earlier age to fulfill the Rabbinic mitzvah of* chinuch, *preparing them for adulthood.*

When does the mitzvah *of* chinuch *begin for the* mitzvah *of* succah? Chazal *ruled that the starting point for the* mitzvah *of* chinuch *regarding* succah *is when a child no longer calls for his mother when he awakens. (see* Succah 28b). *According to Shammai the Elder, however, the* mitzvah *of* chinuch *applies even when a child is too young to comprehend.*

Although the halachah *rules that there is no* mitzvah *of* chinuch *for the* mitzvah *of* succah *at such a tender age, Shammai the Elder is teaching us a momentous message. Our obligation to train, teach, and guide our children begins from the moment of their birth.*

While the obligations of chinuch *may begin as soon as a child is born, there are decisions we, as prospective parents, must make even* before *our children are born. These decisions will have a profound impact on the type of parents we will become and, as a result, the kind of children we will raise.*

Who we choose as a mate to share the mission of parenting is an obvious example. The choice of career and occupation is another decision which will greatly impact our future roles as parents. A less obvious example is the choice of where to make our homes.

This chapter addresses some of the considerations that went through my mind in choosing a community in which to live. You may arrive at very different conclusions and may make a different decision than I did about where to live. But at least you and your spouse would do well to consider the issues my wife and I struggled with in picking a community in which to raise our children. You need to consider these issues because the decision of where to make your home is one of the cornerstones you will be setting down as you lay the foundations for your future parenting.

⎯⎯⎯⎯

I GREW UP OUT OF TOWN, ALTHOUGH I DID NOT REALIZE that my hometown was considered "out of town" until I moved to New York City almost 30 years ago. I'm very glad I made the move and my wife and I have tried to take full advantage of the extra *Yiddishkeit* opportunities available in "the City." But every now and again my wife and I mourn the loss of those *Yiddishkeit* opportunities that were available out of town, opportunities which our children may never know. Let me explain.

The city I used to call home boasted a population somewhat under 80,000 residents, 10 percent of whom were Jews. Although Jews were very prominent in politics and the professions, traditional Jewish life was relegated to the back seat.

We had six synagogues in town: two Orthodox, two Conservative, and two Reform. Unfortunately, the membership in these synagogues was not as equally distributed as their affiliations. The overwhelming majority of Jews did not belong to any synagogue. About a quarter of the Jews belonged to the Reform temples, and 10 percent to the Conservative temple. The two Orthodox *shuls* had a combined membership of approximately 100 families.

In terms of numbers, the Orthodox Jews certainly constituted the minority of a minority. But somehow, the small size of our community seemed to lend to our strength rather than detract from it.

Of course, we missed the opportunities that come with larger numbers. We had no yeshivah in town and my brother and I had to ride over an hour on a school bus, each way, to get to the nearest day school. We were also an hour and a half away, by car, from the closest kosher pizza shop. There was no *sefarim* store in town so all of our *sefarim,* as well as *yarmulkes, tzitzis, hav-dalah* candles and *lulavim* had to be imported from more vibrant Jewish communities, nearby.

So far, it must sound pretty bleak to an "in-towner." But I also gained a great deal from growing up in that town. There were opportunities for *mesiras nefesh* and *kiddush Hashem* that literally knocked at the door every week. Let me list just a few.

- **Shabbos.** We lived two miles from *shul.* In good weather it was about a 45-minute walk through town. In the heat of the summer, the return trip was about an hour. You just can't walk quickly when the July sun shines through a pollution-free sky; and if there had been a snowstorm on or just before *Shabbos,* the walk to *shul* could take almost two hours.

Of course there weren't too many times that it took me two hours to get to *shul* on *Shabbos* morning, but I remember each one with a warm glow of pride. And I can tell you that no *davening* can compare to the *davening* preceded by a two hour walk through the snow — against the wind!

- **Kashrus.** Our choice of stores at which to shop was extremely limited. And we always knew that we couldn't buy everything in the store either. There was only one kosher baker, one butcher shop that was "really kosher," and one appetizing store.

We also learned, at a very early age, in whose homes we could eat and in whose we could not. It was as taken for granted as which streets were one way and which were not. Just as we knew our phone number and address, so too, we knew this necessary information at a young age.

In spite of our many limitations with food, we never felt hungry or deprived. We were proud of our *Yiddishkeit* and never resented its restrictions. But let me tell you, you cannot know what a treat means unless you saw our faces on one of those rare occasions when we were munching kosher hot dogs on toasted buns!

- **Hachnasas Orchim.** Virtually no one traveled through our town. There was only one reason to be there: You lived there. So if you wanted guests for *Shabbos,* you had two choices. Either you could invite a friend or you could try to be *m'kareiv* someone. We did both.

I'll never forget the *Pesach* when we had a particularly difficult time finding a guest. As a last resort, we called a local WASP college and asked them to post a sign: "If you are Jewish and need a place for the *seder,* please call..." Rumor had it that the college did not accept Jewish students, or at least discouraged them from applying. So we were understandably hesitant about making the telephone call. To our surprise, they not only agreed to post the sign but someone called.

The young lady who came to our home that *Pesach* knew only that she was Jewish. My mother befriended her and helped her to make other contacts in our town and elsewhere. Today she is married to a *ben Torah,* and the mother of three.

• **Succos.** How many people use your *esrog* and *lulav*? Just you and your children? Literally hundreds of people used ours. No, they didn't come to our home. My older brother would rush out after the *seudah* on *Yom Tov,* to stop people downtown. He did the same on *Chol Hamoed.*

I can remember standing in the street, a shy, impatient young boy, as my older brother would stop, question and then instruct a passerby. Even on the way home from *shul,* he would be *chapping* these *mitzvos.* But what impressed me more than my brother's bravery was the occasional tear I would notice in the corner of an older man's eye as he looked nostalgically at the odd yet familiar sight of a *lulav* and *esrog.*

"Do you boys go to yeshivah?" We were often asked, "Where? ... Really?" The dialogue was always the same. I could not measure my brother's *kiddush Hashem* then, but I can tell you that the lump in my throat is enormous now, as I recall these events.

Perhaps what was an even greater *kiddush Hashem* was our *succah.* In our town years ago almost no one besides the Orthodox Rabbis had private *succos.* Everyone else used the *succah* in *shul.* It was so unusual for a layman to have his own *succah* that a reporter from the local newspaper came to photograph ours when I was 6 years old. Years later, *baruch Hashem*, there were dozens of private *succos* in town.

Everyone was always invited into our *succah* for *kiddush* after *shul*, on the first day of *Yom Tov*. That may not sound unusual to someone who lives in a vibrant Jewish community, but what would surprise "in-towners" was that everyone came — every year. There was no such thing as only some people coming. In our town, when one person made a *simchah* or gave a *kiddush*, we all came. It was *our simchah*.

Of course, our *succah* wasn't used only for *kiddush*. After the *seudah* we always hosted a *Succos* party for the Jewish children in the neighborhood. We didn't have Pirchei or Bnos but our *Succos* parties grew from year to year. As I got older, I remember that the crowd was so large that we had to break into shifts: 5- to 10-year-olds from 2-3:30 and 11– to 15–year olds from 3:30-5. Who napped on *Yom Tov* afternoon? We were too busy!

Perhaps my greatest thrill was when we decided to build the *succah* on the front lawn, instead of in the back yard. I can't tell you how many cars stopped and how much Jewishness come out of the woodwork. We never felt we were doing *kiruv* work. We just felt we were being Jewish. That's the way it is out of town.

• **Torah Education.** As I mentioned before, we had no yeshivah in our town. My brother and I attended a day school an hour away. But that day school hadn't always been there. In fact, it began in our living room.

When my parents moved into town, there was no yeshivah or day school within an hour and a half of our home. People expressed concern; but no one was doing anything. After we arrived, a parlor meeting was called. Money was raised. A board was formed and officers were elected. My father was the first vice president and I entered kindergarten the following year.

Our home was the scene for meetings not only to raise money, but for other community needs as well. At times *shul* business was conducted in our home. The *Vaad Hakashrus* often met in our home, too. And I always looked forward to our turn to host the *Chevrah Shas*, the Talmud study group, in our home because my mother always baked a lot of special cakes for the men. Our home was not merely involved in *Yiddishkeit;* because of where we lived, the *Yiddishkeit* in town revolved around our home.

As a result, we were never able to take our *Yiddishkeit* for granted, even if we wanted to. We could never forget or become complacent because we were constantly challenged by the world in which we lived. Sometimes these challenges took the form of aggressive confrontations (i.e. "Hey, Jew boy!!"). Other times, they were more lighthearted, such as when the non-Orthodox Jewish proprietor of the local pet store perennially quizzed us, "So when are you boys going to answer my question; are camels kosher?"

These challenges and opportunities strengthened our identity and commitment as a furnace tempers steel. We learned how to defend ourselves — in more ways than one — because we *had* to and I believe we gained enormously from these experiences.

As I grew older, however, I began to long for opportunities to live a Torah life without so many challenges. It was a conscious, albeit gradual, decision to eventually make my own home in town.

During my eighth-grade year of yeshivah, I attended over a dozen *bar mitzvahs.* The principal was invited to all of them, of course, and he attended almost all. His speech was always the same. At the time, I believed that he simply did not want to bother preparing a new speech for each *bar mitzvah.* Now I realize that the message was so important that he felt it had to be repeated, as often as possible.

The message was clear and direct. Not everyone was planning to continue on at a yeshivah high school. For some, this was the end of the line for their Jewish education. Therefore, they should always remember that in order to remain "good Jews" it would be necessary, at times, for us to "swim against the stream." The implication was, "Don't be afraid to stand out from the crowd because of your *Yiddishkeit.*"

It is, indeed, hard to swim against the stream. After growing up out of town, I decided that I would make my home in town so that I could continue my commitment to Torah living *without* having to "swim against the stream." Many of my former classmates also decided not to resist the stream — only they remained out of town and eventually flowed away from *Yiddishkeit.*

Today, I am deeply rooted in town. I have been living here almost thirty years and I am very much an in-towner now. My wife and I are very pleased with our decision. Our children have attended *mosdos* of *chinuch* of exceptionally high caliber. We belong to a *shul* comprised exclusively of *bnei Torah.* There are many *shiurim* available and a plethora of *chessed* organizations in which one can become involved.

In our neighborhood we are surrounded by stores which all sell food with the most reliable *hechsherim.* I can find a *minyan* whenever I need one. And not only are *Shabbos* and *Yom Tov* very noticeably observed, but you can even feel the quickened pulse of *Erev Shabbos* and *Erev Yom Tov.*

Throughout my years in town, I have always tried, and sometimes succeeded, in viewing these many *Yiddishkeit* opportunities as a challenge: Will I sit back and take it easy, remaining stagnant in my old level of learning, commitment, and *avodas Hashem* or will I take proper advantage of these opportunities, utilizing them as tools to help me to grow? I certainly can, and should, do more. And that remains the challenge for all of us who are fortunate enough to live in such exceptional communities.

So what, then, was my dilemma? My dilemma had to do with my children. They have grown up here, in town. As a result, they have never tasted the satisfaction derived from trekking two hours through the snow to get to *shul* on *Shabbos.* They have never felt, at the age of 13, the rocket boost of self-esteem when one is counted as the 10th man on a Friday night. They have never experienced the surge of spiritual adrenaline that comes in response to the challenge of a non-Orthodox Jew with a guilty conscience. And they cannot imagine how good pizza can smell when you have had to drive an hour and a half to get to the kosher pizza store.

My children are not alone in feeling the natural complacency that inevitably arises from the security found in large numbers. They, and even adults who have never known a different world, have not fully experienced the beauty of a *Yiddishkeit* tempered by sacrifice and *mesiras nefesh*. Yet those crucial ingredients are the mortar needed for cementing strong character. We in-towners, in the fortresses of our closely knit and highly structured communities, should help youngsters learn about the preciousness of our heritage. We must teach them to never take for granted that which they have been fortunate enough to inherit. I wanted to prevent my children from feeling that sense of complacency implicit in the Yiddish phrase *"es kumt mir* — it's coming to me!" I also wanted to help them acquire a non-egocentric, more tolerant perspective toward their less religious brethren, especially those who have not had the benefit of a solid Jewish education.

This last point was driven home to me when we were out of town on a visit. We were all sitting around the *Shabbos* table with our hosts and a young man came in to visit. My then 4-year-old son was sitting on my lap at the time and started pulling on my tie.

"What's the matter?" I asked, a bit confused by his behavior. I then recognized the contorted look on his face which meant that he had something to say which he would only whisper. So I bent down and he leaned up to my ear.

"Is that man Jewish?" he whispered.

"Of course! What makes you think that he might not be Jewish?" I replied.

"But he doesn't have a beard — like a *goy*," my son explained.

Needless to say, I set my son straight, as soon as I could, that not *all* Jewish men have beards. I also pointed out that many *frum* Jewish men do not have beards, either. My son accepted the beard lesson, on faith. After all, most of the Jewish men he saw did have beards.

So here, in a nutshell, was my dilemma. I wanted my children to live in a *frum* community, literally surrounded by so many other *frum* Jews that they would not have to swim against the stream. At the same time, I wanted them to accept other Jews with an open, non-critical *ahavas Yisrael*. I also wanted them to be equipped with the strength to swim upstream, should that ever be necessary.

We did not find a solution to our dilemma. My wife and I discussed it often, but we never come up with any real solution. I can only present what have been our partial solutions to counteract the downside of living in town. Others, both in and out-of-towners who share our dilemma, may find our program helpful.

1. Trips to the "wilderness." When our children were young we made a point of going out of town, as a family, at least two or three times a year. During these trips, we visited other Jewish communities which provided the necessary *minyan* and *kashrus* services, but which could be considered Torah wildernesses compared to New York City. These trips gave us the opportunity to teach our children how others live so that they could better appreciate what they have. Hopefully, our children now take their *Yiddishkeit* a little less for granted as a result of these excursions.

Another benefit of these trips was for our children to see other Orthodox Jews who don't look and dress *exactly* as we do. Hopefully, this helped our children to develop a proper tolerance for different expressions of Torah life.

2. Hachnasas Orchim. We made a very firm and deliberate decision to have guests *every Shabbos* and *Yom Tov*. Sometimes, it wasn't easy to find them. My wife has spent literally hours some weeks calling around to find *someone* to invite. *Baruch Hashem*, she has almost always been successful.

As a result, my children have been witness to a veritable kaleidoscope of Jewry parading through our house each week. Our guests run the gamut from the not-yet-*frum*, questioning college students to yeshivah *bachurim* and seminary students.

As they were growing up, our children were delighted with our open-door policy. Every Friday they would ask with excited anticipation, "Who's coming *this Shabbos*?" Of course, there have been times when they felt they would have liked more attention at the table. But then it gave us the opportunity to explain, later, how their sacrifice was enabling them to share in our family's *mitzvah*. It also gave us the opportunity to explain how we were helping our guests and what we were doing for or giving to them.

Yes, I'll admit it was very embarrassing for us the first time my then 8-year-old daughter giggled when a *baal teshuvah* stumbled over a few words of *Kiddush*. But the next time, when a *baalas teshuvah* took 15 minutes to *bentch* and my daughter reminded her, without giggling, to say *retzei*, was I proud of her!

After all is said and done, I know that trips out of town and aggressive *hachnasas orchim* cannot ameliorate all of the undesirable aspects of living in town. So I can only *daven* to *Hashem Yisborach* that my children continue to strengthen their ironclad commitments to Torah *Yiddishkeit*, even though they have not been tempered and tested by the kiln of growing up out of town.

Each set of parents must choose the country, city, and neighborhood in which they will raise their children. As the family grows and grows up, each set of parents may also need to reevaluate their decision in order to take into consideration their children's changing needs. It is not unheard of, for example, for a family to relocate to another country in order to find medical or educational resources which the children require.

Where you choose to make your home will have a major impact on the children you will raise there, *b'ezras Hashem*. Make that choice carefully. Reevaluate it often. It is one of the first of many vital decisions you will have to make as a parent.

3

Picking Priorities:
Planting an AiSHeL in Your Home

Real-estate brokers have a favorite riddle they love to share with new clients.

What are the three most important factors which affect the value of any home or apartment?

The answer: location, location, and location.

While location may play a major role in determining the price of a home or the monthly rent of an apartment, there are other factors which determine the spiritual value of your home.

The monetary value of your home will have negligible impact on the children you raise there. The spiritual values with which you adorn your home, however, will have a profound influence on your children which will reverberate for generations to come.

Thus, in laying the foundations for successful parenting, you need to consider not only where to make your home but also what kind of home you want it to be. And nothing determines the nature of your home more than the priorities you choose to be embodied by your home and family.

A good place to start in setting priorities for your home is to decide that you will include guests on a regular basis at your Shabbos and Yom Tov table. The benefits to you and your family are immeasurable.

Some of the primary benefits of opening your home to guests are the lessons this practice teaches your children. Parents are always trying to convince, cajole, and coax their children into sharing what they have with others. "Let him play, too," "Now, let her have a turn," and, "It's not nice to keep all that for yourself," are comments we constantly hear ourselves making to our children as they are growing up. We want our children to learn the joys and appreciate the value of sharing.

There is no better method of teaching than by example. Our lectures may fall on deaf ears. If we practice what we preach, however, we have a much better chance of being heard. It is for this reason that opening our homes to guests is a most effective way of encouraging our children to share graciously with others.

In case you are not convinced, this chapter details the benefits you and your children will receive if you plant the AiSHeL of Jewish hospitality in your home.

⟡

" **A** ND [AVRAHAM *AVINU*] PLANTED AN AISHEL IN BE'ER *Sheva*" (*Bereishis* 21:33).

What was the *AiSHeL* that *Avraham Avinu* planted? Different opinions have been offered by *Chazal*.

"One said that *AiSHeL* was an orchard. And one said it was a guesthouse" (*Sotah* 10a).

"The word *AiSHeL* is an acronym for *achilah* (eating), *shesiyah* (drinking) and *levayah* (escorting guests)" (*Rashi, Kesubos* 8b).

"These [three] letters [of this word] are the same [as those of] *sha'al* (asking), because *Avraham Avinu* would say to all those who passed by, 'Ask for whatever you want.' Then he would give his guest whatever was requested" (*Rabbeinu Bachye, Bereishis* 21:33).

The word *AiSHeL*, therefore, has come to represent the Jewish tradition of hospitality which was planted so deeply into the soul of our people by *Avraham Avinu* that it still continues to blossom forth today.

Unfortunately, there are some Jewish homes, even very *frum* ones, where the *mitzvah* of *hachnasas orchim* (hospitality) is only practiced infrequently, if at all. These people may have lost sight of the great rewards due to those who regularly practice this *mitzvah*. In addition to the bountiful rewards in *Olam Haba*, which await those who invite guests into their homes, *Chazal* have promised us *peiros* (fruits or profits) of the reward in *this world* (*Shabbos* 127a).

What follows is but a partial list of the immediate, tangible bonuses for fulfilling the *mitzvah* of *hachnasas orchim* that flow from the *mitzvah* itself. Hopefully, after reviewing this list, more people will be enticed to plant an *AiSHeL* in their own homes.

1. A deep feeling of satisfaction and fulfillment.

Anytime you extend yourself to help a fellow Jew, you are immediately rewarded with a deep feeling of satisfaction and a profound sense of fulfillment. While this is true for all acts of *chessed*, it is even more so for *hachnasas orchim*.

For the minimal sacrifice of including a guest at your table or in your *succah*, you may benefit your guest immeasurably. Your guest may have had nowhere else to eat, may have had food but not the warmth of a family, or may have had both but not the Torah-true atmosphere of *Shabbos* or *Yom Tov*. In the latter case, your hospitality could result in bringing your guest closer to *Yiddishkeit*, providing merit for you and your family for generations to come.

2. An opportunity to make new friends.

Even if you have little impact on the lives of your guests, your hospitality is an excellent, fully legitimate vehicle for meeting new people and making new friends. And next to health, few things in life are more valuable than sincere friendship.

Hachnasas orchim not only provides opportunities for developing new relationships with peers, but it also affords unique opportunities to cultivate ties with *Rabbanim* and other Torah personalities whom one might not have otherwise even met. It is quite well known, for example, that the warm, intimate three-decade-long relationship Rabbi Paysach Krohn enjoyed with Rabbi Shalom Schwadron, which led to the now-classic, highly acclaimed "Maggid Series," came about through *hachnasas orchim*.

3. Adding spice to your *Shabbos* table.

Some families have so little to discuss with each other that a typical *Shabbos* meal, *zemiros* and all, is concluded in less than 45 minutes. By adding a guest or two, all sorts of new ideas, information, and points of view are introduced, which can liven up the conversation around your table.

I recall, for example, one particular *Shabbos* meal at our home. We had one guest who was born and raised in South Africa and another who had lived for a year in India. The fascinating conversation that ensued brought the exotic flavor of these far-away places into our dining room.

4. Opportunities to do other *mitzvos*.

Your associations with your guests will afford you countless opportunities to perform other *mitzvos*, which you probably would not have otherwise had. The *chessed* of making *shidduchim* is one example.

Hachnasas orchim also provides opportunities to perform the *chessed* of helping people find roommates, apartments, and even jobs; the latter, according to the *Rambam* (*Hilchos Matnos Aniyim* 10:7), constitutes the highest form of *tzedakah*.

5. Muting family tensions.

Family conflicts that lie dormant all week can easily erupt during the extended interaction of a *Shabbos seudah*. Whether harsh words are spoken between parents, between siblings, or between parent and child, the serenity of *Shabbos* is shattered.

However, when a guest is at the table, everyone at home is on his or her best behavior. "Can't you suggest anyone for me to invite for *Yom Tov*?!" a neighbor once pleaded, desperately, with my wife. "We always make sure to have at least one guest at the table so my boys don't try to kill each other with their dirty looks and comments, and the guest we were counting on just canceled!"

6. Learning from others.

One of the greatest rewards you can receive in this world from practicing *hachnasas orchim* is the opportunity it provides for you to learn from others, thereby improving yourself.

Often, the first thing you can learn from your guests is how much you have to be thankful for. When you see what your guests need, it can remind you of what you have and sometimes take for granted.

You can also learn Torah from your guests, regardless of their level of Torah knowledge. This guest shares a *p'shat* he read in a recently published anthology; that one shares a *vort* she heard at a *sheva berachos*; and still another clarifies an often misconstrued *halachah* about which he just consulted a leading *poseik*. All three have taught you Torah and enriched your life as a result.

Finally, you can become inspired by your guests to increase your own personal growth. In the words of Reb Yochanan, "As a reward for [giving the directive to his daughters], 'Call him [Moshe into the house so that] he shall eat bread,' [Yisro was so spiritually elevated by *Moshe Rabbeinu* that eventually Yisro's] children merited that they sat in the *Lishkas Hagazis* [i.e. they were members of the *Sanhedrin*]" (*Sanhedrin* 104a).

7. Teaching Middos.

As noted above, children learn *middos* best by following the example set by their parents.[1]

Unfortunately, this applies to our undesirable *middos*, as well as to those traits we want our children to acquire.

If we want our children to learn to share their toys and treats with others, we must set an example for them with our own generosity. If our homes are open to guests on a regular basis, one of the greatest rewards is the lesson in *chessed* it will teach our children. Our actions will inculcate them with the value of opening their hearts to others now, as well as when they mature.

After reviewing the list of rich rewards in this world awaiting those who practice *hachnasas orchim*, you may be wondering, "Where can I find guests to invite for *Shabbos* and *Yom Tov*?"

So if you and your family are considering planting an *AiSHeL* in your home, here are ten strategies to employ in locating guests:

1. Borrow your neighbor's guests. Surely you can think of at least one neighbor who has earned a reputation as a *machnis orchim*. Why not ask him to suggest the names of any of his "regulars" for you to invite?

2. Ask your Rabbi. Many Rabbis meet people who would appreciate an invitation for a *Shabbos* — more people than the Rabbi can possibly invite into his own home. He would welcome your request.

3. Call a yeshivah or seminary. Students in a dormitory often come from out of town, and would welcome *Shabbos* invitations each week. Just call the yeshivah and have them put your name on their hospitality list.

4. Contact a *kiruv* organization. Outreach professionals are constantly looking to expand their lists of potential hosts — homes where they can send newcomers to Orthodoxy for a taste of Torah-true living.

---

1. This point is made most forcefully and eloquently by Dr. Bentzion Sorotzkin in his article, "Developing *Middos*: Learned or Experienced?," *The Jewish Observer*, May '99, pp. 6-11.

5. Spread the word you're looking. Let your friends and neighbors know you're "open for business." You cannot succeed in any business if you keep it a secret.

6. Call a Jewish immigrant aid association. All immigrants are eager for social contact with local, established families. In many cases, your *Shabbos* table may be their first opportunity in their lives to encounter authentic *Yiddishkeit*. The thrill of having an adult at your *seder* who has never attended one in his life, for example, is indescribable. And the glow in your home will last long after the *Pesach* dishes have been stored away.

7. Approach strangers in your community. Besides fulfilling the *Mishnah* in *Pirkei Avos* (4:15), greeting newcomers is probably the most effective method to meet people who are looking for a *Shabbos* invitation.

8. Give your guests an open invitation. By giving your guests an open invitation to return, you increase the chances that they will call you on their own, without your having to call them.

9. Let your guests bring their friends. Some of our "best customers" originally came to our home as the companion of a returning guest.

10. Form a *hachnasas orchim* committee. Whether community-wide or only within your *shul*, a *hachnasas orchim* committee can serve as a "matchmaking" service, pairing prospective hosts with those looking for invitations.

The committee need not be run by a potential host. One very active committee in New York City, for example, was managed for many years by a single woman who became quite adept at finding homes for even some hard-to-place guests. (She has since gotten married, perhaps her reward in this world for her active involvement in *hachnasas orchim*.)

PART TWO:
Building Character; Teaching Middos

4

Implanting Self-Esteem
in Children:
How, When, and Why

*One of the first building blocks of character which parents
want to implant in their children is that of self-esteem.*

*In contemporary secular society, however, the trait of self-
esteem has been elevated to a status beyond that of sainthood.
In the Torah world, we reflexively avoid and recoil at anything which is embraced too enthusiastically by the non-
Jewish world. There are sound reasons for that. Seeing how
self-esteem is worshipped by the media, some might have
reached the conclusion that self-esteem has achieved the status
of an* avodah zarah, *or false god.*

*This having been said, is there room in our homes for pro-
moting self-esteem? Is self-esteem something that we really
want to instill in our children; and if so, why? Finally, if self-*

esteem is so important for our children to acquire, how can we accomplish this daunting task in a way which is consistent with our Torah hashkafah? This next chapter will attempt to address these timely questions.

৵৹ ৶৹

SUPPOSE, FOR ONE CHILLING MOMENT, THAT YOU KNEW YOU were about to leave this world. And suppose that you were alone with your 12-year-old son who would have to carry on your life's work after your passing. What could you possibly say to your son at a time like that? If you could bring yourself to speak at all, what final instruction would you want to give before you drew your final breath? And of all the things you wanted to convey, what would be at the very top of your list?

That was exactly the situation *David Hamelech* faced at the end of his 70 years on this world. In his weakened state of old age, David summoned his son, Shlomo, who was only 12 years old at the time. David then spoke to Shlomo, who was minutes away from assuming the full responsibility of carrying on the Davidic dynasty.

David knew that Shlomo would face enormous challenges — both personal and political — in leading the Jewish nation. He would have to deal with internal dissent, with foreign monarchs and his mission would include building the holy Temple. In order to help Shlomo succeed at all of this, David wanted to fortify Shlomo's strength of character. And the one character trait David chose to reinforce first was self-esteem.

"And the day of David's death approached and he charged Shlomo, his son, saying, 'I am about to go in the way of all creatures. Be strong and become a man'" (*Melachim I* 2:1-2).

On this verse, the *Metzudas David* comments, "Albeit that you are only a lad, strengthen yourself to become [as confident as] a mature man since I am dying and I will not be able to guide you on the path that you should go."

While David continued to give other more specific instructions to Shlomo, the very first guidance David offered Shlomo at this crucial time was his encouraging Shlomo's self-esteem.

Why did David consider self-esteem so important? And why should parents today be so concerned about instilling self-esteem in their children?

A good way to measure the true value of something is to examine the impact of not having it. We could easily live without gold, for example. But we could not last very long without air and water.

In order to appreciate the importance of self-esteem, then, let us take a look at what happens to people who *lack* self-esteem, and examine how low self-esteem affects their lives.

People who suffer from low self-esteem are socially handicapped, emotionally at risk, and tend to function far below their full potential. As a result of their low self-esteem, they believe that no one would really want to befriend them, and this becomes a constantly self-fulfilling prophecy. Thus, they have few friends and hardly any close friends. When they do enter relationships, they feel so vulnerable to rejection that they allow — even encourage — others to take advantage of them. These are people who become easily exploited and even abused by their "friends."

Because they feel so inadequate and worthless, such people are most prone to shyness, anxiety, and even depression. Unable to feel good about themselves, they often become overly self-critical, which can lead to feelings of hopelessness.

Convinced of their own inadequacies, people with low self-esteem constantly expect to fail. As a result, they often do not invest enough in themselves to succeed. Since they are so sure they will fail, they don't bother to study enough for exams, to prepare sufficiently for a job interview or even to speak loudly enough to be heard.

Such people stand little chance of finding happiness in marriage. First of all, they often choose spouses who could never satisfy their needs; moreover, they rarely express their wishes and preferences clearly to their spouses. This leads to frustration, disappointment, and, at times, resentment — conditions which fan the fire of marital discord.

If all these negative scenarios can result from low self-esteem, is it any wonder that parents strive to build self-esteem in their children? Is it surprising that parents desperately want to fortify their children with the primary emotional asset which can serve to prevent most or all of the ills listed above? What, then, is the best method to instill self-esteem in children without getting carried away?

There are four practical steps which all parents can take in order to help build self-esteem in their children. While each of these steps is helpful, it is not necessary to do everything listed below. The more steps you take, however, the greater are your chances of succeeding.

1. Praise as often as you can.

The process of acquiring self-esteem (whether high self-esteem or low self-esteem) is similar to the mechanics of learning a language. Confidence, assurance, and a feeling of self-worth can be seen as forms of internal language, or self-talk. People with these qualities think of themselves in positive, accepting, and approving terms. When they judge themselves, they judge favorably. They may think, "I did that well," "That was a nice thing I just said," or, "That was a clever thought I had".

Moreover, when people with self-esteem fail or make mistakes, they are more forgiving of themselves. They tend to overlook their faults instead of criticizing themselves. They give themselves the benefit of the doubt and judge themselves favorably. They may think, "I tried my best," "Under the circumstances, I could not have done any better,"[1] or, "This time was the exception rather than the rule".

How do people learn to think this way about themselves? How do they learn this language of self-esteem, this positive self-talk?

---

1. Of course, every person must take responsibility for his or her actions and make an honest self-assessment. To do otherwise is to be arrogant and would fly in the face of Torah *hashkafah*.

They learn it the same way they learn to speak their primary language: by hearing it spoken to them.

Children learn to speak their "mother tongue" because that is the language that is first spoken to them. Just *hearing* a language is not enough. A child must be addressed in a language in order to acquire fluency. Similarly, in order to think positively about himself, a child must be spoken to in a language of self-esteem — and the language of self-esteem is *praise*.

When parents make it a point to praise every success, compliment every achievement, and acknowledge every accomplishment, a child learns how to think positively about himself. The obvious question is: Won't it spoil the child to be praised so often? The answer is no, not at all. It can, however, actually *spoil* a child not to be praised enough. In over 25 years of clinical practice, I have never once treated a patient who complained that his parents praised him too much.

Often, parents find it easier to criticize their children than to praise them. Perhaps this is because they were more often criticized by *their* parents when *they* were children. Alternatively, perhaps they just see this method as being more consistent with their role as teachers. Or, perhaps, they are simply afraid of an *ayin hara* (evil eye).

Whatever the rationale for not praising, parents must realize that they can much more effectively accomplish their goals of educating and training their children by using praise than they will by employing criticism. Children are always more motivated by rewards than by fear of punishment. Ask any experienced teacher and he or she will tell you what works best to inspire children to learn; the master teachers generally use praise and encouragement, the inexperienced and incompetent teachers most often use threats and punishments.

As *Chazal* understood, when dealing with children, you should always "push away [rebuke and criticize] with the left [the weaker hand] and bring close [praise and compliment] with the right [the stronger hand]" (*Sotah* 47a). So if you want your child to grow up to be a confident, self-assured adult, take advantage of every opportunity now to praise him or her.

2. Spend as much quality time as you can with your child.

What is "quality time" and why is it so vital to building self-esteem in children? Quality time is time that is focused as much as possible on the child. It is not time the child spends with you while you are reading a newspaper, talking to someone else on the phone or balancing your checkbook. During quality time, you are engaged in some pleasurable activity together with your child, such as playing a game, reading a book, baking cookies, riding in the car or even studying.

Interruptions are not allowed at all during quality time — or they are, at the very least, kept to a minimum. Only the most urgent phone calls are taken. Conversations with others are cut short. "I'm sorry. I'm reading (or playing) with my daughter now," is the only excuse you need to offer to others.

Conversation during quality time should be focused on pleasurable topics. This is not an opportunity to reprimand, scold or criticize. Preferably, the child will set the agenda for what is discussed. The form of interaction, however, is not the main ingredient in quality time. What is most important is the two of you being together without other competitors for your attention.

More than anything else, it is the exclusivity of your attention which gives quality time its power to convey to your child how important he or she is to you. For over 3300 years, for example, we have been distinguished as the "chosen people," indicating our unique, intimate, and everlasting relationship with *Hashem*. That special relationship was demonstrated by *Hashem* speaking only once throughout all of history to an entire nation, when He spoke to us at *Har Sinai* (*Devarim* 4:32, 33).

The message that quality time conveys to your child is that you truly value him or her. You show how important your child is to you by virtue of the fact that you are spending time with him or her. Your child knows how precious your time is and how busy you are. So when you find time for your child, when you carve out a piece of your hectic schedule in order to be with him or her, you send your child a very powerful message: He or she is important.

Of course, no children ever feel they have enough time with their parents. Children always wish for more, but the more time we do spend with our children, the more we will build and reinforce their feelings of self-worth and self-esteem.

3. Show interest in your child's interests.

Children, like most other people, identify with their own specific interests. As adults, we usually associate ourselves closely with the things that are important to us. If we feel strong allegiance for an organization or a cause, for example, we feel hurt, even insulted, if someone disparages that organization. Similarly, if we have a hobby or favorite pastime, we naturally feel an affinity towards anyone who shares the same interest.

Children, also, will feel belittled if a contemporary makes fun of their toys, games, collections or friends. If the mockery is coming from an adult, however, the affront is even more severe. But teasing or ridiculing that emanates from a parent has an impact that is truly devastating.

A parent does not have to actually belittle a child's interests to cause deep emotional wounds. Even if the parent only disregards, ignores or is apathetic towards a child's interests, the damage is profound. The message read by the child is, "Your toys (games, friends, hobbies, and collections) are of no interest to me because I don't really care about you, either." The blow to the child's self-esteem is crushing.

On the other hand, it boosts the child's self-esteem immeasurably if parents take a genuine interest in all that is important to the child. This is so because the message to the child is, "I care so much about you that anything or anyone who is important to you is something or someone whom I want to get to know better."

But, some might ask, am I not being dishonest if I show interest in some silly game or childish preoccupation that really does not interest me? Letting your daughter show you her doll collection doesn't require you to have a fascination with dolls. All it requires is that you have an interest in your daughter. Listening to your son's description of how he caught a moth does not require you to be fascinated by insects. It only requires that you highly regard your son.

Children love to talk about their experiences to any adult who has the patience to listen. Perhaps that is one of the main reasons why children usually enjoy coming for individual therapy (after the first appointment, which may be slightly stressful). But if they were given a choice, children would almost always prefer to talk to their parents.

I was once treating a single young woman for mild depression. When I would ask her about her early childhood experiences, she usually skirted the issue, giving me clear signals that she was not ready to discuss that subject. In the middle of one session, after a few months of therapy, she made a passing reference to her father. I seized upon this opportunity to again try to elicit background information. "Could you tell me a little about your relationship with your father?" I asked, gently.

Slowly and softly she described a very estranged relationship with her father, whom she saw as cold, distant, and disinterested. Then she paused and looked down at the floor. There was a brief silence, during which I understood she was wrestling within herself with the dilemma of whether or not to share with me what she was thinking. I gave her the time and space to make her decision. Finally, she looked up. Her reddened eyes were filled with tears. Haltingly, almost in a whisper, she revealed, "One year, at the *seder* — for the *afikomen* — I asked my father for a conversation."

4. Set realistic goals and standards for your children.

A favorite children's book asks, "How big is big? How small is small?" The book goes on to demonstrate through pictures that judgments regarding size are, of course, relative. The lesson is that you need a frame of reference or a standard before you can measure anything.

In Judaism, as well, we know that the fulfillment of many

mitzvos is determined by *shiurim*, or standard measures, for eating, sleeping, walking, etc. Whether or not we have satisfied the Torah requirements for certain *mitzvos* depends upon whether or not the halachic standards have been met.

Similarly, whether or not our children receive our approval depends upon whether or not they have lived up to the standards which we set for their behavior and performance. If we expect a 100 or an A, then anything less will meet with our disapproval and dissatisfaction. If our standards are lower, then it will be easier for our children to win our approval. Setting appropriate standards for children, Harav Shlomo Wolbe writes, "is a major principle of parenting. It is forbidden to demand from a child things which, as a result of his age and development, he can not understand or fulfill."[2]

On the other hand, if our standards are too low, then it will be too easy for our children to win our approval. Consequently, they will not need to make any effort to grow, stretch, and fulfill their potential. Optimally, our standards for our children should be low enough so that they are reachable, but high enough so that our children will be motivated. The following case history will illustrate the importance of achieving the correct balance.

🏵 The Case of Yossi[*]

Yossi always tried to please his parents, but no matter how well he did on his report card, his father always asked why the grades were not higher. After all, Yossi's older brothers had received all A's; why should he not do as well? No matter how carefully Yossi cleaned his room, his mother always managed to find something out of place or not quite tidy enough. Even socially, Yossi did not meet his parents' expectations. His friends were not bad, but he often heard his parents complain that they wished

---

2. My own translation of *Zeriah Ubinyan Bechinuch* (Hebrew) by Harav Shlomo Wolbe (Yerushaylayim Feldheim Publishers, 1995), p.11.

* Not his real name.

he would befriend boys who were "better," even though "better" was never clearly defined.

By the time Yossi entered his teens, he was not doing very well academically or socially; and it should not surprise anyone that he did not feel very good about himself. He did discover, however, that he could temporarily forget his frustrations and feelings of inadequacy by "having fun."

At first, having fun was limited to meeting friends at the local pizza shop; but quickly he graduated from pizza to pool and from malteds to movies. By this time his parents were appalled at his behavior, style and mode of dress, and the company he was keeping. They expressed their disappointment and disapproval openly and with vehemence. Yossi, however, had become desensitized to his parents' criticism. He acted as if he did not care what his parents thought about him because, quite frankly, he no longer did care.

After a number of hostile confrontations between Yossi and his parents, Yossi threatened to leave home. His parents' worst fears were realized when Yossi was expelled from yeshivah. The number of his infractions had escalated until the yeshivah administration felt it could no longer give Yossi "one more chance."

Yossi's acting out and his rebellious behavior were definitely rooted in low self-esteem and feelings of inadequacy. His defiant attitude won him notoriety at yeshivah and gave him a false sense of bravado. His tough-guy exterior was only a cover up for his underlying feelings of worthlessness, and it took many years of patient outreach to bring Yossi back into the mainstream of Jewish life.

In Yossi's case, the downward spiral of disobedience, disrespect, and disregard for parental authority was caused by his feelings of hopelessness and low self-esteem. But the feelings of low self-esteem originated from the unrealistic expectations and impossible standards set for him by his parents. Had the goals Yossi's parents set been based on his abilities rather than on their dreams and fantasies, the entire debacle of Yossi's odyssey off the *derech* (Torah path), and then finally back, may have been avoided.

As Rav Wolbe explains, "More than once we met parents who attach great importance to those things which they lacked in their own childhoods ... But the unfortunate child has a natural inclination in another direction ... What ensues is that what the child is good at, he is not allowed and what he is given, he does not want. Consequently he fails."[3]

For example, Rav Wolbe adds, "There are some normal boys who because of their natures are not cut out to learn *Gemara* for all three *sedarim* of the day in yeshivah high school."[4]

Considering the devastating impact of Yossi's parents' unrealistic expectations, we have to ask why his parents made so tragic an error. Why could they not see how destructive their high standards were for their son? Why would they not be more accepting of Yossi's limitations?

The root causes of Yossi's difficulties go back beyond the parenting he received. They go back to the parenting his parents received. Both of Yossi's parents came from homes where praise was doled out more sparingly than water during a drought. Both of them grew up in environments where excellence was not only expected but also demanded, and both of them experienced situations where anything less than perfection was treated as failure.

Both of Yossi's parents were highly successful, highly accomplished individuals. But, coming from such homes, each harbored underlying feelings of inadequacy. Their own constant successes helped allay the nagging doubts they had about themselves, but without a continuous flow of accomplishments to reinforce their fractured self-images, they were vulnerable to feelings of insecurity about themselves.

As long as their children were at the top of their classes, everything was fine. However, as soon as one child failed to

---

3. My own translation, op. cit., p. 30.
4. Loc. cit. p. 48.
.

meet their unrealistic standard of excellence, the parents began to doubt themselves and felt compelled to badger Yossi, crushing his ego and passing their torch of low self-esteem on to the next generation.

The lesson to be learned from Yossi's tragic example is that, frequently, the main reason parents set unrealistic standards for their children is that they have actually set unrealistic standards for themselves. If we as parents can learn to be more accepting of our own limitations and more aware of our own imperfections, we can then learn to be more accepting of our children. This, in turn, can help build within our children that most essential and vital character trait: self-esteem.

Building self-esteem in children is a long-term project for parents. It requires considerable time, patience, and attention at all stages of a child's development. But since there is no greater gift parents can bestow upon their children, all of the effort to build self-esteem is more than worthwhile.

Ultimately, if we raise our children to feel good about themselves, they will become better students, workers, friends, and spouses — and they will be far better equipped to build self-esteem in our grandchildren.

5

Candyman for a Day:
Teaching Hakaras Hatov

If middos *were politicians, millions of dollars would have already been spent on public-opinion polls to determine which* middah *is currently in vogue. But even without the "benefit" of such surveys, it is safe to assume that the* middah *of* hakaras hatov, *thankfulness, would top the list of* middos *parents most want to instill in their children.*

Why is thankfulness so favored by parents and educators alike? And why does our children's lack of this trait cause us so much frustration and disappointment? The answer lies in the very name of our people. Let me explain.

The Jewish people are called Hebrews, Israelites, and "the chosen people." But the name most commonly used now and throughout history has always been "Jews." Why are we referred to that way? Why do we refer to ourselves that way? Where, for that matter, did the term "Jew" originate?

Upon the death of Shlomo Hamelech, *the kingdom of Israel was divided into the Kingdom of Judah, comprising the tribes of Yehudah and Binyamin, and the Kingdom of Israel, comprised of the other ten tribes. The Kingdom of Israel was exiled before the Kingdom of Judah and was not heard from since.*

All Jewish people today, therefore, descend from the Kingdom of Judah, and thus its people are called Jews.

The Kingdom of Judah was named after the progenitor of the largest of the two tribes, Yehudah, the fourth son of Yaakov Avinu. *Why was the name Yehudah given to this son? The Torah tells us:*

> *"And she [Leah] conceived again and gave birth to a son and she said, 'This time I will thank [odeh] Hashem,' therefore she called his name Yehudah..."* (Bereishis 29:35).

Rashi comments, "This time I will give thanks because I took more than my share. Now I truly have for what to be thankful."

Leah knew through prophecy that there were destined to be twelve tribes of Israel. Since Yaakov had four wives, that meant that each wife could expect to mother three of the sacred tribes of Israel. So when Leah gave birth to her fourth son, she was overwhelmed with gratitude. She eternally preserved her appreciation in the name she chose for that son, Yehudah.

Throughout the ages, the hallmark of our people has always been our keen appreciation for the benefits we receive from Hashem and our fellow man. Our name serves to remind us of this noble calling, even when this middah, *at times, becomes tarnished.*

The following chapter contains a personal anecdote which not only highlights how often children today are lacking in the middah *of* hakaras hatov, *but also suggests why this* middah *may not be as prevalent now as it once was — and should be.*

WHEN I THINK OF THE "CANDYMAN" IN *SHUL*, MY MIND conjures up patriarchal images of *zaidie*-types with flowing white beards, soft puffy palms and eyes that twinkle with close to a century of experience. As a man who is barely middle aged, I don't quite see myself fitting the bill.

In spite of this poor type-casting, a few years ago I did experiment with the role of candyman for a day, on *Simchas Torah*. The initiative came from my then 4-year-old son, Yeshaya, who began working on me shortly after *Rosh Hashanah*, "*Tatty*, why don't you buy candies to give out to the kids in *shul* on *Simchas Torah*?" he asked, almost rebukingly.

"We have a candyman in *shul*, already. He gives you a candy every *Shabbos*," I replied defensively.

"But Tatty, on *Simchas Torah* kids are supposed to get *lots* of nosh, not just one piece!"

"We'd feel special if all the kids had to come over to you to get a candy," chimed in then 8-year-old Sarah with that special smile daughters reserve for manipulating their fathers.

And so it went until *Hoshana Rabbah*, when Sarah played her trump card: "Tatty, if you want, I'll take Yeshaya with me to the candy store to buy the candies for you to give out on *Simchas Torah*. O.K.?"

So I was drafted. I had been reluctant to play the role for admittedly selfish reasons. How would my performance be received by the other men in the *shul* where we *davened* at that time? Would I be the butt of their jokes, however harmless? But by the time Sarah returned with her two-pound bag of hard candies, I was already looking forward to my new role.

My children decided that I should divide the candies into three bags: one for the *hakafos* at night, one for the *hakafos* the next morning — and one for them to keep for after *Simchas Torah*. I was beginning to feel that I'd been had!

All during *Shemini Atzeres*, the pre-*Simchas Torah* excitement was growing by geometric proportions. My children started prepping me like Olympic coaches, giving me strict and detailed instructions regarding the procedures for candy distribution.

"Give only one candy to each child."

"Be sure you don't let anyone take two."

"Don't forget to give the girls as well as the boys."

"Wait until the second *hakafah* before you give out any candies."

"Keep the candies in your pockets so you won't have to go back and forth to your coat."

"If I see a friend who has a baby brother or sister at home, I'll tell you and then you can give two."

By the time *hakafos* started, even I was eager to begin giving out the candies. My strategy (or M.O., as detectives refer to it) was simply to approach each child I passed and extend my hand, with a candy. Although I followed the same procedure with each child, the responses and reactions elicited from the children — not to mention those of their parents — varied greatly. What began as an effort to simply add joy to *Simchas Torah* quickly turned into a Rorschach test of attitudes, *middos*, and plain ol' courtesy.

Some of the children simply froze. They stared at the candy in my hand, then looked at my face, back at the candy and otherwise remained motionless. Others also cast a quick glance at a nearby parent. It was only after I directly asked if they would like the candy that they took it from my hand, albeit gingerly.

Other children seemed to have been training all year for this "event." I had barely opened my hand before those children literally swooped over, grabbed the candy, and darted halfway across the *shul*. A variation of this response was to scoop the candy out of my palm and immediately look away, as if nothing had happened.

After a while I couldn't help but wonder: *What happened to "Thank you," "Sh'koach," or even a smile? Did these children expect me to be giving out candies? Did I owe it to them? Were the candies too small, perhaps, to warrant any old-fashioned appreciation?*

To be fair, there were some children who did not run or look away. And with a little coaching of, "What do you say?" I did manage to eke out a few inaudible grunts which I wholeheartedly accepted. Occasionally, one or two children even volunteered a whispered word of gratitude.

But then, I thought, most of the children were under 9 or 10 years old — As they get older, they'll learn to behave differently.

❧ The Parents' Reactions

And then there were the parents. First they approached me with their requests. Some were almost apologetic, others were more assertive.

"Do you, perhaps, have another candy? My little one was in the bathroom before when you gave one to his brother."

"Could I take one for my daughter? She already went home with my wife, but I'll save it for her for tomorrow."

"You wouldn't happen to have a red one, would you? Maybe my son could exchange this?"

I was more than happy to comply with their requests. After all, my purpose was to please, so I appreciated people letting me know exactly what they wanted. Nevertheless, I was a bit surprised when parents walked away, offering little more than a nod. At this point, I felt like saying, "The least you could do is say, 'thank you.'"

But I decided to maintain my silence. These parents are surely distracted by the commotion of *hakafos*. Surely in a less hectic setting, they would be much more appreciative.

Had my experiences as candyman for a day ended there, I probably would not have been sufficiently perturbed to transcribe these events. But as the *hakafos* progressed, I encountered much more unsettling parental responses.

One parent began to chide me, in harsh tones. "You know, all that sugar is unhealthy and bad for their teeth. I try not to give my children candy at home, and I'm sure there are other parents here who feel the same way!"

Another parent was more critical. "I know these candies have a *hechsher*, but not everyone relies on that particular *Rav*. If you're giving them out in *shul*, you should have selected candies with a more reliable *hechsher* that everyone would accept. I don't really know the details, but I heard there could be a question that his *hechsherim* — " (The Rav referred to was one of the most highly respected *poskim* in the New York area.)

One parent was openly antagonistic. "Are *you* the one giving out these candies?" began the interrogation, as this parent held up one of my candies. Although I wanted to deny it at this point, I nevertheless found the courage to nod.

"Well, you really should stop! Do you know how dangerous these candies are?"

I naively thought this parent was referring to the time bombs of tooth decay that I was so ruthlessly planting around the *shul*. But this angry parent blamed me for much more serious recklessness.

"Don't you realize that these candies could get caught in the children's throats, *chas v'shalom*, and they could choke? Believe me, I saw it happen once." This last sentence was uttered in a tone of authority matching, "I even read about it in *Reader's Digest!*"

My level of irritation finally passed the threshold of restraint. "The regular candyman gives those same candies out every *Shabbos*," I pleaded. "Why don't you tell *him* to stop? I'm only giving these candies out tonight."

This parent then surprised me by answering my question. "He's an older man and probably wouldn't listen to me, anyway. But you're right, someone should speak to him. Nevertheless, it is still worse to give out these candies on *Simchas Torah*, when children are more likely to be running around than they would be on a regular *Shabbos*."

Now, don't feel sorry for the children in that *shul*. They did not miss out on receiving a treat from this candyman the following year. I bought lollipops (with soft sticks) that were endorsed by another *hashgachah*. So, my efforts to brighten the *Simchas Torah* celebration in *shul* the next year met with less disapproval, opposition, and criticism.

I couldn't help reflecting on the varied responses I had encountered. The children in that *shul* were, for the most part, unappreciative. While there were some notable exceptions, most of the children treated me with a "Well, it's your job!"-attitude. Of course, my experiment quickly led me to trace the roots of this attitude, straight back to their parents.

We hear a lot today about placing greater emphasis on *middos* in Torah education. We read articles about the weakening of adherence to the *bein adom l'chaveiro*, interpersonal conduct, among children. And rare is a parenting workshop, conference or gathering that doesn't decry the lack of *derech eretz* among our youth today. But who is really to blame?

True, children don't automatically pick up *middos tovos* that they see their parents have. But one thing is certain: If parents are ungrateful, unappreciative, or rude, their children will definitely imitate *that* behavior.

Perhaps parents could begin to correct their children's *middos* by improving their own. When people adopt an attitude of, "Well, it's your job," they generally treat a favor as if it were deserved. After all, they reason, if he is paid to serve me, then I don't owe him any appreciation. This attitude allows people to criticize "unsatisfactory" service to their hearts' content, while permitting "satisfactory" service to go by without any acknowledgement whatsoever. One example: When was the last time you sat at a wedding dinner and said, "Thank you," to the waiter?

To some, the idea of expressing gratitude for paid services sounds farfetched. But there are so many examples of *gedolim* who have gone far out of their way to thank the most highly paid Jewish and non-Jewish workers, such as physicians and surgeons, or lower-status workers, such as aides or orderlies, for their services.

One need not look outside of the home for opportunities to model *hakaras hatov* for children. Within the family itself are countless often-missed chances for parents to teach appreciation by example. Does the father thank the mother for serving supper each night? Does the mother express gratitude to the father for chores he performs at home? Do the parents thank the children for things the children do? If we want to raise children who appreciate what they receive from others we may just have to set the proper example ourselves.

We parents can begin by exercising our own appreciation muscles whenever we receive service from someone, whether or not it is that person's job. Another way we might try to help counteract the "*es kumt mir*" attitude is to become "candyman for a day" this year. I really don't think children would object to a few additional candymen on *Simchas Torah*. By practicing this form of giving, the new candymen may come to be more appreciative about receiving. The results may then help them to set the proper example for their children to learn the true meaning of *hakaras hatov*.

6

My Child the Collector:
Two Sides of the Coin
of Tzedakah Campaigns

*Many teacher-training workshops, seminars, and confer-
ences have been devoted to developing curricula for teaching*
middos *in our yeshivos and Bais Yaakov schools. The educational institutions in our community are working hard at designing programs to instill proper* middos *in our children.*

*But children learn more by doing than by listening. That is
why all successful teachers know that children must actively
participate in the learning process, not just passively absorb
knowledge. If this is true for* chumash *and* halachah, *it is even
more vital for the learning of proper* middos, *character traits.*

*While all of our instruction is important and well inten-
tioned, however, we may be undermining our own efforts to*

teach middos *if we allow children to participate in projects which bring out improper* middos.

Children's tzedakah-*collection campaigns are designed to inculcate an appreciation for the* mitzvah *of* tzedakah. *Unfortunately, these campaigns can, at times, become a vehicle for acquiring the wrong* middos.

There are more than two sides to the coin of children's collection campaigns. Whichever side of the coin you are on, you should at least consider the opportunity such campaigns provide for parents to teach, or neglect, the middos *of their children.*

✑ᔆ ᔆ✑

"THERE THEY ARE. THEY JUST SPOTTED ME. IT'S TOO LATE to turn around or go another way. Now they're approaching me. Another few seconds and I'll be surrounded. Here they come!"

Are these the last-minute thoughts of a celebrity being pursued by a band of photographers? No, not at all. These are the private apprehensions of many a sidewalk pedestrian being approached by a dozen yeshivah boys and Bais Yaakov girls armed with *pushkas* and receipt books.

Nowadays you hardly need a calendar to know when *Yom Tov* is coming. All you have to do is check the local street corner after school hours. If you see a cluster of eager children waving receipt books in people's faces you know *Yom Tov* is almost here.

But do we ever stop and think whether this development is really welcomed and whether or not it enhances our children's *middos*? After careful consideration, as well as consultation with Rabbanim, what follows is one man's point of view, which just may be a view that is shared by others.

As has been mentioned, it is often argued that seasoned *tzedakah* campaigns teach children to appreciate the importance of *tzedakah*. If so, we should question whether that goal is always met.

Let's eavesdrop on a typical sidewalk conversation between two fifth graders: "I think you need to collect $50 to get the walkie-talkie set. That's what I really want."

"Oh, I got that set after last year's *tzedakah* drive. It broke in a week. They give such junky prizes for *Keren Hachesed* Fund. I'm just going to collect $10 so I can get the key chain. That, for sure, won't break."

"Yeah. Maybe I shouldn't work so hard either, collecting for *Keren Hachesed.*"

"I'm going to work hard for the *Aniyei Ircha* drive this year. They give out really good stuff and you don't have to collect as much money to win the top prizes as you do for *Keren Hachesed!*"

Yes, children do learn from these *tzedakah* campaigns. But they may learn more about which groups give out the best prizes than they do about the importance of *tzedakah*.

Some proponents of using yeshivah and Bais Yaakov students as volunteers argue that children acquire a sense of responsibility through their participation in these *tzedakah* campaigns. The children see themselves as sharing in the community obligation to support the poor and needy. Even though these students have little or no money of their own, they can still contribute to these worthy organizations by collecting money from others.

But do these *tzedakah* campaigns always encourage responsibility? Let's eavesdrop on another conversation, this time in the hallway of a Bais Yaakov.

"When is the last day?"

"I think *Morah* said all the money's gotta be in by Friday."

"I don't think I'll make it."

"Waddaya mean? All ya gotta do is bring whatever you have by Friday."

"But I don't know where it is. I know I put it away at home in a safe place. I just can't remember where I put it."

"Why don't you ask your parents to help you look for it?"

"I'm afraid they'll yell at me. I lost some of the money I collected once before and my parents said I better not let it happen again."

While these conversations are hypothetical, the circumstances are not. Anyone who organizes *tzedakah* campaigns in elementary schools will admit that *some* of the money collected at *every* drive is lost, misplaced or forgotten. It may not be a large percentage, but it does occur with disturbing frequency.

"Hey, what's all the fuss?" some readers may wonder. "What's so terrible about kids going around with *pushkas* and receipt books for a few weeks a year? So what if they don't always learn responsibility? They're having fun and the yeshivos make a few extra dollars. What could be wrong with that?"

Plenty. Let's take a look at what these fund-raising campaigns might really be teaching our children. Doubtless, many principals give fiery warnings to their students not to succumb to the behaviors outlined in the following list, as it could tarnish the reputations of their schools. In spite of these severe and well-intentioned appeals for proper *middos* prior to the campaign, just take a look around on your street corner or inside your *shul* and judge the efficiency of prewarnings for yourself.

• **Disregard for *tefillah*, prayer.** A *shul* or *beis medrash* is supposed to be a place primarily for *davening* or learning. During a *tzedakah* campaign, *shuls* are sometimes transformed into collection centers for our junior fund-raisers. At times, they will not only disregard their own *tefillos* but they will disturb others as they make their rounds. This one jingles the change in his *pushka*, making it sound like a *Purim gragger*; that one waves receipt books disrespectfully in the faces of men, some of whom are still *davening Shemoneh Esrei*; still another collector combines both techniques by jingling a fistful of change as he waves his receipt book.

• **Aggressiveness training.** I always used to think that a refined demeanor, what we call *aidelkeit*, was a universally valued Torah virtue. But one day the *menahel* of an elementary school advised a father, "You really should try to toughen him up." The *menahal* was responding to the father's concern about the excessive use of corporal punishment on other boys in the yeshivah, and the impact it was having on his son. The following year the father registered his son in a different yeshivah because he also believed *aidelkeit* is a Torah value, albeit not a universally recognized one.

Perhaps in many communities, children gently and modestly display their *pushkas* and receipt books to passersby on the street. But in some neighborhoods that I've visited, children armed with *pushkas* and receipt books surround, jostle, and otherwise disturb every adult who is not in uniform or walking a dog.

Furthermore, since the more experienced would-be-prize-winners have found that change purses are not bottomless and that only the first few "in line" will be "served," they quickly learn that only those who push ahead of the competition will prevail. This may be a valuable lesson for the business world but, quite frankly, it's a lesson I prefer my children did not learn.

When it comes to questions of *chinuch* and child rearing it is best not to make decisions based on purely subjective, gut reactions. So although it struck me as poor parenting to allow my children to "go collecting," I decided to consult Torah authorities before setting any official policy in my home.

Since I was dealing more with *hashkafah* than *halachah*, I felt free to consult with more than one Rav.

The first Rav, Grand Rabbi Levi Yitzchok Horowitz, *shlita*, the Bostoner Rebbe, asked, "Will you or your wife accompany your children as they go collecting?"

I replied that for these *tzedakah* campaigns, the children generally go around the neighborhood on their own.

"How will you know whether your children are properly safeguarding the money they collect if you do not supervise them?" the Rebbe wanted to know. I had no adequate reply.

The second Rav, Rabbi Eliezer Ginsburg, *shlita*, Rav of Agudas Yisroel Snif Zichron Shmuel and Rosh Kollel of the Mirrer Yeshivah, seemed to weigh the pros and cons carefully. He asked how I felt and what my considerations were. He wanted to know why I felt that my children *should* participate.

I explained that all of the other children "go collecting" and eagerly look forward to the prizes. If I deny my children the opportunity to join in the fun, how could I possibly justify it to them?

There was a long pause. Then Rabbi Ginsburg said, "I'll tell you what I have advised other parents. I told them to ask their children to tell them what the average amount collected was, and that the parents should then write out a check to the organization for that amount. In this way the children do not lose out on their prize. But you are right to be concerned about them collecting in the streets. Explain your objections to your children and they will surely accept them."

In essence, that is how I resolved this dilemma in my home. My purpose here is not to imply that every Rav would agree with the *Rabbanim* with whom I consulted. My purpose is only to point out that, as parents, we do have alternatives to having our children go around collecting.

❧ Addressing the Other Side of the Coin

The issue of young children collecting *tzedakah* in the street is not a simple two-sided coin, but rather a multifaceted gemstone. Reactions to the view I have expressed could range from surprise and disappointment to dismay and outrage. Because some will object to what I have stated thus far, I would like to address specific arguments which may be raised against my contention that the current collection campaigns clamoring for our coins on every corner of the community instill negative *middos* in our children.

Some might claim that enlisting children to collect *tzedakah* in the street is a time-honored practice which has been endorsed by leading *Gedolim* of previous generations. In fact, it has been practiced for so long that it may even have achieved the status of a *minhag Yisrael* — an accepted Jewish tradition.

To address this objection, it should be noted that there is a phenomenon, which is not new, called "getting out of hand." Simply stated, even honorable practices with sacred origins can sometimes be taken to excess. One illustration should suffice: Initially, it was an accepted practice to dress deceased people in expensive clothing before burial. Although this and other lavish expenditures during mourning had become the norm, these customs were eventually modified after they had gotten out of hand. (See *Moed Katan* 27a and 27b.) Similarly, I believe that reforms are now needed in the practice, however time honored, of children taking to the streets to collect *tzedakah*.

Others could argue that just because there is *potential* danger to our children's *middos* by collecting publicly does not mean that we should modify the practice any more than we would prohibit our children from lighting a Chanukah *menorah* because of *potential* safety hazards.

This viewpoint only strengthens my case, because I seldom see these junior collectors accompanied by their parents as they roam the streets and *batei medrash* of my neighborhood. Perhaps if more parents chaperoned their *gabbaim*-in-training, just as they oversee the lighting of Chanukah *menorahs*, we would see less change bouncing out of young pockets and getting lost as the youngsters run about their rounds. In this way, all of the money which had been donated would actually reach the intended recipients. Additionally, the rudeness to which some people are subjected would be eliminated.

Finally, some might contend that collection campaigns are the best vehicle for children to learn about the important value of *tzedakah*, so for all their shortcomings, these campaigns should not be tampered with, in any way.

Enlisting children to solicit funds does not automatically teach children the value of *tzedakah*. As noted, it may even teach children bad *middos*. Among the more obvious problems is that on more than one occasion, children have been tempted by the astronomical (to them) sums of money in their pockets to "borrow" some for nosh or other personal uses. Without careful, close adult supervision, such misappropriation of funds is inevitable.

These youthful indiscretions make the most irrefutable argument for collection-campaign reform.

Children do need to learn about *tzedakah* through active participation, just as they learn about all other *mitzvos*. But revisions are sorely needed in our current collection code for children.

A good place to start would be to require closer parental supervision. If that is not possible or practical, then the campaigns could be focused on raising the funds from the children themselves, so that they can learn the true meaning and joy of giving to others.

Whether you encourage or discourage your child from participating in the current *tzedakah* collection campaigns which are being sponsored in our communities, you need to consider the impact of your decision on your children. The position you and your spouse take on this issue is but one of many which will have a profound impact on one of the most important aspects of your child's development: his or her *middos*.

PART THREE:
Establishing Structure and Setting Limits

7

Shabbos:
The Benefits of Family
Routine for Children

It is practically impossible for adults to imagine what a toddler experiences in a world almost devoid of language. As adults, we communicate all of our ideas, feelings, and information through language. Without fluency in language, a small child experiences the world as an unstructured, confusing, and unintelligible place.

Parents try to establish structure for children. Imposing order and routine help greatly in all of the many tasks parents need to manage for and with their children. But as much as these routines help the parents, they help the children even more.

While young children may resist structure when it is initially imposed, they nevertheless welcome the predictability and order it brings to their otherwise random lives. Structure gives children a feeling of reassurance which supports and encourages their growth and development.

The most natural and common structures parents provide for their children are the routines of family life. Mealtimes, nap-times, and bedtimes anchor the child's day in a way which is vital to a child's sense of security.

One of the most valuable routines for children is the weekly observance of Shabbos. An understanding of the benefits that Shabbos offers to small children can help us to appreciate the advantages of establishing other structures in their tender years.

～◈◈～

J UST AS *SHABBOS* CAN BE DIVIDED INTO STAGES AND PHASES which may differ in degree, theme, mood or intensity, *Erev Shabbos* also has its own subdivisions. Perhaps the best-known and most respected (and feared) stage of *Erev Shabbos* is the final stage, ushered in with those familiar words, often uttered in shrill tones of urgency: "It's almost *Shabbos!*" From that signal until the onset of *Shabbos*, the pace of preparations picks up steadily and the sun seems to descend more rapidly; voices are sometimes raised and expectations for what can still be accomplished before *Shabbos* are sharply reduced.

During one such *Erev Shabbos* finale, my family and I began our usual race against the clock. Everyone over the age of 4 was automatically conscripted into compulsory *Shabbos* preparation and everyone's leisurely weekday gait was replaced by a more frantic pace. In the midst of this flurry of activity, my then 3-year-old son, Yeshaya, rushed up to me and demanded to know, "It's *Shabbos* now?"

"No. But it's almost *Shabbos!*" I answered as I flew by. I was down the hall by the time I completed the sentence. A short while later, Yeshaya repeated his question and received a similar reply, a few decibels louder.

What I had neither the time nor the patience to realize then was that my son was feeling totally swept up in the family's collective anticipation of *Shabbos*. Freed from the concerns of responsibility, he was able to experience this anticipation with unadulterated glee. His excitement was marred only by his undeveloped, 3-year-old's awareness of time. He was frustrated by his inability to discern just how much longer it was until *Shabbos*.

So Yeshaya took what must have been an enormous risk — considering my volatile emotional state at the time — and he approached me again a few minutes later. "Tatty, Tatty," he pleaded desperately, "when is it *Shabbos*?!"

"Soon, very soon!" came my wholly inadequate reply. A lengthy diatribe was prevented only by the lateness of the hour.

Later on that evening when the commotion of the *Erev Shabbos* finale had been replaced by the serenity of the *Shabbos* table, I began to reflect on the implications of my hallway encounter with Yeshaya.

In adult terminology, the proper answer to his third question would have been, "Approximately 37 minutes." But to a 3-year-old, 37 minutes means about the same time as "37 months" or "37 miles." Three-year-olds are simply not able to comprehend time or distance in quantifiable, adult terms.

Most of us cannot even imagine what life would be like without an awareness of time, a perception which we take for granted. Of course, in a spiritual sense, there is no limit to the sensitivity to time an adult can achieve through prolonged and diligent Torah study and observance. But since the most elementary level of grasping the concepts of minutes, hours, and weeks usually comes in the fourth or fifth year of life, most adults cannot remember what life was like before these fundamental lessons were learned.

Just try to imagine a trip by car to a beloved relative whom you have not seen in many years. Your preparation for the trip is effortless, as you are buoyed along by your eager anticipation of the long-awaited reunion. Once you are finally on the road, you follow the travel directions with the precision of a watchmaker.

"Take Interstate 91, north to Route 86, east," you repeat to yourself as your car gobbles up the miles. After 20 or so miles you begin to wonder, "How many miles on 91 is it until we hit 86?" After a half-hour, you wonder out loud.

"The directions don't say," comes the helper's reply. After an hour, everyone begins to wonder if Route 86 was passed, and accusations for not being more observant are now exchanged between the driver and passengers.

After two hours on Interstate 91, without the aid of maps or the reassurance of a gas-station attendant, you would probably begin to experience the same frustration of uncertainty that 3-year-old children live with every day.

Reassurances of, "You can have the candy in an hour," "Mommy is coming back at 2:30," or "*Bubbie* and *Zaidie* will be here on Tuesday," are as useless to a 3-year-old as a sextant would be to a lost motorist.

Small children never really know what to expect or when to expect it — but don't be fooled by their apparent calm. They are constantly groping, struggling, and searching for any clues that can help them order, structure, and comprehend their somewhat chaotic worlds, lives devoid of an awareness of time.

Their thirst and yearning for structure, order, and predictability are familiar to anyone who has experienced the joy of playing with preschool children. The games they enjoy most are always those that involve an inordinate amount of repetition. While this may bore an adult, it offers an oasis of security, stability, and reassurance for the very young child.

In short, small children look for any recognizable order in life which they can use to orient themselves in a world of time, until they develop their own awareness of the units of time.

"No, Mommy! I wanted the milk *before* the chocolate!" a 3-year-old will complain.

"What's the difference?" Mother protests. But her child cannot possibly explain that the routine of milk first and chocolate second provides a tiny source of security to a 3-year-old.

Robbing a child of that security would be tantamount to stripping a prisoner of his calendar and wrist watch. Just as that prisoner would pay greater attention to the setting of the sun or the changing of the guards, so too small children become preoccupied and seemingly obsessed with routine and repetition.

So how can parents assist young children in their struggle to bring order to their lives? The best way is to provide and impose structure, limits, and routine — all within reason, of course. One of the best ways to provide that for children is with rituals. Rituals are so important for children that, in addition to religiously meaningful rituals taught to them by their parents, children often create their own rituals. Milk first and chocolate second, a drink of water before going to sleep, or avoiding cracks in the sidewalk are some typical examples of children's rituals.

Thus, the repetitive daily *mitzvos* — *berachos*, *negal vasser*, and *krias shema*, for instance — provide children with invaluable signposts which help them navigate through the world of time without a mature awareness of time. Even before reaching the age of *chinuch* (according to any halachic opinion), observing and imitating their parents' performance of daily *mitzvos* can give small children many anchors to balance themselves in the waves of temporal confusion.

Perhaps the greatest temporal anchor, for people of all ages, is *Shabbos*. That island of tranquility and sanctity provides reassurance and hope to adults as well as children. As the humorous bumper sticker proclaims, "Hang in there: *Shabbos* is coming!"

One day passes like another to a small child who has not yet learned the meaning of "Monday" and "Tuesday." But *Shabbos* is so unmistakably unique that even preschool children can recognize its presence.

When Yeshaya's older sister, Sarah, was 3 years old, she overheard a discussion of a plan to spend *Shabbos* with *Bubbie* and *Zaidie*. "When are we going?" she asked with unabashed excitement.

"Not for another two weeks," came the reply.

"But I mean, how long until we go?" she persisted, showing me how much off target my answer had been.

"Not this next *Shabbos*, but the *Shabbos* after that," I explained, trying a different tack.

"You mean in two *Shabboses?*" Sarah asked, to confirm the date.

"Yes," I explained, "we'll be going to *Bubbie* and *Zaidie* in two *Shabboses.*"

Sarah walked off with a perturbed look, shaking her head, as if to say, "Then why didn't you say so in the first place!?"

I had learned my lesson. I learned that well before children understand the meaning of days and weeks, they can grasp the difference between weekday and *Shabbos*. It is a distinction which can help them, on their level, with their developmental needs.

So, returning to that *Erev Shabbos* finale described above, when Yeshaya looked up at me as my wife lit *Shabbos* candles, and he asked with confidence in his voice and a smile on his lips, "*Now* it's *Shabbos;* right, Tatty?" I learned my lesson all over again.

8

Preventing a Chol Hamoed Fiasco: How to Entertain Children Successfully

The Torah tells us, "The inclination of a person's heart is evil from his youth" (Bereishis 8:21). *Rashi explains, "From the time a child moves to leave his or her mother's womb, the* yetzer hara, *or evil inclination, is placed into him or her."*

The yetzer hara *represents a person's physical lusts, desires and impulses. The* yetzer tov, *or good inclination, which enters a child at the age of maturity, represents a person's self-control, frustration tolerance and spiritual strivings.*

Young children have a seemingly unsatiable desire for the physical pleasures of recreation and entertainment. They would play forever if they were given the opportunity.

Children do need to have fun. Parents must provide recreational opportunities for their children. These are necessary for the children's proper physical and emotional growth and development. As Harav Shlomo Wolbe emphasizes[1]:

> *"Playing is a very serious matter for a child ... One who disturbs a child at play is actually stealing something from the child."*
>
> *But parents must also provide proper limits, otherwise even a long-awaited* Chol Hamoed *excursion can turn into a fiasco.*

But the need for parentally imposed limits is nowhere as prominently pronounced as it is in the area of entertainment. This chapter will spell out the significance of developing structure and setting limits which will help enable children become happily adjusted and contented rather than discontented, disgruntled and unappreciative.

LET US EAVESDROP ON THE COHEN[*] HOUSEHOLD ABOUT A month before *Yom Tov*: Mr. Cohen, a yeshivah alumnus, is now a computer analyst for a large data-processing firm. He has just returned home from *Ma'ariv* after his *daf yomi shiur*, and he is settling down at the kitchen table with his wife for a little snack.

The conversation leapfrogs from topic to topic and then, referring to the upcoming *Yom Tov*, Mr. Cohen muses, "I think I have a few vacation days coming to me."

"Do you think you could take off on *Chol Hamoed*?" Mrs. Cohen asks. "The kids would be thrilled if we could all go out together. *Yom Tov* is still four weeks away, and Shloimie is already asking what plans we're making for *Chol Hamoed*."

"Well, it's not going to be easy," Mr. Cohen replies with a deep sigh. "So much piles up at the office over the two days of *Yom Tov*.

---

1. My own translation of *Zeriah Ubinyan Bechinuch* (Hebrew), op. cit. p.16.
* Not their real name

But, I suppose, it's worth the effort so we can give the kids a good time on *Chol Hamoed*." Finally the Cohens decide to go "somewhere special" with the children on the first day of *Chol Hamoed*.

Three weeks later, Mrs. Cohen is busy cleaning for *Yom Tov* while 8-year-old Shloimie peppers her with questions. "Where are we going on *Chol Hamoed*? Are we going to an amusement park? Can we each have our own ticket-book for rides?"

"Now, wait a minute," Mrs. Cohen interjects, urgently. "We don't even know for sure whether or not we'll be going to the amusement park. We'll see."

"But you promised we'd go 'somewhere special,'" Shloimie protests, with the determination of a veteran litigation attorney. "Only the amusement park is 'special.' That's the only place with rides. And we wanna go on rides!"

"Wides! Wides!" chimes in 3-year-old Suri, picking up on the cue.

"Can I go on the fire truck this time, Mommy?" asks 5-year-old Yanky. Then, turning to Suri, he adds, "You can come on the fire truck with me, too, if you're good."

"Fire twuck," Suri responds approvingly.

Ominous weather forecasts finally give way to a surprisingly sunny first day of *Chol Hamoed*. The Cohen children wake up an hour earlier than usual, as Mr. and Mrs. Cohen give up their dream of sleeping an hour later. The same children who are always late for the school bus miraculously manage to negotiate *negel vasser* and breakfast unassisted.

"I thought we might visit the historical museum," Mr. Cohen suggests. "I just read in the paper that they have a special exhibit for children on...."

"A museum?" Shloimie interrupts. "A museum?! What's so great about a museum? You just look at old stuff. That's not for children. You promised we'd go 'somewhere special' on *Chol Hamoed*. We wanna go on rides!"

"Wides! Wides!" shouts Suri, with impeccable timing. Yanky begins to cry.

"I don't want to go to any dumb museum," Shloimie continues his offensive. "My whole class is going to the amusement park." Finally the *coup de grace*, "This isn't just any day; this is *Chol Hamoed!*"

On the way to the amusement park, the Cohen children seem to be oblivious of the rides as they openly speculate about the refreshments of the day. "When we get the chocolate bars, let's have half right away and then save the rest for later," Shloimie counsels his protégés.

"Who said you're each going to get a chocolate bar?" Mrs. Cohen demands.

Falling back on his earlier successful ploy, Shloimie reminds his mother, "But it's *Chol Hamoed!*"

Three minutes into the amusement park, the Cohens accept the impossibility of preserving the unity of their family. So Mr. Cohen takes Shloimie on the Devil's Slide, and Mrs. Cohen takes Yanky and Suri to the fire trucks. But Yanky wants to go on the Turbo Wheel first and Mrs. Cohen thinks he's too young for that ride …

At 3:30 the family meets at the entrance gate as planned. Mr. and Mrs. Cohen agree that they've had enough. They disagree only as to how much earlier they really should have left the park.

All three Cohen children begin shouting simultaneously. Each one cites the ride he or she *really* wanted to go on but which was missed, so far. Mr. Cohen is firm, Mrs. Cohen waffles. Shloimie proposes a compromise. They should stop at the souvenir stand and each pick out something "small."

Mr. Cohen agrees, albeit reluctantly, as his patience wears paper thin. The negotiations that then take place at the souvenir stand make nuclear disarmament talks sound simple. Suri grabs for anything within reach. Yanky and Shloimie display bargaining tactics with their parents that would impress a vendor in the Arab *shuk.*

After 20 frustrating, unproductive minutes at the souvenir stand, Mr. Cohen announces that his offer to buy souvenirs has been rescinded and the car is leaving, with or without the rest of the family. At this point it is difficult to determine exactly who is shouting at whom. What is clear is that on the way home, Mr. and Mrs. Cohen are sitting silently in the front while all three children are crying in the back. What was planned as a joyous *Chol Hamoed* outing has ended in a total fiasco. The children's disappointment is matched only by their parents' frustration and sense of having been abused.

🍀 What Went Wrong?

Mr. and Mrs. Cohen are, unfortunately, not alone. In fact, when they left the amusement park on *Chol Hamoed*, they received minor consolation from the shouts of protest and crying emanating from many of the other cars pulling out of the parking lot.

Lots of parents begin with plans and expectations similar to the Cohens', all motivated by the desire to go "somewhere special" on *Chol Hamoed*. Somehow, more often than not, it doesn't work out quite as "specially" as everyone would have liked. So perhaps we should review the scenario to analyze just what went wrong.

In analyzing the Cohens' expectations, it is important to separate those of Mr. and Mrs. Cohen from those of Shloimie, Yanky and Suri. Let us begin with the parents:

Mr. and Mrs. Cohen had the right idea when they wanted their children to look forward to *Yom Tov* and *Chol Hamoed*. But they had the wrong idea when they thought in terms of "somewhere special."

The enjoyment a person has from any experience is inversely proportional to his expectations. The more he expects before the experience, the greater the chances are that he will be disappointed later. *Increased expectations drastically reduce the enjoyment actually experienced.* Or, to put it more simply, the most fun is often had when it is least expected. If this is true for adults, it applies even more so to children.

So returning to the senior Cohens, their *first* mistake was thinking that to insure a good time for Shloimie, Yanky and Suri, they had to go "somewhere special." Had they lowered their own expectations of what constitutes a good time, perhaps they would have planned for *Chol Hamoed* with a better perspective.

Chazal, of course, recognize the importance of including children in plans for *simchas Yom Tov*. As the *Shulchan Aruch* states (*Orach Chaim* 529:2): "A man is obligated to be happy and with a joyous heart on *Yom Tov* together with his wife and children," to which the *Mishnah Berurah* (529:16) adds: "*Chol Hamoed* is included with *Yom Tov* regarding *simchah*."

The *Shulchan Aruch* then asks, "How does one make them happy? For children, he gives them toasted grain and nuts."

That's all? Perhaps these are guidelines only for the poor? Surely those who could afford to should provide more for their children than simply toasted grain and nuts!

The *Shulchan Aruch*, however, goes on to explain that, "for his wife, one should buy clothing and jewelry, *according to his financial ability*." The latter qualification is stated regarding purchases for his wife, but not regarding those for his children. How are we to interpret "according to his financial ability"? Do these words come to suggest that clothes and jewelry are minimum requirements and if he can afford more he should spend more? Or are these maximum guidelines, implying that one with limited financial means may spend less? The *Bi'ur Halachah* answers these questions quite definitively: "According to this, 'financial ability' [means that] if he cannot afford [to buy clothing and jewelry] he should at the very least buy new shoes [for her] in honor of *Yom Tov*."

By contrast, we can assume that toasted grain and nuts are not simply minimum guidelines for children's *simchas Yom Tov*. Of course, it would not be prohibited to provide more, but that goes beyond the expectation of *Chazal*. Perhaps *Chazal* are trying to teach us this basic principle of human nature — that *enjoyment is increased when expectations are reduced*.

There is another principle we can infer from the words of

Chazal. Expectations, especially for children, should be clear and specific, not vague and open to speculation. *Chazal* knew that whenever children are given general promises, their wild and creative imaginations will inevitably lead them to expect more than was intended. "Toasted grain and nuts," however, leaves little room for speculation.

This leads us to Mr. and Mrs. Cohen's *second* mistake. By telling their children that they would go "somewhere special on *Chol Hamoed*," they were planting the seeds for future disappointment. And by leaving the plans up in the air for weeks in advance, they were watering those seeds every day.

Instead, the Cohens should have planned something modest and promised something as clear and specific as possible. "We haven't decided, yet," is better than "something special"; — and "We're going out to Hartley Park for a picnic," is even better. The picnic trip may include a stop along the way, but that is not included in the contract; and, if an extra stop is made, it would be the proverbial icing on the cake.

Suppose Mr. and Mrs. Cohen had immediately decided on a trip to the amusement park and promised that to their children. Would spelling that out in advance have prevented their *Chol Hamoed* fiasco? It certainly would have helped, but that alone would not have guaranteed a successful outing.

❧ Setting Limits

All people need structure in their lives; children even more than adults. Adults, hopefully, have internalized many forms of self-regulating structure that, as was discussed previously, children have not yet developed. For instance, adults can *sense* the passage of time, even without a clock or a calendar, while children cannot. As a result, children can enjoy any experience much more if elements of structure are provided for them by their parents. This will minimize the chances for disappointment later on and will help the children to fully delight in the experience.

Certain questions, therefore, should be answered in advance of a trip to the amusement park. How long will we stay? How many rides will we go on? Will we be given refreshments? If so, how much? Will we come home with souvenirs? How much money can we spend? Of course, sound judgment would dictate that the age of the children be taken into consideration when addressing such questions, and not every question needs to be answered in advance. What is important is the principle: *The more children know what to expect and where the limits are, the less likely they are to feel deprived and disappointed later on.* So the *third* mistake Mr. and Mrs. Cohen made was not to offer their children *any* limiting guidelines for the trip to the amusement park.

Parents should always spell out some clear limitations to their children in as concrete a fashion as possible. It will take some forethought and planning and it may reduce spontaneity, but it's well worth the price. "We will stay for two and a half hours or for six rides each, whichever comes first," might sound funny to some parents. But after all the " What if ...?" questions subside, it's amazing how relaxed the day can be.

As mentioned, all children possess an underdeveloped awareness of time, especially when they are having fun. To be told abruptly, "It's time to leave," literally shocks their systems. They need gentle reminders — even a 3-year-old can grasp the meaning of, "This is the next-to-the-last ride."

"Isn't it mean to remind children that the trip is almost over?" some parents might argue. "Why not let them enjoy themselves fully while they're having fun?"

In fact, however, it is not reminding children of the time that is cruel. Just listen to all those crying children at the exit of the amusement park — they've all just been told that it's time to leave. Adults do not throw a tantrum when they must end their own entertainment or vacation, because they have been cognizant all along of the impending end. Why not give children the same opportunity to adjust?

The Cohens' *fourth* mistake, therefore, was not helping their children to anticipate and thereby adjust to the eventual conclusion of the trip to the amusement park.

❧ Teaching Appreciation

Nothing rankles parents more than extending themselves to make their children happy — and receiving no appreciation for their efforts. What parents need to realize, however, is that appreciation is not a genetically transmitted trait; it must be acquired. Children must learn to exercise their appreciation muscles, and we must teach them using the same methods employed for teaching any other skill.

No one teaches a child to ride a bike by giving a lecture on the principles of physics. Parents simply put the child on a bike and walk him or her through the motions, offering tips here and there, until the child can pedal independently.

Learning to exercise appreciation muscles is no different. Parents have to help guide their children through the motions until they become automatic.[2]

This brings us to the Cohens' *fifth* mistake. Whenever Mr. and Mrs. Cohen take their children on a *Chol Hamoed* trip, or any other outing, they wait for their children to express gratitude. If no appreciation is forthcoming, they may sulk quietly, castigate themselves for not giving their children a good enough time, or simply tell themselves, "What can you expect? They're only children."

That's precisely it: Now they are children, and they will never acquire adult appreciation skills tomorrow unless they start learning them today! On the way home, the Cohens should have insisted on hearing some words of gratitude from their children, not to reward themselves, but to fulfill their obligation of *chinuch* with their children.

---

2. More about teaching children to appreciate and express gratitude can be found in Chapter 5. "Candyman for a Day: Teaching *Hakaras Hatov.*"

Of course, considering the circumstances, the Cohens could only expect to have heard the most begrudging "Thank you," uttered in barely audible tones. But that would be enough for the time being. No child learns how to ride a bike in one day, either.

Hopefully, with years of practice and training, several years hence, on the way home from a *Chol Hamoed* outing, Mr. and Mrs. Cohen just may hear a "Thank You" *before* the children are reminded. And, oh, how sweet that will be!

9

Spare the Rod:
Designing Discipline for a
Torah Home

Even though to many parents the responsibility of disciplining their children seems like a curse, discipline is not a four-letter word.

Some of the parents who feel this way were disciplined harshly when they were children. As a result, they are only clear about what they do not want to do with their children. They are totally lost, however, about how they should discipline their children.

Other parents who have an aversion to disciplining their own children were not disciplined at all when they were growing up. Consequently, they have absolutely no frame of reference on which to rely when the need for setting limits at home arises.

Finally, some parents find themselves confronting behavioral problems in their children for which the techniques of discipline used by their own parents simply do not apply. Methods of discipline which were extremely effective a generation ago may appear as anachronistic today as trying to replace your cellular phone with a phone that has a rotary dial.

No aspect of parenting strikes as much uncertainty and doubt in the hearts of parents as does discipline. Many parents feel overwhelmed, intimidated and inadequate to the task. Unfortunately, far too many parents give little thought as to how to go about designing discipline for a Torah home. This chapter, then, may be, "just what the doctor ordered."

⌒∕⊘ ⌒∿⌒

T HE DISTRAUGHT FATHER OF A PARTICULARLY OBSTREPEROUS teenaged boy once began a counseling session by posing the following question to me. "In your professional opinion, which is a better form of discipline for my son, hitting him with a baseball bat or with a chair?"

Although his question was somewhat tongue in cheek, this father's feelings of helplessness and frustration were quite real. He had not been in any way physically abusive toward his son, but he had endured so many nasty, verbal confrontations in such a short time that he and his wife were prompted to come for help.

Over the course of our work together, I had the opportunity to correct some glaring misconceptions this father had about parenting in general, and the meaning of his son's behavior in particular. And the father's misunderstanding of the word "discipline" was certainly not the least significant of his misconceptions.

To this father, "discipline" was synonymous with "punishment." He used the two words interchangeably. But what he did not realize is that "discipline" is related to "disciple," meaning "student," and is more correctly defined as "teaching" or "instruction."

In Hebrew as well, words that sound alike often have similar or related meanings. And we can better understand one word by examining the meaning of other words which sound the same.

Take, for example, the Hebrew word for discipline, *mussar*, as in the following verse: "To know wisdom and [self-] discipline (*mussar*), to understand discernment" (*Mishlei* 1:2). *Mussar* has the same root as *mesorah*, tradition, and *mesirah*, transmitting.

These three Hebrew words, then, are interrelated, suggesting that the true meaning of discipline is to transmit the tradition. And the principles which apply to teaching and transmitting tradition from one generation to the other are the same principles which apply to discipline.

If we want to know how best to discipline our children, we must analyze how best to teach and instruct our children, and we must try to understand what conditions are most conducive to learning. Just as good rebbei'im and teachers must understand what promotes learning most effectively, so, too, parents who want to succeed in teaching *middos*, good behavior and proper conduct at home must understand these same principles of education.

Suppose your son or daughter reported to you that his or her teacher regularly comes to class unprepared, in a horrible mood, and spends all day impatiently finding fault with the students, only to wind up imposing grossly unfair punishments on the entire class. And suppose you had no reason to doubt your child's report because many of the parents of your child's classmates corroborated the account.

Would you not be incensed at this teacher's poor performance? Would you not question the judgment of the principal who hired such a teacher? And would you not consider calling the school, at least to ask for an explanation? Who wouldn't be upset?! For you to be unconcerned about this teacher's poor performance would be a gross dereliction of your responsibility as a parent.

While we would be quick and unanimous in giving this teacher a poor grade, how well would we do if we measured ourselves by the same standards? Are we, as parents, not teachers in our homes? Are we not responsible for conveying lessons on manners, behavior, attitudes and *hashkafah* to our children? Should we not use the same criteria to gauge our performance as parents at home as we use to evaluate the performance of our children's teachers?

Let us then examine what we expect from our children's teachers and see how that applies to our handling of discipline at home.

🌸 Preparation

We want our children's rebbei'im and teachers to come to class prepared for each day's lesson. We expect them to be well versed in the material being taught. We also presume that they have given proper thought and advance planning to the methods and techniques which will be utilized to convey the information to the class. Finally, we trust that they will consider the age, intelligence, maturity and attention level of the class in setting realistic standards that are in reach of, rather then beyond the grasp of, the students.

What about us? Are we as prepared as we would expect the *rebbi* or the teacher to be? Firstly, are we clear about the lessons we want to impart to our children? Have we thought through exactly what it is we want to teach and how we ought to convey it? Or do we simply react impulsively, spontaneously and without consideration for consequences?

Consider the following scenario. You had a particularly difficult day. Anything that could go wrong did go wrong. You are tired, irritable and drained. All you want now is some peace and quiet to unwind and relax. Your 3-year-old son, on the other hand, has just made the delightful discovery that banging on an empty pot with a spoon creates a sound similar to that of a drum. Exploiting this creative breakthrough, your son composes a *Percussion Symphony for Chulent Pot* which is quite allegro.

"Shmully!" you erupt, in frazzled-nerve shock. "You're making too much noise!"

Your son pauses, momentarily, as he tries, unsuccessfully, to decipher your cryptic message. A few moments later, the banging resumes.

"Shmully!" you repeat, this time in a voice considerably raised. "What did I just tell you?" you ask, rhetorically.

Your son stops what he is doing. Again, he pauses apprehensively. Eventually, he returns to his musical composition.

Now you've had it. You rise from your chair, convinced that more forceful methods of communication are required. You let Shmully "have it" in one form or another until he bursts into tears. Then you slump back into your chair feeling guilty, as the possibility of your relaxing vanishes like a dream.

Were you prepared to teach? Were you clear about your lesson? And more importantly, did you convey your instruction in a simple, direct and age-appropriate manner? Obviously not. Poor grades for teaching, here.

What should have been done differently? You could have been more concrete, specific and unambiguous in your "lesson." Especially when trying to modify a child's behavior, regardless of the age of the child, parents must adopt the approach of Yaakov *Avinu* when he spoke with his sly future father-in-law, Lavan.

Lavan asked Yaakov what wages he would request in exchange for his labor. Yaakov asked to be able to marry Lavan's daughter, Rachel. But he referred to her as, *"Rochel bitcha haketanah,* Rachel your younger daughter" (*Bereishis* 29:18). Rashi asks: Why were all of the extra words necessary? Didn't Lavan know who Rachel was? Rashi answers that when dealing with someone who could distort your words, it is necessary to be very specific.

Now a 3-year-old is not out to *deliberately* distort your words, as Lavan was. But he may nevertheless misunderstand exactly what you want from him. So instead of telling him that he is, "making too much noise," it may have been much more effective if you told him, "Please go into your room if you want to bang on the pot," or, "You cannot bang on the pot now because I'm trying to rest. I'll let you know when you can start banging again."

Of course, the need to be clear in communicating our directions applies not only to small children, but to older ones as well.

Statements such as, "You are acting too immaturely," "You are not talking with proper respect," or "Why won't you help more at the table?" are all much too vague. They are open to misinterpretation, distortion and even debate.

These same messages would be more effectively conveyed as follows: "I think you are old enough, now, to eat with a knife and fork, like a grownup." "Raising your voice is not a nice way to talk to your parents." "When Mommy gets up to serve the next course, I would like you to get up to help her."

❦ Age-appropriate Expectations

Once we are clear in our minds about what we want and have found a concrete way to articulate our message, we also must be sure that our expectations are age appropriate. Just as we would be appalled if a 6-year-old were assigned to write a book report for homework, we should be equally upset with ourselves if we insist on behavioral control that is beyond the ability and maturity of our child. Harav Shlomo Wolbe puts it this way:

"Parents must adjust their demands to the ability and developmental level of their child. If the child is not mature enough to understand or fulfill that which is expected from him, great damage can result from such parenting."[1]

When assessing whether our expectations are age appropriate, we should use the widest frame of reference for comparison. Just because your older daughter was able to do her own laundry at 12, does not necessarily mean that her younger sister, who is now 12, will be capable of doing the same. And just because you were able to go to an out-of-town yeshivah at 13 does not mean that your son is ready for a dormitory right after his bar mitzvah.

Each child's individual needs, strengths and weaknesses must be taken into account when judging what he or she is capable of

---

1. My own translation of *Zeriah Ubinyan Bechinuch* (Hebrew) by Harav Shlomo Wolbe (Yerushalayim: Feldheim Publishers, 1995), p.15.

doing at any age. Perhaps that is what Shlomo *Hamelech* had in mind when he advised, *"Chanoch l'naar al pi darko,* educate the child according to *his* way" (*Mishlei* 22:6). (Emphasis added.) Or, as *Metzudas David* interprets that verse, "according to his intellectual ability, whether more or less."

✿ Even-tempered Teaching

If your child's teacher is impatient, short tempered and irritable in class, you would have a valid reason to worry about the quality of your child's education. Similarly, if you are exhausted, stressed out, or testy, you will not be very successful at getting your message across to your children.

Of course, we cannot be expected to always be in a good mood. Everyone has good days and bad days. But we do not expect to accomplish our most important tasks when we are in a bad mood. We don't work on our taxes or balance our checkbooks when we are on edge. We don't begin building the *succah* or start washing the windows when we are exhausted. So why would we expect to communicate the most important lessons to our children when we are at our lowest point? When tempers flare and patience runs out, our message will get lost among the static. *After* the dust settles or *before* you reach the end of your rope is the best time to be heard.

Setting limits and clarifying consequences will be much more successful if you attempt to do so when both you and your child are calm and relaxed. If you missed the chance before a confrontation, then at the very least, sit down with your child later or the next day and go over what happened. At such times, a short apology can go a long way toward accomplishing your goals.

For example, instead of shouting, "Why don't you ever listen to me?!" or "What did I tell you?!" you might try approaching your child later, or the next day with, "I'm sorry I raised my voice last night. But I would like you to understand that you simply may not play ball in the living room (or, cannot be on the phone on week nights after 10 p.m.; or, should always call if you see that you will not be home by 11 p.m.)."

Rav Wolbe quotes Harav Chaim of Volozin as follows, "Whoever does not have a nature to speak softly and is quick to anger at those who do not obey him is exempted from the *mitzvah* of reproof."[2]

Right now you may be thinking, "Sounds wonderful. But what do you do when you have spelled out your expectations clearly, in a calm tone of voice, and your child *repeatedly* disregards, disobeys or disrespects you? Is there any way to *enforce* your rules at home? Or must parents be treated like doormats for the children to walk all over? Is there ever a time and place for punishment? If so, when and how should it be administered to be most effective?"

❧ Punishment

Just as teachers at times need to punish in order to maintain proper control in the classroom, parents also need to occasionally administer punishments. But just as a teacher who *constantly* punishes his or her classes is demonstrating his or her ineptitude, so too a parent who frequently resorts to punishments is revealing his or her helplessness and inadequacy as an effective parent.

The first lesson parents need to learn about punishment, therefore, is that it is a strategy which must be used as a last resort. All other methods should be utilized first because, like strong medicine, it causes numerous undesirable side effects. It can generate resentment; it can alienate children; and, it can quickly lose its effectiveness if utilized too often. Even antibiotics will cease to be helpful if taken too frequently.

Secondly, punishment must be placed in the proper context. It is a cardinal law of physics — and life — that every action has a reaction. And we must teach this lesson to our children. As Jews,

---

2. Op. cit. p. 26.

we have a special appreciation for this fact of life. (See #11 of the *Rambam's* "Thirteen Articles of Faith," codified in the *Ani Maamins* found at the end of *Shacharis*, in most *siddurim*.) We can best instruct our children about the consequences of behavior by demonstrating that their behavior at home will result in consistent, clearly anticipated consequences.

Children need to know that their behavior matters to their parents. If parents adopt a totally laid-back, nonchalant attitude, their children will get the message that "anything goes." They will assume that their actions should be guided only by their whims and desires. And, most significantly, they will grow up without learning the vital trait of self-control.

Addressing mothers, whom he saw as tending, at times, to be less willing to set limits than fathers, Rabbi Shmuel Matzin writes (*Even Sheleimah* Ch. 6, note A), "And mothers are commanded to reprove their children just like fathers, and even more so because they are at home more. And it is said, 'How are women worthy [of their share in *Olam Haba*, the World to Come]? By bringing their children to yeshivah.' (See *Berachos* 17a.) And since the nature of women is soft, women must, at times, adopt a firm hand [with their children]. Perhaps this lesson is alluded to by the verse, 'The hands of compassionate women have boiled their own children' (*Eichah* 4:10) [i.e. the misguided compassion of parents who refuse to set limits will ultimately cause the destruction of their children]."

On the other hand, parents must not overreact to misbehavior with excessive punishment. First and foremost, extreme measures of retribution simply do not work. They are ineffective at correcting misbehavior. Ask any experienced educator and he or she will tell you. I know — because I did just that. I consulted a highly respected *yeshivah* principal, and former *rebbi*. And this is what he told me:

"I was certainly opposed to hitting my students. Simply, that was not the atmosphere I wanted in my class. But some children were so completely unruly that they seemed to be expecting me to use corporal punishment. These were always the children who had come to us from other yeshivos which had encouraged the rebbei'im to hit the children. It generally took until Chanukah each year for these new boys to be 'deprogrammed' and to calm down."

In addition, excessive punishment, as well as excessive criticism, causes children to lose the ability to discriminate between major crimes and minor offenses. As my friend and colleague, Dr. Bentzion Sorotzkin, has pointed out, when all misbehavior is met with heavy-handed retribution, children learn to blur distinctions between major and minor incidents.[3] Often it is these same children who later grow up and become indecisive adults who cannot decide which dress to buy, which yeshivah to attend or which *shidduch* to marry because they have become desensitized to distinguishing between major and minor factors. To them, all factors are major because that is how they were treated by their parents as they were growing up.

Finally, when parents impose drastic penalties on their children, they usually do so in anger, when they are feeling most frustrated and helpless. Certainly, that is the worst time to try to teach or instruct anyone about anything. And just as your children will learn little from an angry teacher in school, they will not learn very much from an angry parent at home.

This fundamental principle of family life was articulated hundreds of years ago by the Vilna Gaon, long before the word "psychology" was even dreamed of.

❧ Corporal Punishment

The Vilna Gaon addressed a question which is obvious to any parent. Shlomo *Hamelech*, the wisest of all men, stated, *"Choseich shivto sonei v'no,* One who spares his rod hates his child" (*Mishlei* 13:24). The implication here seems to be that when it

---

3. Sorotzkin, Ben, "Understanding and Treating Perfectionism in Religious Adolescents," *Psychotherapy*, Spring '98, pp. 87-95.

comes to corporal punishment, more is better.

Our experience, however, suggests otherwise. The more children are hit, the more they rebel, disobey and disrespect their parents. Regular corporal punishment teaches children to act out their own impulses, settle disputes with aggression and take advantage of those who are weaker — all lessons we do not want our children to learn.

How do we explain this apparent disparity? Is our perception of the effect of corporal punishment distorted? Did Shlomo *Hamelech's* advice not apply to our generation? The Vilna Gaon explains that the resolution of this apparent contradiction can be found in the manner in which Shlomo *Hamelech* wanted us to utilize corporal punishment.

In the words of the Vilna Gaon, "When a parent hits a child, he [or she] should not hit in anger, as one would hit an enemy, for actions the child has done in the past. Rather, the intention of the hitting should only be to save the child from misconduct in the future. Therefore, do not hit the child a lot, but only a very little bit, according to his age, level of maturity, and what is appropriate for him. And when the parent sees that his or her anger is escalating, the parent should not hit the child *at all* at that time" (free translation of *Even Sheleimah* Ch. 6, paragraph 4). (Emphasis added.)[4]

According to the Vilna Gaon, therefore, Shlomo *Hamelech* is recommending the use of corporal punishment only when parents are not angry and not out of control. If parents will hit their children in defiance of this advice, the punishment will prove ineffective and counterproductive, as we see from our own experience.

Perhaps the best argument against the use of corporal punishment comes from the following observation: Parents who do hit their children almost always hit their first children more often than they hit those born later. Apparently, these parents have

---

4. I am grateful to Harav Yaakov Perlow, the Novominsker Rebbe and Rosh Agudath Israel of America, for sharing this reference with me.

either learned from experience that corporal punishment is ineffective or they have learned that there are more effective methods of discipline.

Rav Wolbe quotes his rebbi on this subject. "Harav Eliyahu Lopian used to tell us always: 'With children, use only pleasant ways.' He said that in his old age he regretted each slap he gave his own children when they were younger."[5]

Now, if parents are not to ignore misbehavior yet avoid hitting when angry, how else should they attempt to guide, correct and mold their children? Once again, *Chazal* understood the dynamics of family life better than psychologists — and long before the field of child psychology even acquired its name.

❧ Positive Reinforcement

Especially when dealing with children, *Chazal* advised nearly 2,000 years ago, *"Le'olam tehei se'mol do'cheh ve'yemin me'kareves*, Always push away [i.e. chastise and rebuke] with the left [i.e. the weaker force] and bring close [i.e. praise and approve] with the right [i.e. the stronger force]" (*Sotah* 47a).

Going one step further, the Nirbater Rav, Rabbi Aaron Teitelbaum, cited this quotation from *Sotah* in a public address and pointed out that compliments, positive regard and positive reinforcement must precede any criticism, because one can only "push away" that which has already been brought close.

The message of *Chazal* is clear. Parents will be far more effective if they encourage their children with positive, rather than with negative, reinforcement. All forms of punishment such as criticism, scolding and hitting will not get the job done as well as the positive rewards such as affection, approval and compliments.

Rav Wolbe offers the following insight into the impact of corporal punishment. "When the child is 14 years old, the shocked parents come crying, 'I do not understand what it is with my child.

---

5. Op. cit. p. 24.

He does not speak to me at all. He does not tell me anything. I have no idea what is going on with him.'

"When the parents come to me and ask what to do, I ask them, 'Tell me, did you hit the child when he was 3 years old?'

"'Of course, after all we had to teach him,' they reply.

"Then I respond, 'Now you are getting paid back for all the smacking you gave him then.'"[6]

This sounds wonderful. But what do you do when your 2-year-old starts to run into the street, picks up an expensive vase or tries to lean out of the window? How do you control such behavior with only positive reinforcement?

When dealing with young, preschool-age children, limits must be enforced with a firm (not angry) tone, often buttressed with physical intervention. You simply have to grab 2-year-olds to prevent them from running into the street. You also need to take expensive or dangerous objects away from them or remove such objects from their reach. With firmness, disapproval and repetition, 2-year-olds can, and do, learn to refrain from potentially hazardous or harmful activities. It takes time, but it happens.

With older, school age children, the expectation of reward or the fear of losing that reward can be extremely effective motivations for modifying their behavior. Parents can, for example, work out "deals" with their children to encourage their compliance with parental expectations.

When negotiating "contracts" with children, the parents should keep in mind that the reward must be meaningful to the child and the task should be reasonable, realistic and reachable for the child. In addition, the goal must be concretely defined so that there is little room for debating whether or not the goal was, in fact, reached. With somewhat younger children, literally charting their progress with checks or stars helps them maintain motivation for good behavior the same way yeshivos motivate students to memorize *mishnayos* by charting achievements.

An alternative strategy is to withhold an expected reward as a

---

6. Op. cit. p. 17.

consequence for noncompliance with parental expectations. Once again, the expectations need to be spelled out clearly in advance so there is no misunderstanding and resentment later on. Here too, the consequence for noncompliance must be within reason and not excessively harsh, otherwise it overloads the child's circuits and shuts down his or her capacity to absorb the lesson you are trying to teach.

One of the most commonly utilized rewards with children is money. While money, as any other reward, can be misused, it nevertheless represents a most effective teaching tool for parents. And the most common venue for dispensing money to children is by granting a weekly, daily, or monthly allowance.

Children need and should have some money of their own. To children, as to adults, money signifies power. If you have money, you have power. To have no money means you are powerless. Seeing everyone around them, including their friends, having money, all children will want and ask for some money of their own.

Giving children an allowance provides a valuable opportunity for parents to teach children that all-important lesson of "the value of money." It also provides an opportunity for children to learn how to manage their money, as well as their desires and impulses, in a safe, controlled and supervised manner.

Providing a regular allowance to children also enables parents to convey both forms of approval: conditional and unconditional. When children receive an allowance regardless of how they behave, they get the message that they are entitled to certain benefits by virtue of who they are and not what they do. This is a valuable message which all children should receive in order to feel truly loved by their parents.

But children also need to know that some approval is conditional and very much tied to their behavior and performance. This teaches children to confront the reality that they must live with the consequences of their actions.

If children receive *only* unconditional love and approval, they grow up to be self-centered, selfish and narcissistic adults who always expect more than others can provide. (Perhaps you know some people who fit that description.) On the other hand, if children receive only conditional rewards, they grown into insecure adults who lack confidence, feel inadequate and always belittle their own accomplishments. (Perhaps you know some people who fit that description, as well.)

Ideally, then, children should receive both unconditional and conditional rewards. This can be accomplished when dispensing an allowance.[7]

A practical example will illustrate how this works.

Let's say Dovi is 9 years old and has been stubbornly uncooperative about making his bed in the morning, and his parents are eager to find a way to motivate him. He might receive $1 allowance per week, regardless of his behavior. But he could be earning an additional 10 cents per day if he makes his bed. Morever, if, at the end of the week, he had a perfect record of making his bed every day, he would earn a 30-cent bonus, giving him a grand total of $2 dollars.

This "contract" can motivate Dovi in a number of ways. Firstly, he has the ability to double his income with good behavior. In addition, he sees that while he earns only 10 cents for each time he makes his bed, he risks *losing* 40 cents for any single day he fails to make his bed. Finally, instead of his parents scolding him whenever he does not make his bed, Dovi's behavior is "silently" modified by the firm enforcement of the contract to which he agreed. This frees his parents from feeling the need to coerce Dovi with increasingly violent threats of retribution.

Parents who prefer not to give their children an allowance can substitute trips to the pizza shop, playground or pickle factory instead of money. But more creativity is required to provide both conditional as well as unconditional reward. ("Regardless of whether or not you make your bed, we will go on the tour. If, however, your bed is made every day this week, I'll allow you to

---

7. I am grateful to my friend and colleague, Dr. Rashi Shapiro, for sharing this formulation with me.

accept the sample pickles they offer at the end of the tour.")

But what can be done with an out-of-control school-aged child who is terrorizing his siblings, provoking his parents and disrupting the entire family on a daily basis? What do you do with a child who seems to totally disregard his parents' disapproval? How do you deal with an older child who just never seems to learn his lesson? These were the questions posed to me by the totally exasperated parents of a third-grade boy; let's call him Chaim.*

🍂 The Case of Chaim

Both of Chaim's parents were mild-mannered, even-tempered people who spoke softly, both as a result of politeness as well as embarrassment at having to consult a professional about the behavior of their child.

Chaim's father was a hard-working computer programmer who made sure to find time each night to spend with his family as well as learn with his *chavrusa*. Chaim's mother was a busy housewife who sold costume jewelry at home in her nonexistent spare time.

Chaim's mother shouldered the brunt of his outbursts, tantrums and disruptions at home. She dreaded his return from yeshivah each evening and could not wait until he was finally in bed at night. He would taunt his younger siblings and annoy the older ones. He would whine and beg for special favors. He would erupt in fury if his needs were not met immediately. In a word, he was a nightmare.

Chaim's parents tried bribes. They tried treats and prizes. They used charts and stars. Nothing helped. Then they tried scolding and rebuke. They tried ignoring him and paying no attention to his tantrums. They even tried hitting. Nothing worked. In desperation, they asked their pediatrician if he thought consulting a therapist might help.

The pediatrician advised against consulting a therapist. "You'll

---

* Not his real name.

just waste your money," the doctor warned. Instead the physician suggesting being more firm and giving Chaim time to outgrow this "stage." But Chaim's parents felt they could not survive this stage. So they consulted with me anyway, against their doctor's recommendation.

At our initial meeting they appeared shell shocked, battle scarred and ready for surrender. They confided in me that they were even considering the drastic step of placing Chaim in foster care, although they knew they would never actually go through with it.

"Maybe he's just trying to get more attention," Chaim's mother suggested. "But he's already taking up 90 percent of the time we have for our six children and he's still terrorizing us."

My first recommendation was to bring Chaim in for an in-person, in-depth evaluation. It was a suggestion to which his parents readily agreed. The evaluation revealed that Chaim was above average in intelligence, suffered from severe sibling rivalry, felt he was not getting enough attention from his parents, had no friends and had a severely low opinion of himself.

After sharing these findings with Chaim's parents, his father asked the obvious question, "How can we give Chaim more approval when he is constantly misbehaving? We would love to compliment him more often because we know he would thrive on that, but how can you praise a child who is always misbehaving, acting up and disrupting the peace at home?"

I explained to Chaim's parents what you now know if you have read this chapter from the beginning. Then I pointed out to them that to an attention-hungry child, punishment and rebuke, however repugnant, is still preferable to being ignored and overlooked. Chaim needed so much attention that when things were too quiet he would act up just to get noticed. All of this backfired, of course, when he would earn his parents' disapproval, because this made him even more starved than he had been for positive regard.

In order to break this cycle, his parents had to do two things. First, they had to ignore, downplay and overlook Chaim's tantrums, as much as possible. Second, and even more importantly, they had to "catch him in the act" of not acting up. Any quiet, peaceful play on Chaim's part had to trigger affection, hugs and expressions of pride from both his parents. At the very least, these short "doses" of intense attention and approval had to be administered every half-hour from the time Chaim came home until he went to bed.

This plan sounded bizarre to Chaim's parents, but they were so desperate that they were willing to try it, anyway. A week later they returned and sadly reported they were right … the plan did not work. We carefully reviewed their implementation of the plan and it was clear that they had followed my instructions religiously. Now they felt even more hopeless than when they first met with me.

I empathized with their frustration, but discouraged them from declaring defeat. If Chaim was still acting up at home, I explained, it means that he is so needy of attention that they have to reduce the interval to 15 minutes.

Frankly, I never expected them to agree to stop whatever they were doing, search out Chaim in his room or wherever he was, and hug him, telling him how proud they were that he was playing so nicely, *every 15 minutes!* But I had no other advice for them. It was such an extreme measure that I really expected them to reject the idea out of hand. Certainly, what I was asking was not going to be easy.

To my surprise, Chaim's parents agreed to the revised plan. And they were cautiously optimistic when they returned two weeks later to report that Chaim's behavior had improved, significantly. They were relieved and grateful. A follow-up meeting one month later proved that the progress was maintained. Once again, the timeless wisdom of *Chazal* had been demonstrated.

Chaim was, of course, an extreme example of disruptive behavior. And some disruptive children may have neurological or psychological disorders which require medication or other therapies to correct. But most misbehavior does not require the intense, painstaking program that Chaim's parents had to implement. Nevertheless, the case of Chaim illustrates just how much can be accomplished when parents make a concerted effort to discipline with *positive* reinforcement ... rather than with hands, bats and chairs.

PART FOUR:
Managing the Dynamics of Family Life

10

Coming Home:
An Opportunity and a Challenge

Even an "only child" does not live in a vacuum. He or she lives and relates to you, your spouse and any other extended family members who live in or visit your home. And when there is more than one child at home, the possible interactions increase geometrically.

The way in which two family members deal with one another in a specific instance affects all other family members, even those not directly involved in that particular episode.

The dynamics of family life are complex, and a detailed analysis of all areas of family interaction would be well beyond the limitations of a single volume.

There is one arena of family dynamics, however, which can underscore the power and potency of all the rest, while highlighting the need for constant vigilance and preparation: the daily point of reconnection, when each member of the family crosses the threshold coming home. On the one hand, it is an opportunity to find the warmth, comfort and security of family life. On the other, it is also the time which presents a constant challenge to attend to and be aware of the needs of others.

❧ ❧

W ITH THE EXCEPTION OF SAILORS AND TRAVELING SALESMEN, coming home is something we all do almost every day. In fact, virtually every member of the family over the age of 3 or 4 comes home each day from school, work, shopping, etc. Coming home is so much a part of "every day" that we usually take it for granted, for ourselves and the other members of our families.

Nevertheless, coming home represents the initial encounter, after separation for a brief or extended period, with home and family. As such, it is fraught with expectations, anticipations, and hopes, as well as surprises, demands, and responsibilities. Perhaps, however, the most important feature of coming home is the way in which it sets the tone and atmosphere for that which follows.

If the father comes home angry, it is very hard for the mother to feel affectionate. If the father comes home and finds the mother hostile, it is hard for him to feel caring towards her. And what about the children? What happens when they come home? What do they find waiting for them when they get off the school bus? What tone is set when they walk in the door? And how does all that make them feel about themselves, their brothers and sisters, their homework, and everything else that is going on?

Certainly, parents are not totally in control of the environment that exists when the children come home. It may be that both parents are not there. One parent may come home very late. And the child often comes home with his or her own *"peckalah"* of trials and tribulations from school.

But there are many things parents can do to enhance the experience of coming home. There are a few rules of thumb which, if implemented effectively, can help make coming home a positive, constructive, and tension-free experience.

1) Anticipate and prepare yourself for coming home. Ask yourself, "What will I find and what will be expected of me?"

On one of his tapes, Horav Avigdor Miller cites the verse from *Mishlei* (28:14), "*Ashrei adam mefacheid tamid*, Happy is the man who is always afraid," and he elucidates it as follows: Happy is the person who is always on guard, anticipating any possible trouble that may be lurking ahead, so that he can be properly prepared.

Rav Miller goes on to present the following illustration: Suppose you are about to come home after attending his lecture. As you put your hand on the doorknob, pause a moment before opening the door. Ask yourself what you think you will find waiting for you when you enter. Will your parents scold you for coming home later than they expected? If so, how will you react? Will you lose control and lose your temper? Or, will you respond with due respect?

The point Rav Miller was making could apply to us all. We should try to imagine, for a moment, what will greet us when we enter the doors to our homes. Will it be just as we wanted and hoped? Or, will things be different from what we expected? How should we respond in either case? Just taking a few seconds to prepare ourselves can prevent untold hardship for ourselves and our families.

2) Keep the responsibilities placed on family members immediately after coming home to a minimum. Don't demand X, Y or Z from someone until that person, adult or child, has had a few moments to relax.

This applies to the one coming home as well as the one already at home. Often, we can not wait to get home to ask, tell, or request something from someone at home. But the moment of being reunited at the end of the day is usually the worst time to bombard someone with your agenda. Delaying for even just a few minutes can mean the difference between a pleasant evening and a night full of conflict and tension.

3) Tune into others. Pay attention to *their* needs. What was their day like and how do *they* feel?

4) Encourage a brief refreshment when coming home. This can take the form of food, drink, music, mail, or just a few moments in an easy chair.

Let's peek in on the Shiffman* home one Friday afternoon, as Jack is about to come home from work. Jack keeps long hours at his insurance office. His wife, Linda, has lately been complaining that Jack comes home too close to *Shabbos* each week. She really would appreciate Jack's coming-home a bit earlier, so that he could give her a hand. But even if he could not manage that, the least he could do, she feels, is not to make it into *Shabbos* just under the wire.

Today, Jack is feeling quite proud of himself. He's made it home a full hour earlier than usual. He's planning to offer to help Linda when he gets home. He's also looking forward to having a quick bite with Linda as soon as he walks in the door so he won't go into *Shabbos* famished, as he usually does.

Now Jack has just arrived on the scene at home. He can smell all of the *Shabbos* goodies simmering on the stove, and he asks Linda to join him for a snack.

But Linda is in the middle of bathing the kids, so she calls to him over her shoulder to take something for himself from the fridge.

Jack is miffed. He barks at Linda. Linda feels overwhelmed and hurt. She snarls at Jack. The children feel anxious and start to cry. The tension lasts through the afternoon and ruins the first few hours of the Shiffman *Shabbos*.

Had Linda remembered that Jack had asked her to prepare a bite for him when he got home, she might have had something

---

* Not their real name.

ready for him this week. Had Jack considered that Linda would be busy when he arrived, he never would have even expected company with his snack. But because neither Jack nor Linda gave much thought to the other's end of the coming-home equation, the week-long wait for the serenity of *Shabbos* was made even longer.

Now let's look in on the Tauber* home, late one weekday afternoon. Mrs. Tauber is on the phone with the caterer, making final arrangements for her son Sender's *bar mitzvah*. Sixteen-year-old Fraydie is about to walk in the door, after a particularly disappointing day at school.

Fraydie was hoping to win a part in the school's annual play. She had not tried out in her freshman year because she was too shy. Last year, she did try out, but was not accepted. This year, she thought she would do better since she had been in the play at camp during the summer. In addition, all of her friends received parts in the school play. Fraydie had no intention of missing the fun and excitement of rehearsals, performances and the big party at the end.

But, as you may have guessed, Fraydie learned today that she did not get a part. And she can not wait to unburden herself to her mother. But Mrs. Tauber is on a very important call.

Let's see what happens:

Fraydie bursts into the house, scattering her books, coat and scarf on the floor. She runs into the kitchen and finds Mrs. Tauber on the phone.

"Ma!" Fraydie begs, almost in tears.

Mrs. Tauber does not acknowledge Fraydie. She sees her, but figures that since the conversation with the caterer is almost over, she will wait and then devote her full attention to Fraydie.

"Ma, I have to talk to you!" Fraydie insists, already starting to cry.

"Mr. Green, please excuse me for one minute. I'm terribly sorry," Mrs. Tauber says into the phone. Then, covering the mouthpiece with her hand, she says to Fraydie, "Can't you see I'm on the phone?"

---

* Not their real name.

Fraydie erupts into a torrent of tears, storms upstairs and slams her door. Mrs. Tauber is disgusted with her daughter's impatience. She concludes her conversation with Mr. Green. Then she goes up to Fraydie's room to scold her for being so rude.

You don't want to know what happens next. Trust me. It isn't pretty.

Both Fraydie and Mrs. Tauber could have easily prevented the conflagration which ensued if they each followed Rav Miller's advice. Fraydie should have considered that Mrs. Tauber might not be available to soothe her hurt feelings at just the moment she walked in the door. In addition, Mrs. Tauber could have considered that Fraydie may need at least some acknowledgment when she comes home from school, and she might have made that important call either a little before or a little after the time Fraydie usually comes home each day.

But even if the caterer had called Mrs. Tauber, she still could have asked him to hold on while she briefly acknowledged Fraydie's arrival.

These suggestions apply to children and adults, both to the "comer home" as well as the "waiter at home." If implemented, these suggestions may minimize some of the tensions, frustrations, and *disappointments* so often associated with "coming home."

11

The Shabbos Table:
An X-Ray of Family Interaction

The function of an X-ray is to enable a doctor to see past the outer layers of clothes and skin into the bones and internal organs of the body. With this noninvasive procedure, a doctor is able to examine the inner workings of the body to help him arrive at a definitive diagnosis of an illness.

Because of the great insight it offers into the inner dynamics of a family's life, the Shabbos table of a family is a virtual X-ray of that family's interaction. And just as a medical X-ray enables one to see many of the strengths and weaknesses of a person's body, so too a family's Shabbos table can expose both the strengths and weaknesses of that family.

A doctor who needs to diagnose an ailment may carefully examine a patient's X-ray. Similarly, parents who wish to gain a deeper understanding of their family's interaction should take a closer look at how their Shabbos table is conducted and what transpires there.

꒜꒱꒜

MOST PEOPLE THINK OF WINE, CANDLES, AND *CHALLAH* WHEN they hear the phrase, *"Shabbos* table." Mental pictures are drawn of a large dining room table, spread with a clean white tablecloth and adorned with the family's finest silver and dinnerware. Places are set for all the members of the family, as well as relatives and guests who may be visiting that week.

The *Shabbos* table, of course, includes not only what is set *on* the table in honor of *Shabbos*, but also what happens *around* the table during *Shabbos*. Much of the very observance of *Shabbos* itself takes place around the *Shabbos* table. It is there that the mother lights the *Shabbos* candles, the father makes *Kiddush*, and *Shabbos* meals are enjoyed.

In addition to the prescribed routines of the *Shabbos* table, there is also ample opportunity for family members to relate to one another in their own unique and special ways. And each family has its own "traditions." Some tell stories of family history at the *Shabbos* table; other families engage in informal Torah study or say *divrei Torah*; and many families use the time to catch up with each other about the weekly goings-on.

Because of the long working hours many parents have, long days in yeshivah for the children, and all of those *simchos*, meetings and *shiurim* at night, many families hardly gather all together *as a family* except at the *Shabbos* table. When the *Shabbos* table is the only experience shared by the entire family *at the same time*, it takes on an even greater significance, and is anticipated all the more by parents and children alike.

Since the experience of the *Shabbos* table is common to all Orthodox Jewish homes, it is an opportunity to reaffirm one's sense of belonging to his or her family. For this reason, when someone is away from home and family, he feels most lonely while sitting at someone else's *Shabbos* table. Furthermore, there are those who live alone and must be invited to someone else's *Shabbos* table each week. These people often feel most alone when they are making arrangements for *Shabbos* or waiting to be invited to someone's *Shabbos* table.

The *Shabbos* table not only brings out the best of family life, but it can, at times, bring out the worst, as well. Families that are disorganized and frenzied, for example, find that coordinating a full-scale *Shabbos* table is as daunting as planning the invasion at Normandy. With so many courses, plates, trips to the refrigerator, and different requests all at once, unless a family has a fairly good system of cooperation and organization, the *Shabbos* table can feel like a three-ring circus!

Some families with latent hostilities find that they can prevent open outbursts of anger during the week by avoiding each other and maintaining a "cold war"-type cease fire. At the *Shabbos* table, however, with the entire family present, these dormant hostilities can emerge into full-blown confrontations. Considering all of the effort that goes into preparing the *Shabbos* table, when such arguments spoil the pleasure and tranquility of the *Shabbos* table, everyone feels deeply disappointed.

I often ask the families with whom I work to describe the *Shabbos* table at their home. I find that each family's *Shabbos* table tells the story of what the family's life is really like.

The *Shabbos* table, of course, is much more than a diagnostic tool which can be used to assess the quality of family life. The *Shabbos* table is, most of all, a great *opportunity*. As with any great opportunity, if it is exploited fully, the rewards can be enormous. If, however, it is misused or abused, the despair and disappointment are intensified.

❧ Enhancing Your Shabbos Table

How can a family improve or enhance its own *Shabbos* table? The best way is to play musical chairs — but only figuratively, of course. Let each member of the family imagine sitting in someone else's "chair." How does it feel now? What would the *Shabbos* table be like for the father, for example, if he had to sit in the mother's seat? What would it be like for the mother if she had to sit in one of the children's chairs?

Viewing the *Shabbos* table from someone else's vantage point gives each family member an idea of what the *Shabbos* table means to others. The children, for example, may look forward to the delicious food and happy *zemiros;* but are they aware of how hard their mother works to prepare the *Shabbos* table? Is the father aware of how bored and restless the small children can get?

Playing virtual musical chairs, as described here, does not automatically *guarantee* a happy, pleasurable *Shabbos* table. Much time and effort are required to make significant improvements in the quality of family life. Improvements, however, can be made. Even so, there are some families in which the conflicts are so great, the difficulties so chronic, and the disappointments so deep that professional help is necessary to help them get back on the right track.

🐚 An Exemplary Shabbos Table

Whenever anyone makes an effort to improve in a specific area, it certainly helps to have a clear goal in mind. More specifically, if parents want to improve their *Shabbos* table, they should have a clear mental picture of what a *Shabbos* table can become when its potential is fully realized.

When I try to think of an exemplary *Shabbos* table, one particular family I know immediately comes to mind. There is so much one can learn about the beauties of Torah life just by sitting at this family's *Shabbos* table. While their sense of modesty would be violated by public identification, I do not think they would mind if I presented a brief description of their *Shabbos* table.

This *Shabbos* table is set like any other. Nothing is especially fancy; in fact, much of the table setting is quite plain. Only one feature stands out: the number of place settings. Nobody has *that* many children! Even before the dining room fills with people, you already know that this is a *Shabbos* table that includes many guests.

The family and guests file in together with a mixture of solemnity and anticipation. By just watching the way people gather around the table, you know that this is an experience that takes place regularly but never feels repetitious.

The father and mother are unquestionably king and queen. While no formal coronation has taken place and neither one wears a crown, the royal stature of the parents is evident in the respect reflected in the faces of all who sit around this *Shabbos* table.

When the stirring sounds of *Shalom Aleichem* are heard, a joyous journey begins, as each individual forges into the uncharted depths of his or her own soul and reaches for private heights of *ruchnius*.

The father recites *Kiddush*. It is the same *Kiddush* that is said in every home, and yet it is not at all identical. The father recites it alone but everyone is with him, hanging on to each word. No one has to make an effort to pay attention, no one's mind has wandered.

The *zemiros* are sung with no unique musical talent. In fact, some of the men are definitely off key! No one cares. The melodies fade into the background as the words take on special meanings. The *zemiros* are not simply pleasant tunes but become more like joyful *tefillos*.

The food is tasty, but does not meet any gourmet standards. Different criteria, however, are used at this *Shabbos* table. Here the food is seen as an opportunity to serve *Hashem Yisbarach*. Although such a concept sounds somewhat ethereal and abstract, here it becomes a concrete reality.

Boundaries between "family" and "guests" melt away at this *Shabbos* table. In tone and manner, words and actions, all is done to create a larger family atmosphere that makes everyone feel included.

No one can be given an abundance of attention here. There are just too many people. The quality of attention, though, more than makes up for whatever may be lacking in quantity. By the time the wine goblet is raised for *Bircas Hamazon*, everyone has been made to feel more than just noticed.

The *divrei Torah* spoken here are an integral part of this *Shabbos* table. They are not an addition to the meal, or an appendage arbitrarily imposed. Instead, they flow from the meal as smooth as honey and just as sweet. No earth-shattering novellae or brilliant Torah insights are offered. Nevertheless, the words of Torah are cherished by all who sit around this *Shabbos* table. What is special here is the unusual way in which the *divrei Torah* seem to speak to each individual, on his or her own level, in a most personal and intimate fashion.

Sitting at this *Shabbos* table even once opens up a whole new world of what *shemiras Shabbos*, in general, and the *Shabbos* table, in particular, can accomplish. Like the sweetness of wine which lingers on long after being swallowed, the impact of this *Shabbos* table lingers on long after *Havdalah*. People who have had the *zechus* to sit at this *Shabbos* table carry the inspiration on to other parts of the week and other parts of the world.

The inspiration of this *Shabbos* table has changed people in many ways. Some have gone on to make deeper personal commitments to *limud Torah*. Others have come away motivated to *daven* with greater *kavanah*. Still others experience a recharge of their spiritual battery which permeates every aspect of their *Yiddishkeit*.

When I left this *Shabbos* table, I felt that I had gained new insight into what it means to be part of the *Am Segulah*. In addition, I had a better grasp of what the home of Avraham *Avinu*

must have been like. Finally, I came away with a burning resolve to try to emulate this experience at my own *Shabbos* table.

In the final analysis, what makes the *Shabbos* table so special is something so obvious that it can, at times, be overlooked: The *Shabbos* table represents a regular weekly experience in Torah living which is shared by *the family*. As such, each family's *Shabbos* table reflects the uniqueness of that family's *Yiddishkeit*. It is a kind of "family signature."

What do you think of *now* when you hear the phrase, "the *Shabbos* table"?

12

A Parent's Survival Guide
to Sibling Rivalry

*Part of the excitement of living through today's explosion
of technological advancement is watching the size of appliances shrink each year. Tape recorders, which used to require
two hands to lift, now fit into a shirt pocket. Phones, which
used to sit on tables, are now smaller than the palm of your
hand. And calculators, which used to fit into shirt pockets, are
now carried in wallets.*

*But as the appliances, themselves, are getting smaller, the
instruction booklets which come along with them are growing
exponentially. The instructions for most appliances used to be
printed on the packaging. Occasionally, an instruction card
was included. Now appliances come with lengthy books that
barely can be read in one sitting.*

*Unfortunately, there are no instruction books that come
along with children. If there were, they would probably include*

many volumes and we would never have the time to read them, anyway. But there is one aspect of childrearing which would prompt every parent to run for the manual: sibling rivalry. It is safe to say that no other facet of parenting confounds parents more. And no other area of questions sends parents scrambling with such desperation for answers.

In lieu of a "manufacturer's manual," the following chapter represents a compact guide to help parents survive one of the most difficult ordeals of parenting.

∽∂∾

"**A**ND RABBAH THE SON OF M'CHASYA SAID IN THE NAME OF Rav Chama the son of Gurya who said in the name of Rav, A person should never [treat] one son differently from his other children because as a result of the two *selah's* weight of silk which Yaakov *Avinu* added to Yosef above [that received by] his brothers (i.e. for the cloak of many colors), his brothers became jealous of him and it led to our forefathers descending [into exile and then slavery] in *Mitzrayim*" (*Shabbos* 10b and *Megillah* 16b).

Tosafos (*Shabbos*, loc. cit.) notes that Avraham *Avinu* had already been told (*Bereishis* 15:13) that a foreign nation shall subjugate his children. That being the case, how can the *Gemara* attribute the Jews' enslavement in Egypt to the jealousy of Yosef's brothers? *Tosafos* answers that had it not been for this episode, the Jews would have been subjected to less affliction.

From these words of *Chazal*, we can glean at least four valuable insights into the Torah view of sibling rivalry.[1]

---

1. It must be noted at the outset that the spiritual levels of Yaakov *Avinu* and his children are completely beyond our ken. When *Chazal* discuss their "errors," "jealousy," or "rivalry," they refer to microscopic character flaws which affected their halachic decision-making by hairsbreadths. That having been said, the Torah and *Chazal* have chosen to teach us of these shortcomings so that we might learn from them in our own experience. That is what we aim to do here.

First and foremost, we see that *Chazal* ascribe to Yaakov *Avinu* the blame for provoking the jealousy between Yosef and his brothers. *Chazal* are highlighting then, that parents are often the ones responsible when jealousy among siblings reaches extreme levels. This is true even when the siblings are all adults, as was the case with Yosef and his brothers.

In addition, *Chazal* emphasize the far-reaching consequences of sibling rivalry. The extreme and extended suffering of *Klal Yisrael* in *Mitzrayim* could have been prevented, had it not been for the jealousy of Yosef's brothers.

Furthermore, we can infer from this episode that the phenomenon of sibling rivalry is quite universal. If *tzaddikim* of the stature, prominence and maturity of the adult sons of Yaakov *Avinu* were capable of experiencing a degree of jealousy toward their brother Yosef, then we should not be surprised or disappointed if our children demonstrate such feelings toward each other, albeit in a much more basic way.

Finally, *Chazal* do not simply assign blame to Yaakov *Avinu* for his sons' rivalry. Rather, they explicitly teach us what to avoid in our own homes. They identify what they see to be the root cause of sibling rivalry: differences in the way the parents treat one child. This difference is perceived by the other children as grossly unfair.

Let us see if we can apply these four lessons of *Chazal* to the battles with sibling rivalry which takes place on the front lines of our own homes.

1. Parental Responsibility

It is well known that President Harry Truman kept a sign on his desk in the White House which read, "The buck stops here." This no-nonsense attitude of accepting responsibility helped him earn his honored place in American history.

Not all parents today share Truman's willingness to accept

responsibility. I recall, for example, Seymour and Toby Gold,* who met with me to arrange for an evaluation of their 12-year-old son, Simcha.*

For the past few years, Simcha had been fighting with his brothers, both older and younger. More recently, the clashes had become physical and the Golds were concerned that Simcha might be suffering from some deep-seated emotional problems.

"We're ready to pay for therapy, if that's what he needs," Seymour assured me. "It has gotten so out of hand lately that my wife and I are willing to do practically anything to help Simcha."

The evaluation revealed quite unremarkable findings. Simcha had ample friends, good social skills, solid self-esteem and above average intelligence. If anything, he was suffering from "middle-child syndrome," feeling that his younger brother earned indulgence as the baby, his older brother wielded the status of *bechor*. He felt left out in the cold.

When these findings were shared with the Golds, they were stunned to hear that Simcha did not require therapy.

"Then what would you recommend we do about Simcha's problem?" Toby asked, incredulously.

I explained to the Golds that they would accomplish far more for Simcha by looking for ways to make him feel special than they would by sending him for therapy.

❧ Helping "Middle Children" Feel Unique

Children who are sandwiched in between more accomplished older siblings and cuter younger siblings often struggle to achieve their own unique niche in the family. While parents cannot pretend that their middle child is as advanced as an older child or as immature as a younger child, there are still ways they can help a middle child carve out his or her own exclusive identity.

---

* Not their real names.

A few examples are:

• Praise any talents or skills, however small, even when they are not being demonstrated (i.e. saying during the week, "You add so much to our *Shabbos* table by the beautiful way you sing *zemiros*").

• Assign an important but realistic task at home. (*Shabbos* preparations are especially well suited for this.)

• Devote a special time to be alone with the middle child or allow only him or her to join you while you complete a weekly errand or chore, designating the middle child as your "helper." (This can be used for older as well as younger children.) Of course, when parents take these steps they must be sure not to completely ignore the older or younger siblings.

2. The Far-Reaching Consequences of Sibling Rivalry

Chazal saw an unbroken chain of events which began with the rivalry between Yosef and his brothers and ended in the servitude and suffering in *Mitzrayim* generations later. As a therapist, I have seen the unbroken chain of events which begins as sibling rivalry between children and ends as destructive competition between adults.

Take, for example, the case of Mrs. Rochel Solomon,* the veteran assistant principal of Netzach Bais Yaakov* in Parktown Heights.* Mrs. Solomon initially consulted with me regarding some minor marital discord between her husband and herself. That later shifted to some parenting questions regarding her adolescent children. By the second year of treatment, she began bringing up administrative challenges she was facing in her running so large a girls' school.

One day, Mrs. Solomon came late to her session, explaining that she had been detained by a stressful meeting with a teacher

---

* Not their real names.

who was causing problems at school. This teacher was well liked by students and parents, but failed to complete some minor administrative duties in a timely fashion.

Mrs. Solomon wondered out loud how strict should she be with this teacher. She certainly wouldn't want this teacher to leave the school, but on the other hand, perhaps this teacher was undermining Mrs. Solomon's authority. Then, again, perhaps, as assistant principal, she was being too harsh.

I asked Mrs. Solomon to describe the teacher. Her description revealed some feeling that seemed to play a subconscious role in the conflict. Mrs. Solomon went on at length about how well dressed this teacher was and how good her marriage seemed to be. Touching on what appeared to be a recurrent theme in her life I observed, "It sounds as if you might be feeling a bit jealous of and competitive with this teacher."

Mrs. Solomon dabbed a tear from the corner of her eye. She then described how fiercely competitive she had always felt toward her sisters as she was growing up. Even now, as a grandmother, she was amazed and saddened that the old rivalries of her childhood were still haunting her now, many years later.

Uncovering these hidden motives in herself eventually led Mrs. Solomon to put her dealings with this teacher into proper perspective. Her struggle to gain insight into her feelings highlights how much effort is required, at times, to break the chain of destructive events which can begin with unbridled sibling rivalry in childhood.

3. Universality of Sibling Rivalry

"*Tza'ar rabbim, nechamah*, the fact that many share the same suffering is itself a source of comfort" (*Sefer HaChinuch* 331). When people realize that they are not alone, unique or abnormal, it can ease the burden of any misfortune. Sibling rivalry is no exception.

Parents who believe that everybody else's children get along smashingly and that it is only their children who squabble with each other are more likely to blow minor bickering out of proportion, and overreact with extreme and inappropriate measures. Once these parents realize that *some* sibling rivalry is a fact of family life, they can relax, calm down and deescalate their rising emotional stress and tension.

Take Shaya Zucker,* for example. He runs a tight ship at the office and tries to do the same at home. He even conducts his *Shabbos* table as if it were a staff meeting. When the serenity is disturbed by his children's mutual taunts, Shaya spins out of control. He loses his temper and raises his voice, frightening his children and embarrassing his wife.

After a few parental guidance sessions with Mr. and Mrs. Zucker, they were helped to understand how universal sibling rivalry really is. As a result, Shaya learned to feel less helpless and inadequate as a parent, and more tolerant of his children's behavior.

When a child does not behave just the way the parent would like, all too often the parent takes it much too personally. The parent translates the child's misbehavior into a personal failure for him or herself. It is as if the parent thinks, "If my child can act that way, then I must be at fault. I'm just an inadequate parent."

If parents blame themselves for all of their children's deficiencies, a vicious cycle can develop. A typical reaction is that the parent tries to "correct" the child. These frantic efforts place an enormous burden on the child, who seldom responds positively. When the child's behavior deteriorates further, in spite of the parent's efforts, the parent often becomes enraged, turning his or her anger at the imagined cause of his or her feelings of incompetence: the child. If these parents could feel less totally responsible for all of their children's behavior, they would not be so angry at their children.

That is exactly where Shaya Zucker began. Instead of seeing himself as a failure, and lashing out at his children for triggering

---

* Not his real name.

these feelings, he was able to adopt a more laid-back attitude. This defused many potential confrontations even before they flared up.

It was, perhaps, just for people like Shaya that *Chazal* felt it necessary to highlight for us the jealous feelings which were aroused between Yosef and his brothers. If sibling rivalry existed, to some degree, even in the home of Yaakov *Avinu*, then Shaya did not have to feel like a failure if his children contended with each other across (or even underneath) the *Shabbos* table.

4. Treating Siblings Fairly

One of the most difficult and universal challenges parents face is how to respond to allegations of unfairness. There is perhaps no accusation more frequently leveled at parents by children of all ages than, "You're not fair!" Children will hand down this indictment with all the moral authority they can muster. They will invoke this "fairness doctrine" as if it carried the weight of constitutional law. And they will even succeed, at times, in intimidating their parents into making concessions which go well beyond the parents' better judgment.

Generally, the complaint of unfairness follows some limit setting, punishment or assignment of responsibility by a parent. "How come *I* have to and *she* doesn't?!" "Why do *I* get punished and *they* get away with it?! "You always ask *me* to do it but you never ask *him*!" These are some of the many forms in which the fairness doctrine is invoked.

But aren't parents supposed to treat their children fairly? Isn't that the message of *Chazal* and the lesson we are supposed to learn from the story of Yosef? Is there never any legitimacy to children's grievances that their parents are unfair?

Certainly, parents must always attempt to treat their children fairly. Fairness, however, is not synonymous with equality. Just because parents do not treat each child in an identical manner does not mean they are being unfair. This is a critical lesson for both parents and children.

Often in school or camp, fairness is defined as equality. If children do not get equal opportunities, privileges or treats, their complaints of unfair treatment may be justifiable.

At home, however, it is neither possible nor advisable to treat all children identically, all the time. One child is older, the other younger. One child has special needs or unique abilities, the other does not.

To be fair, parents must give each child equal *consideration*, but not necessarily equal treatment. Whenever possible, children should receive equal favors. When treats are measured out evenly, for example, fairness is clearly demonstrated. (With extremely competitive siblings, however, even such efforts may be challenged with, "His piece is bigger than mine!" In such cases, it is advisable to let one child divide the goodies while the other has first pick. That way the division will be scientifically precise and you will be freed from accusations of unfairness.)

But when equal treatment is not possible, then the fairness doctrine must not prevent parents from doing what needs to be done. At the same time, however, efforts must be made to explain why the unequal treatment is, in fact, impartial.

A brief interchange between my good friend, Eli, and his son, Yaakov, should suffice for illustration. When Yaakov was old enough to have a bedtime, he soon noticed that he was going to bed earlier than his older sister, Dinah. Naturally, he complained to his father that this was unfair. Eli asked him to propose a solution. Yaakov readily suggested that both he and Dinah should go to bed at the same time.

"But Dinah is already in school and must do homework at night," Eli pointed out. "If she goes to bed when you do, she will not have time to complete her homework. And if you go to bed when she does, you won't have enough sleep and you'll be tired all day."

Yaakov could not argue with his father's logic so he reverted to the bedrock of his case. "But it's not fair!"

Eli admitted that the different bedtimes *appeared* unfair. Then he reflected Yaakov's feeling that he would prefer across-the-board equality. Finally, Eli played out Yaakov's wish a bit further so that the boy could grasp the true meaning of fairness.

"I guess you're right," Eli began, appearing to have been swayed by Yaakov's invocation of the fairness doctrine. "In order to be treated fairly, both you and Dinah must be treated exactly the same. So if she gets to stay up later, you should be allowed to stay up, too."

Yaakov was beaming, now, feeling very gratified that he had been heard ... until Eli continued.

"Of course, if we're going to treat you both the same, that will have to be for everything. Otherwise it wouldn't really be fair. So I suppose we'll have to skip making a *bar mitzvah* for you when you get to be 13, because Dinah won't have a *bar mitzvah*. You'll be the only boy in your class not having a *bar mitzvah*, but we'll just tell everyone that we are treating you and your sister the same."

Yaakov contemplated what his father had just told him and weighed the loss of a *bar mitzvah* as compared with accepting an age-adjusted bedtime. Eli knew his son got the point when Yaakov asked, "But if I go to bed now, will you still read me a story?"

This discussion was repeated, often, between Eli and his children as they were growing up. (He used the forfeiture of her later bedtime as the negotiating point with Dinah.) At times, these dialogues even took on the flavor of a familiar family ritual, as both parent and child came to expect the other's arguments. The fact that each child has distinct needs which may require disparate treatment is a difficult concept for children to grasp. Therefore, it requires ongoing reinforcement. But if parents hammer long enough and hard enough, the notion will penetrate.

Some parents can handle the different-needs issue with aplomb. Where they really get stuck, however, is when they are called upon to take sides in a sibling quarrel.

Being drawn in to adjudicate between siblings is among the most common of scenarios which lead to accusations of unfairness. Trying to mediate between adversarial siblings is a classic no-win situation for parents for a few reasons. First and foremost, parents will never be able to determine all the facts. Even with subpoena power to ask anyone and everyone, "What happened?" parents will never learn the whole story. And even if parents actually witness an episode themselves, they do not know what events *preceded* and precipitated the episode.

Thus, when parents try to right the wrongs and "settle" disputes between their children, at least one child will feel unfairly treated. At times, both children will feel that way — the apparent victim will feel inadequately defended and the apparent perpetrator will feel unjustly accused. Therefore, attempts to arbitrate disputes between siblings are more likely to exacerbate conflicts rather than diffuse them.

Suppose, however, a parent *does* have a good idea what transpired, or at least he or she thinks they do. Will they still lose if they attempt to arbitrate the sibling conflict? Isn't it a parent's responsibility to maintain peace and harmony among children?

The reality is that the triangle involving two siblings and the parent(s), by its very nature, creates competitive conflict. All children want to be loved and approved of by their parents, all the time. Nevertheless, all children are sometimes ignored or criticized by their parents. This creates a constant concern in the minds of children that perhaps they are no longer loved and appreciated. As a result, children need repeated reassurance that they are, indeed, still loved and cared for by their parents.

The concern about the parents' love is generated not only by parents' disapproval. It is also generated when approval, praise or love is bestowed upon the other children. It is as if a child says to him or herself, "Since I was just scolded, maybe Mommy doesn't really love me like she used to yesterday. But when I see how much attention my sister is getting, now I'm really worried about what Mommy thinks of *me!*"

So how can a child find out his or her current popularity rating at home? Without the advantage of a pollster, like those used by politicians, a child is left with no option other than to test the parent. And what better test could there be than to lure the parent in to adjudicate a dispute? The child is thinking, "If Mommy takes *my* side, then I'll know I really am loved more than my sister!"

Since both children in a dispute may think this way, it means that at least one child will leave the arbitration hearing feeling even more unsure of the parent's love than before. This, in turn, could prompt the child to provoke another opportunity to test the parent's preference by instigating yet another confrontation with the same sibling. And so we now have so vicious a cycle of teasing, taunting and tattling that any parent will be driven to the bookstore to buy the latest ArtScroll book on parenting!

Harav Shlomo Wolbe sums it up this way. "When brothers and sisters are quarreling among themselves ... it is necessary to let the children work it out themselves ... As the Rosh says: Do not interfere in an argument in which you are not involved. The result is likely to be that the two sides will settle matters between themselves while the one who tried to intervene will be at odds with both sides in the dispute."[2]

If parents should not intervene in sibling arguments, how will the skirmish be resolved? This was the question I was asked by the timid, frustrated parents of 8-year-old Shimshy.[*]

❧ The Case of Shimshy

Shimshy was constantly getting into fights with his two brothers, who were not only older, but bigger and stronger as well. Shimshy really took a beating from both of his brothers and his parents were at their wits' end to figure out how to prevent these verbal and physical attacks.

Shimshy's parents acknowledged that it was Shimshy who

---

2. My translation of *Zeriah Ubinyan Bechinuch* (Hebrew) by Harav Shlomo Wolbe (Yerushalayim: Feldheim Publishers), p. 43.
* Not his real name.

provoked the attacks. He would act in ways which practically invited a showdown. Nevertheless, his brothers were older and more mature. Shouldn't they be able to control themselves, the parents asked? In addition, since the older boys were both athletic, either one could potentially hurt Shimshy.

Shimshy's parents tried everything. They encouraged the older boys to avoid Shimshy. They tried reasoning. They even resorted to punishing the older boys whenever battles ensued. Nothing helped. The parents also tried to coach Shimshy on how to avoid behavior which would antagonize his brothers. To the parents' utter amazement, however, Shimshy continued to goad one or both of his older brothers. Finally, in desperation, Shimshy's parents brought him for an evaluation to help them solve the puzzle of his continued self-destructive behavior.

The evaluation revealed that Shimshy was insecure, with low self-esteem and an abiding desire for parental approval. Although he was receiving considerable attention, affection and approval from both parents, he wanted still more. While the beatings he received from his brothers were not welcomed, they seemed to him well worth the "reward" of his parents rescuing him from his brothers whenever the combat escalated.

After explaining all of this to Shimshy's parents, I pointed out that as long as they broke up the wrangling and reprimanded the older boys, Shimshy felt rewarded for his provocative behavior. Therefore, I advised them to resist any and all provocations and to refuse to intervene between Shimshy and his brothers.

I also suggested to the parents that they could justify this non-intervention policy by saying that they did not see what happened; they don't know what really went on; or, they simply don't have all the facts so they are unable to determine who was really at fault.

"But maybe it will get even worse if we don't try to stop them," the parents objected, almost in unison.

"It probably will," I told them. "But if so, that will be just to test your determination. When they see you are committed to not getting involved, they will learn to resolve their disputes by themselves."

Then I went on to explain that *children learn important social skills when they are forced to figure out how to settle their differences on their own.* And these lessons are important, and learned, for life. Parents just cannot always be there when children confront each other. And children must learn how to negotiate differences with each other independent of their parents.

Parents certainly should not become indifferent to these negotiations. But their role must always be that of coach or cheerleader, not pinch hitter. As with other developmental learning tasks, parents can help children best by rooting from the sidelines, not by jumping out onto the field.

Another area where this coaching role is valuable is homework. If you do your children's homework for them, they will never acquire the skills they need to learn. But if you offer only guidance or suggestions, and you allow your children to do the rest, you demonstrate concern and caring while you also exhibit the kind of trust which can build confidence and pride.[3]

The only exception to the principle of nonintervention articulated here would be the case of toddlers and very young children. Below the age of 3 or 4, it may be necessary for parents to step in when hitting starts. In such cases, the parents should only try to separate the combatants, *without taking sides* in the fighting. While limits must be set for such young children, parents still need to avoid the sand trap of sitting in judgment between adversarial siblings. A firm, "You play there and you play here," may be all that is needed to deescalate the conflict. A disputed toy, for example, can be removed from both children so that neither gets the impression that the parents took sides. In this way, the stakes are lowered and the children learn that they will not win points in the competition for parental love by drawing the parents into the adjudication of sibling rivalry.

Oh, yes. Whatever did happen to Shimshy?

His parents went against their better judgment, disobeyed

---

3. (The subject of homework is complex, and is discussed in a chapter of its own. See Chapter 14: "Whose Homework Is It, Anyway?")

their instincts and followed my advice. They were pleasantly surprised to discover that in a relatively short time, Shimshy gradually eliminated his irritating behavior. This, in turn, reduced the friction between him and his brothers, and brought peace and harmony to their formerly embattled home.

Chazal, in their infinite wisdom, understood that sibling rivalry is universal and can be found in any home with more than one child. They also realized that it is up to the parents to ensure that the competition between siblings does not escalate beyond normal bounds. Finally, they taught us that whenever sibling rivalry does spin out of control, it is up to the parents to examine their parenting and make whatever adjustments are necessary to reduce the corrosive competition.

Extrapolating from what *Tosafos* suggested, we may not be able to completely alter the course of history by minimizing sibling rivalry in our homes, but we just may be able to reduce a great deal of pain and anguish for ourselves and our children. Considering what we have to gain, it may be well worth the effort.

PART FIVE:
Dealing With School and Camp

13

The Home and the Yeshivah:
Shifted or Shared Responsibility

Many years ago, I took issue with one of my children's mechanchim *over the way in which a certain matter was handled in class. He told me, "He is your child at home. But when he is in my class, he is my child and not yours!"*

This mechanech *was trying to convey to me how much he loved each student in his class. In fact, he went on to say that he treats his students the same way he treats his own children at home.*

In spite of the fact that this mechanech *was trying to impress upon me how much he cared for my son, his words alienated me somewhat by making me feel that we were adversaries rather than allies. I think I would have felt better if he had said, "He is not your child or mine. He is* our *child. And we must try to work together, as a team, to reach our shared goals."*

When parents and mechanchim *see each other as team-mates sharing the responsibility for* chinuch, *then everyone reaps the rewards. But when parents and* mechanchim *see each other as adversaries, the educational process is doomed to fail.*

ᘯᕤ ᕥᘰ

HOW MUCH CHARACTER BUILDING AND TEACHING OF *MIDDOS,* character traits, should parents expect their children to receive in the yeshivah or *bais yaakov,* and how much is the parents' responsibility?

Today, *Baruch Hashem,* there are more yeshivos and *bais yaakov* schools in this country than ever before. The number of yeshivah students is growing at an even faster pace. While this proliferation of Torah study is cause for celebration, the frequency with which the above question is being asked is cause for alarm.

Years ago, the division of responsibility between home and yeshivah was much clearer than it is today. The yeshivah was seen as the center of Torah authority. *Middos* — values and character building — were seen as the responsibility of *both* the home and the yeshivah.

Sit in on any informal gathering of pedagogues today, however, and you will learn a lot about what ails yeshivah education in America. After commiserating for a while about work conditions and salary scales, the subject of *middos* is invariably raised. *Rebbei'im* bemoan the lack of respect, self-discipline and *derech eretz* among many yeshivah students today. This is true for the girls' schools, as well.

The finger of blame, of course, is often pointed at the home:

> *"The parents are not doing their job; they are abdicating their responsibility."*

Others put it this way:

> "What these parents cannot accomplish in 16 hours a
> day and on weekends, they expect us to accomplish in
> only eight hours a day, five days a week!"

Many parents are themselves very dissatisfied. They, too, are concerned with the character development of their children. In fact, they usually agree with their children's educators on all but one point: Who is to blame? Many parents feel that the responsibility rests with the yeshivah to develop and teach *middos* to their children.

This is what the parents have to say:

> "After nine years in the yeshivah, I would expect that
> they would have instilled a little more derech eretz *and*
> kibud av v'aim *than this!*" (a reference to some disre-
> spectful behavior)

Others go even further with their criticism:

> "What's the good of all the Torah study if they (the
> yeshivah faculty and administration) can't teach him
> (her) how to act like a decent human being."

It is not my purpose here to fix the blame for eroding discipline, *derech eretz* and *middos* on either the home or the yeshivah. My purpose is rather to help encourage greater collaboration between the home and the yeshivah. The result of the controversy described above is that both yeshivah personnel and Torah homes are, at times, experiencing an overwhelming sense of helplessness and frustration.

When people feel helpless, they tend to respond to that feeling with efforts to make themselves feel more secure. At times, they will attack and blame others. They might reach too quickly for simple, superficial or inadequate solutions. Finally, they might just give up any efforts at rectifying the situation and hope that everything will work out all right anyway.

To put it quite simply, when people feel helpless, they sometimes cope with these feelings in ways that can make the situation even worse than it had been.

The most critical casualties when there is conflict between parents and yeshivah educators are the children themselves. Children, as we all know, are extremely perceptive and aware. While they might not be able to articulate their perceptions, they are, nevertheless, very well aware of what goes on around them.

I have been consulted regarding many cases involving troubled yeshivah students. In the vast majority of those cases the most pervasive feeling about the child — at home and in the yeshivah — was one of helplessness; the *mechanchim* and the parents just say, "We just don't know what to do anymore with this child. We've tried *everything!*"

Children expect adults to know what is right, good and helpful. They look to adults for direction and guidance — even when they appear to want the opposite! When children begin to sense that the adults around them are confused, uncertain, doubtful or even just hesitant, they can become insecure and frightened.

Think of it this way. Most people today take bus and train travel pretty much for granted. We all know that a bus has a driver and a train has a conductor; but we hardly pay attention to them. We expect them to be doing their job efficiently, all the time. Suppose we were to hear the bus driver or train conductor begin to wonder, *out loud*, which controls to manipulate next, or what route to follow. Or suppose we were to hear the motorman arguing with the conductor. One need not have a vivid imagination to picture the frenzied bedlam that would result.

In spite of what we would like to think, children *do*, often, know when adults are unsure of themselves. Nothing communicates this more strongly than when parents openly criticize yeshivos and yeshivos openly criticize parents. When children grow up in such an atmosphere they can adopt an attitude of "anything goes." In addition, they could become frightened, insecure, misguided, or Heaven forbid, easy prey to whatever foul wind may be blowing in their direction. Is this what we want for our children?

Let us take a look at Mendel,* a young man from a wonderful family who has now moved out of his parents' home.

Mendel now insists on being called Mark. Although the name Mark does appear on his birth certificate, he was always "Mendel" at home and in yeshivah. And his new attitude towards his name is not the only thing that disturbs and frustrates his parents.

In dealing with the problem, the following pattern emerged: At home, when Mendel was growing up, Mendel often heard his parents criticize the yeshivah for his own poor behavior. He heard similar comments made by his rebbei'im about his parents.

Certainly a much more positive prospect would be if parents and yeshivos allied more closely — as they often do — to fortify yeshivah students against the alien winds blowing around them outside. Parents and *mechanchim* can, must, and generally do, provide each other with mutual backup and support for the other's efforts. Helplessness on either side must be acknowledged and overcome instead of attacked and denied. Only then can the problems be addressed effectively.

Many yeshivos, for example, have taken concrete, constructive steps and are already leading the way. These yeshivos are sponsoring workshops and discussion groups for the parents of their students on all aspects of childrearing and child development. These groups have been specially designed for all parents, and help to deal with the everyday trials and tribulations of parenting. Groups formed only for parents of "problem children," often bear the stigma of shame and embarrassment and participation is thus reduced. On the other hand, stigma-free parenting workshops for all enable parents to learn effective child-rearing

---

* Not his real name.

skills which can translate into more well-behaved children. In addition, the fact that these workshops are offered *at the yeshivah* serves to enhance the parents' loyalty to, and feelings of partnership with, the yeshivah.

Many of these very same yeshivos are also addressing their own needs. They have engaged part- and full-time guidance counselors and professional consultants who are on hand *in the yeshivah*. These consultants are available to both faculty and administration, as well as to parents. They are there to provide assistance and advice, not only for the all-too-frequent "impossible cases," but also for the less serious cases, many of which are "nipped in the bud" *before* they reach crisis proportions.

Hopefully, if these efforts gain momentum, parents and yeshivos will be working so closely together that questions like the one raised at the outset, will become out dated and old fashioned.

14

Whose Homework
Is It, Anyway?

Most parents only come to school twice a year: once at the end of fall for P.T.A. and once at the end of spring for registration. Aside from these two evenings, there is often no direct contact between the parents and the school, unless there is a problem.

Although parents hardly set foot into their children's school, they confront their children's education every night through the medium of homework and review.

For some parents and children, homework is a relaxed, pleasant, nightly experience which blends smoothly into the rhythm of the evening schedule. Who these people are is no secret. Their names are listed in the Guiness Book of World Records.

For the rest of us, homework can become a nightly ordeal. It causes parents and children to lock horns, raise voices and gnash teeth. The passionate drama is so intense, at times, that it makes a Greek tragedy look like a comedy by comparison.

Before we, as parents, indict the school administration and before we whisk our children off to the nearest educational consultant, perhaps we should first examine some of our own attitudes about homework and ask ourselves, "Whose homework is it, anyway?"

⟡

I DON'T CONSIDER MYSELF MIDDLE AGED, YET. BUT IF YOU'D ASK MY children, they'd probably tell you that I went to school during the Middle Ages. Of course, some things *were* different when I attended elementary school yeshivah. We were discouraged, for example, from watching the now ineffable "box," but we were not excommunicated for doing so. (While community standards have risen, the media's have plummeted!) And the only "uniforms" were "*yarmulkas* and *tzitzis* for the boys, and skirts or dresses for the girls."

But, while some things have changed, I have always assumed that others would not, and should not, change. One of those Rock-of-Gibraltar components of yeshivah education is homework, or more properly, the "h" word.

Now don't get me wrong. I HATED homework. I dillydallied and then dillydallied some more. I complained and mumbled and then complained some more. But I did it. In retrospect, I don't believe that it did me any harm. In fact, I benefited greatly from all of those chapters I reviewed, verses I memorized and words I looked up. And if not for all of those compositions I had to write, I might not have been able to write this book!

However, this generation's homework situation is very different from the way it was when I went to yeshivah. Oh, sure, my children still came home with loads of *sefarim*, books and stencils, just as I did; and yes, they did launch into the same impassioned oratory on the injustices of homework, just as I used to do. But ... they didn't *do* the homework, as I did. Instead, my wife and I ended up doing a lot of the homework for them!

My parents were certainly there for me when I needed help with my homework, but that usually consisted of little more than giving me the spelling of a word that I might have otherwise had to look up in the dictionary or helping me cut a piece of cardboard in a straight line. Today, it is increasingly difficult for children to complete many of their homework assignments unassisted; and in some cases, it is even necessary for the parents to complete the assignments *unassisted by their children!*

I would not lift pen to paper on this sensitive subject had I not surveyed dozens of other yeshivah and *bais yaakov* students. Both my wife and I have had experiences which, unfortunately, have been shared by others as well.

"How long did it take you to answer those Navi questions last week?" I once asked a father.

"Are you kidding?" the other father snapped in disgust. "I let my wife do those questions. She went to seminary; I never learned Navi in yeshivah."

"How long did it take you to complete the Chumash homework last night?" I asked another father.

"I'm ashamed to admit it, but I couldn't finish that one. I put in about an hour and a half and then I just gave up. So I wrote my daughter's teacher a note that she didn't feel well."

My wife once asked another mother how she managed the difficult social studies homework which was due the day after a wedding.

"It wasn't easy," the other mother explained, triumphantly. "But we had a long drive to the hall. So I took the social studies book with me in the car. As my husband drove to the wedding, I dictated the answers to my son over the car phone."

And so it goes. More often than we would like to admit, *chavrusos* are kept waiting, suppers are served late, and *shiurim* are missed as parents hassle with their children's homework. In some extreme cases, invitations to *bar mitzvahs* or *sheva berachos* are declined as parents are held hostage at home because of homework. Invariably, tension mounts, patience runs out and at least one person ends up crying. And it is not always the child!

Hopefully, all would agree that this situation cannot continue. Firstly, our children are simply not learning from the homework we do for them, denying them the education they need and deserve. In addition, we cannot keep up under the strain. Our relationships with our children are suffering the most as we become the targets of each other's tempers, which have been shortened by accumulated frustration.

As a parent, I found myself singing the all-too-familiar chorus, "Whose homework is it, anyway?!" How did this happen? When did it start? Who is to blame?

To answer the last question first, we have to blame ourselves, not our children. It is our fault for putting grades above learning and "success" above genuine achievement. If our daughter did not understand her teacher, if the *rebbi* went over our son's head, or if our children cannot get all the answers right, that does not mean that we are supposed to do the work for them. *They will gain more from accepting the responsibility for their own limitations than they will by passing the buck to us.*

But parents do not bear all of the guilt for this homework nightmare; the *yeshivos* and *bais yaakov* schools are at least partially at fault, as well. The drive towards "excellence" in education has gone too far. Competition is no longer just a problem among students but also among schools. Some *yeshivos* are trying to outdo each other while some *bais yaakov* schools are attempting to set ever-higher standards. Every few years the level for starting *Mishnayos* drops one grade, as does the grade for beginning *Ramban*.

Let's look in on the Bergers,* now, as the supper dishes are being cleared away. Supper started about a half hour later than usual tonight, so everyone is a bit behind schedule.

---

* Not the real name.

"If all the traffic lights are green, I can still be on time for my *daf yomi shiur*," Sol Berger calls over his shoulder to his wife, Esther, as he bolts out the door.

"Shoshanah, don't go into your room until you've helped clear the table," Esther instructs her 15-year-old daughter.

"But, Ma, you know I have a *major* math test tomorrow. I need every minute to study. As it is, I'll probably have to stay up past midnight."

"Just give me five minutes and then I'll let you go," Esther insists.

After everything has been cleared away from supper, Esther looks for 7-year-old Yitzy. She finds him in the den, on the floor, surrounded by his Lego.

"Yitzy, it's time to review your *Chumash* homework. Remember what your *rebbi* said about the contest?" Esther coaxed.

"Oh, Ma, not now. I'll do it with you later," Yitzy protests.

Esther now looks for the book she was reading and settles into an easy chair in the living room. No sooner does she find her place than 11-year-old Ruchie runs in, breaking the peaceful silence.

"I just can't do this book report! I don't understand what the teacher wants. I don't know how to do book reports. And I couldn't even understand what the book was all about," Ruchie pleads to her mother.

"Would you like me to help you?" Esther asks in a calm, soothing tone.

"I don't even know how to begin!" Ruchie continues her whining.

"I'm offering to help you, Ruchie," Esther repeats. "Bring me the sheet your teacher gave out in class, together with the book you read for the report. Let's try to work on it together."

Once Esther and Ruchie are sitting across from each other at the kitchen table, Esther peruses the book-report requirements. "When is the book report due?" she asks her daughter.

"Tomorrow," Ruchie replies, cautiously. "And if we give it in late, points are going to be taken off."

A few moments later, Shoshanah appears in the kitchen doorway. She is practically breathing fire from her nostrils.

"This math is just *impossible!*" Shoshanah announces. "I did five of the review problems at the end of the chapter and I got them all wrong. There's simply no way I'm going to pass that math test tomorrow. I know I'm going to fail. If I average in the 67 I got on the midterm, it will take a miracle for me to pass math this year. I might as well give up now."

"Shoshanah," Esther begins, calmly, "What would you like me to do about this?"

"Maybe you could show me how to do this stuff," Shoshanah asks sheepishly. "I can usually figure it out when you explain it to me."

Now the phone rings. Esther picks up the receiver.

"Hello? ... Yes ... Oh, hi, Chavy... Congratulations. That's wonderful. I never win anything in Chinese auctions. Your husband must be thrilled ... I'd love to hear all about it but I'm busy with homework now. Let me call you back tomorrow."

Now Yitzy runs through the kitchen holding a Lego airplane and making the appropriate engine sounds.

"Yitzy," Esther shouts. "I thought you were going to review *Chumash* with me."

"Later, Ma," he shoots back. "V'room, V'room," he intones, allowing the toy plane to carry him down the hall.

"Ma, you said you'd help *me* with my book report," Ruchie objects.

"You know you really could do that report yourself," Shoshanah chides her younger sister. "But I don't stand a chance of passing this *major* math test tomorrow unless Ma studies with *me.*"

Esther Berger steals a glance at her watch, quickly calculating how much longer it will be until Sol gets home. Her next thought is, "How on earth did I get myself into this mess in the first place? Whose homework is it, anyway?!"

Obviously, the problem began well before tonight's supper. Once Mrs. Berger accepted upon herself the responsibility to fill in all of the gaps in her children's knowledge, she was planting the seeds for tonight's crisis.

Months and years earlier, when Mrs. Berger agreed to compensate for any deficits of memory, knowledge, comprehension, or frustration on the part of her children, she laid the foundation for tonight's dilemma.

Parents can and should assist their children with homework. It supports the educational process and sends a message that parents do care about their children's *chinuch*. But parents must make it very clear right from the outset that assistance does not include last-minute, 11th-hour bail outs.

Children can, at times, be quite manipulative. That is their birthright. But parents must not allow themselves to be blackmailed with such comments as, "You don't want me to fail, do you?" "If you don't help me, I just won't be able to do it myself" and, "But I'm no good at this and it's so easy for you."

It takes courage, at times, to resist children's pressure. They can be very insistent and unyielding. In response, many parents just feel it is easier to do the homework themselves rather than go through the hassle of confrontation.

The issue here, however, is more than a book report or a math test. It goes way beyond that. The issue is whether or not your child will learn to be self-reliant and accept responsibility for his or her own shortcomings.

No, it doesn't feel good to fail a test or lose points on a book report. But that bad feeling may motivate your child to prepare in advance next time. If you bail your children out today, they will never learn the more important lesson of how to plan ahead, tomorrow.

This may sound like a radical approach to some of the parents who have been picking up, cleaning up and fixing up after their children for many years. In fact, it might even sound downright revolutionary.

But that is just what we need. What we need is a revolution! We need a return to traditional family values! We need to make homework a job for children, not parents! And we need to end this hostage crisis so that I can get to my *shiur* on time!

15

"I Don't Want To Go To School": Faking or Phobia?

Baruch Hashem, *many childhood diseases have become merely historical footnotes as a result of inoculations and vaccines which have virtually eliminated these illnesses from our children's lives. Other less serious, but nonetheless unpleasant, ailments remain to temporarily disrupt the lives of our children, as well as our own.*

Just as few children can expect to reach adulthood without contracting chicken pox, hardly any child makes it through 12 - 14 years of formal education without announcing, at least once, "I don't want to go to school today."

When that happens, the parents are immediately confronted with a host of serious questions. Should they allow the child to remain home from school or not? What is the best way for parents to handle this situation? The answers depend very much on why the child wants to stay home.

Is the child not feeling well? Is he or she suffering a medical problem? Or, is this more likely an example of malingering? Is there a psychological problem here or merely a social problem between classmates? Is this a symptom of a serious emotional problem or is there a test the child would like to avoid? In short, is the child simply faking an illness or has a genuine phobia developed? This chapter will offer some practical guidelines to help parents make these distinctions.

ONSIDER THE FOLLOWING SCENARIO: YOUR ALARM RINGS. YOU reflexively reach over to your clock and hit the "snooze" button. You fall back to sleep even before your head hits the pillow. Your alarm rings, again. You check the time to convince yourself that you had better get up, now. You drag yourself out of bed, thinking, "Tonight I really must get to bed earlier." Sound familiar so far?

It is time to wake your children. You make the rounds, waking them each shortly before they have to get out of bed, acting as a human "snooze" button. You return, a few minutes later, to let them know that now they really have to get out of bed.

"You'll be late for the school bus," you warn them, prodding them out of the comfort of their warm beds. Eventually, your children drag themselves out of bed, starting their morning routine.

This morning's script, however, has been altered dramatically. One of your children announces in a plaintive tone, "I don't want to go to school."

You may have heard this before or, perhaps, this is the first time you are confronted with this challenge. Why is your child starting the day this way? What does this mean? How should you respond? What is the best approach for you to take?

This is one of those situations in which you cannot fully assess the circumstances until you have more information. To try to intervene, at this point, would be premature. The proper response, therefore, is to gather more data.

"Why don't you want to go to school today? Is there anything wrong at school? Does anything hurt you? What is bothering you?" Any or all of these questions convey the message that you are really interested to know what your child may be facing. These questions also signify that you are more interested in your child's welfare than in school attendance for its own sake. Finally, they help your child focus more on the underlying problem rather than the immediate symptom.

Your child's reply will usually fall into one of two categories. Either your child will express a specific complaint or else, a more nonspecific protest will be voiced. In each case, you will need to probe further, but the eventual responses will differ greatly.

I. Specific Complaints

When a child expresses a specific complaint which is prompting him or her to want to stay home from school, the parents must first try to understand fully the nature of the objection. Initially, all specific complaints about school should be taken seriously. Children need to feel their parents really care.

The second step is to address the problem directly. If your child is experiencing worry, pain or fear, the source of the stress must be identified and then a plan should be formulated to ameliorate the stress.

This problem solving should be done together with your child for two reasons: First, if a plan is offered which makes sense, it will help to calm your child immediately. Of course, the problem does not have to be solved before the school bus arrives, but your child needs to know that it will be worked out eventually. The second reason children need to be included in the problem-solving process is to teach them coping skills so they will be able to solve their own problems one day.

While there are countless specific complaints a child could present as a rationale for not wanting to go to school, most of them fall into one of four categories.

1. Physical/Medical Problems

The most frequent justification for not wanting to go to school is a physical complaint. "This hurts," or, "That aches," are common refrains.

As with all specific complaints, considerable judgment is needed in evaluating physical ailments. Is this the first time that particular body part has been identified as hurting? Are there other corroborating symptoms? Does this sound serious? Is this a child who is always crying 'wolf'?

If you feel concern may be warranted, tell your child that you will consult the pediatrician over the phone during the next calling hour. If you feel concern may not be warranted, write the symptom down in a "doctor's notebook" and tell your child you will monitor the situation for three days. If it stays the same or gets worse, you will call the doctor. Otherwise, it may prove to be insignificant. Either way, you have laid out a plan.

Staying home from school, however, should not be considered as an option unless your child is bleeding, vomiting, running a fever, has a history of this ailment, or is suffering another readily apparent symptom. Allowing your child to stay home from school under any other circumstance is to risk that he or she will be encouraged to repeat the same complaint in the near future.

2. Teacher/Schoolwork Problems

The next most common specific complaint expressed by children who do not want to go to school is a problem related to schoolwork or a relationship problem with a specific teacher.

Once again, the problem should be taken seriously and a plan must be presented which could lead to a solution.

Suppose, for example, your child complains that he or she cannot keep up with the workload or is unable to understand what is being taught. You might offer to call the teacher, spend some time that evening assisting your child with homework, or arrange for tutoring.

If your child accuses a teacher of unfair treatment but asks you not to speak to the teacher for fear of exacerbating the problem, you could suggest alternative strategies. You could offer to speak with the principal, other parents, or an experienced outside party. In addition, you could offer to sit down later that evening to discuss what has been going on in greater detail, so that the two of you can come up with an effective plan of action.

Once again, staying home from school is simply not an acceptable resolution to teacher or schoolwork problems.

3. Bus/Bus-Driver Problems

Sometimes the problem has nothing to do with school, itself, but involves difficulties with getting to school. For example, the other children on the bus may be picking on or teasing your child. If so, you need to hear exactly what has been going on and then decide whether your child needs to learn how to protect him or herself or whether some adult intervention is warranted. Depending upon the nature of the problem, you may want to contact the bus teacher, if there is one, the principal, or even arrange alternate transportation temporarily.

If the problem is related to the bus driver, you may want to consult parents of other passengers to verify your child's account of the objectionable behavior. Depending upon the seriousness of your child's accusation, you may not wait for confirmation and might consider alternative transportation immediately.

4. Social Problems

Although social problems do not relate to school directly, they are extremely important in the life of a child, and these issues play a much larger role in academic performance than some parents realize. Having conflicts with classmates could be so stressful for your child that he or she feels that school attendance is unbearable.

While you must not belittle your child's concerns, you must also teach your child that avoidance is not a valid solution to relationship difficulties. Once again, offering to sit down later that evening to discuss the entire matter may be enough of a plan to get your child on the bus.

Later that evening, of course, you would have to deliver on your promise to help. You could do so by sharing stories (only true ones) of when you were a child and how you overcame similar obstacles, or by recommending steps your child could take to appease, confront or befriend the aggressors. If the problem is related to an overall lack of friends, then concrete suggestions for reaching out and socializing with others would be most welcomed, and offering to contact a teacher for assistance may be in order.

II. Nonspecific Complaints

Clearly the most challenging scenario is when a child is not able to articulate any specific objections to school. Instead, the child simply whines, cries or protests without providing any justification for wanting to stay home. When that happens, you have to use other indicators to help you assess the underlying meaning and message of this most disturbing behavior.

One indicator is tone of voice. Is your child tentatively hinting at the idea of not going to school or violently insisting? Is the crying a whimper or more like wailing?

Another indicator is body language. Is your child curled up in a ball, hiding under the bed cover, or is he or she simply dawdling on the way to the school bus? Does your child appear to be feeling panicky or just discouraged?

Finally, you need to consider this episode in the context of the your child's age level and prior performance at school. Is this your child's first week or month of school? Has your child happily attended school in the past, and if so, for how long before today's scene? Are all separations difficult for this child, or is today's fussing out of character for him or her?

As you evaluate your child's protest, you should bear in mind a number of different possible explanations and underlying causes.

1. Fear of Reprisal

You've just asked your child, "What's the matter? Why don't you want to go to school today?"

Your child takes a deep breath, as if to begin to explain, and then simply repeats the protest. While no specific complaint is expressed, you get the distinct impression that your child does have a clear reason in mind for refusing to go to school.

If your child has had a good attendance record and going to school has never been a problem before, you may need to consider whether your child is withholding some important information from you because of fear of reprisal.

One simple possibility is that your child has done something for which he or she feels terribly guilty. Now your child not only wants to avoid school but also wants to hide the truth from you. He or she may be frightened about how you will react if you discover the impropriety. If you suspect that this is the case, you should point out to your child that if he or she has done something wrong, you will probably find out about it sooner or later, so he or she might as well tell you and get it over with.

Another possibility is that your child has been, or is currently being, victimized or abused in some way by another student or even an adult at school. Your child may be fearful of reporting this to you because the perpetrator has threatened your child with even worse consequences if he or she reports the abuse or harassment, or because the child assumes that you will not believe him or her.

In one case, for example, an academically weak 8-year-old boy was being molested by a tutor who was taking him out of class for remedial work. The boy withheld this information from his parents for months because the tutor had convinced the boy that he would be able to know, through his special abilities, if the boy reported the tutor to his parents or teachers.

If you do suspect that your child has been or is the victim of abuse, by anyone at any time, you should contact your pediatrician immediately for guidance and instructions.

2. Limit Testing

Did you ever watch a child step gingerly on an ice-covered puddle during the winter? Why take the risk of getting your foot wet and freezing cold, you wonder to yourself. The answer is that children constantly feel the need to test limits — the limits of the ice covering a puddle as well as the limits of their parents' patience and endurance.

You can therefore expect that every rule at home will be tested at least once by at least one of your children. The rule about going to school every day is no exception.

If you determine that your child's refusal to go to school today represents a test of your ability to set limits, then by all means do not fail this test. Remain calm yet firm. Do not sound tentative or unsure. Clearly and unequivocally explain to your child that daily attendance at school is absolutely mandatory in your home.

All of this should be done without anger in your voice, on your face or in your heart. Remember, it is your child's birthright to test limits. And it is your responsibility to enforce them.

3. Rebelliousness and Anger

At times, children who are frustrated and angry with their parents act out their rage by refusing to go to school. They suspect (and rightly so) that their parents will be more than mildly disturbed by even the prospect of a child staying home willfully. It is the shock value they are seeking.

If you determine that your child is balking at going to school as a means of provoking your anger, do not play into your child's hand by blowing your stack. Remain calm; but remain firm.

In this case, however, it is especially necessary to address the underlying feelings. If you fail to do so, your child will continue to try to act out his or her emotions by stubbornly refusing to go to school, or worse.

You address your child's feelings simply by acknowledging them. For example, you might say something like this. "Yenty, I know you are still upset about the disagreement we had last night. I can tell that you are feeling angry about what I said. I am perfectly willing to discuss this further with you tonight, after school. You do not need to stay home today to show me how angry you are. I can see that already."

4. Attention-Seeking

Some children seem to crave attention. Like dry sponges, they soak up as much of their parents' time as they can. They seem to always need to be noticed by parents and teachers alike.

As a result of their insatiable thirst for attention, these children often devise creative schemes to place themselves on center stage both at home and at school. And nothing puts a child into the spotlight at home any quicker than that age-old line, "I don't want to go to school today."

Now you are placed in a double bind. If you try to ignore your child, he or she will simply crank up the volume, trying even harder to get your attention. If you sit down now for a heart-to-heart talk about the "problem," you will already be reinforcing and rewarding this undesirable behavior. So what should you do?

The best approach would be to hold out the prospect of greater attention, but only during the evening after school. For example, "This seems serious, Shmully. We are going to need a lot of time to discuss this with you so we can understand exactly what it is that is bothering you and why you are so unhappy.

"Your father and I, however, simply do not have that much time right now. I assure you that we are going to be thinking about this all day until you get home tonight and we can talk about this together."

5. Work Overload

As children grow, their academic responsibilities and homework also increase. And by the time they enter high school, some children feel overwhelmed by the pressure of the workload.

Especially in high school, the academic year can be compared to a marathon race. Those students who expend all of their energy in the beginning will find themselves totally spent before they reach the June finish line. To succeed, students need to pace themselves by taking breaks each day, week and month.

Some children, however, need help in learning how to pace themselves properly. These students find themselves only halfway through a test when the time is up. And they need a vacation weeks before one is scheduled. As a result, they may try "to take a break" by skipping school occasionally.

They may argue that they really need a break because they have been studying so hard for so long. And they may be right. But to let them stay home from school today is to set a bad precedent for the future.

If you let your children stay home from school today, you will be sending the wrong signal. You will be saying, in effect, that whether or not children go to school is up to them; that if they need a break or feel they deserve one, they should simply take off a day whenever they please.

This is not the message you want to give your children. Instead, you want to recognize the effort they have been expending. You also want to acknowledge that breaks are needed and important. But that is why weekends and vacations were invented.

If additional time off is, in fact, necessary, it should only be considered when it is planned in advance, as opposed to on a sudden I've-got-to-have-it-now basis. For example, parents could discuss allowing a child once or twice a year to take a "mental-health day," but only if it is negotiated and agreed to *in advance* (preferably in consultation with the child's school).

In this way, parents are not being blackmailed by threats of, "If you don't let me stay home today, I'll fail this year, for sure!" In addition, your teenager will be granted the increased autonomy he or she is so desperately seeking. Moreover, by "giving in" a little, you will avoid a full-scale power struggle and confrontation which you can never really win, anyway. Finally, this approach will reduce your chances of being faced with another "I don't want to go to school" dilemma in the future.

6. Elevated Anxiety

So far, most of the scenarios and complaints described have been the garden variety encountered in every home since compulsory education was devised. This last category is less common and much more difficult to manage.

Suppose your child expresses no specific concern but still protests, with extreme intensity, going to school. You rule out fear of reprisal, testing limits, acting out anger, seeking attention or work overload as the underlying cause. And you are, quite frankly, baffled as to why your child is so adamantly and vehemently opposed to going to school today.

Your child may be crying tears of anguish which appear to you to be genuine. Your child seems frightened, as if gripped by panic. He or she pleads, often in bone-chilling tones, to be allowed to stay home. Your child is literally begging for your mercy. The crying is so intense that involuntarily vomiting may be induced. What is going on here? Why is this happening today? And what should you being doing about it?

If your child is acting this way, he or she may be suffering from an anxiety disorder. Two of the more common such disorders among children are Separation Anxiety Disorder and School Phobia. Since they are two distinct syndromes, they need to be discussed separately.

7. Separation Anxiety Disorder

Some children function normally, play amicably and learn well in school. Their one difficulty is that they experience intense anxiety whenever they are separated from their parents.

All children experience some anxiety when they are separated from their parents. That is natural and healthy. In addition, most children are distressed, initially, by the new challenge of starting school. In fact, crying on the first day of nursery school or kindergarten is so common that the sounds which assault the teacher on that day may sound like a cacophonous chorus.

Most of the time, children are able to achieve a successful adjustment to school in less than a week. If crying persists and the child is under 4 years old, attending a play group, it may mean that the child is simply too young to make a healthy adjustment to school. If the child is over 5 and crying continues for two weeks or more, the parents should consider consulting a child-development expert.

In order to be most helpful during that first stressful week of school, parents need to be supportive and caring, while also being firm and confident that their child will adapt. In addition, parents should avoid becoming alarmed by their child's tears, which will only serve to convince their child that a real catastrophe is taking place. Finally, parents should try to coax their child to express his or her fears and then offer appropriate reassurances.

For children who are having a difficult time, transitional objects can be sent along to school to provide comfort. A few good examples are a picture of the parents, a small article of a parent's clothing, a special snack or a favorite toy.

But when children suffer intense anxiety — well beyond the bounds of what would be considered normal for their age level — a diagnosis of Separation Anxiety Disorder needs to be considered. If so, professional help may be necessary.

❧ The Case of Bracha*

Bracha, for example, was a sad, withdrawn first grader. She had taken a long time to adjust to kindergarten and then pre 1-A. By the time she reached first grade, she was a fair student who was slightly behind in reading. In addition, she had few friends, preferring to play by herself during recess.

Whenever Bracha and her two older siblings were left with a babysitter, Bracha would cry hysterically and cling desperately to either parent. In fact, when she was brought to me for consultation, she refused to enter my office unless one of her parents held her hand on the way in and stayed inside the room for the entire session.

After a few months of play therapy, Bracha learned to express her feelings, gained self-confidence, and mastered her fear of separation. She also improved her reading and social skills.

I knew we had succeeded in our work when Bracha calmly informed me one day that her mother was planning to travel to *Eretz Yisrael* without her. Bracha related this to me in such a matter-of-fact tone that I realized she was no longer terrified of

---

* Not her real name.

separations. (She had also long since allowed her parents to sit outside, in the waiting room, during our sessions.)

🌊 School Phobia

Some children can cope with separations from their parents better than Bracha did, but they experience the same degree of panic and fear when it comes time to go to school. One of the most perplexing features of School Phobia is that it can crop up at any age. Most often, however, it happens sometime during the elementary school years. It can even occur suddenly, without any early warning signs whatsoever.

A child can calmly, happily and uneventfully attend school for months or years without expressing or feeling any opposition. Then, quite abruptly, this former model child will refuse to get on the school bus or set foot in school.

No manner of bribing or threatening helps, as the child digs in his or her heels in stubborn resistance. No specific complaint or explanation is offered to justify this bizarre behavior. And what appears as a temporary "phase" can drag on for weeks and months, trying the nerves of the most patient parents.

Cases of School Phobia tend to call forth an extremely wide range of suggested solutions from well-intentioned but misguided advisers. Some advocate giving the child monetary bribes. Others encourage one parent to briefly sit in class with the child and then sneak out. Then there are those who recommend hitting, or threatening to hit, the child. Some even think they can convince the child to attend school by explaining to him or her the damage that will ensue to his or her social standing. My all-time "favorite," however, has to be the suggestion to deprive the child of solid food until school attendance resumes!

In over a quarter of a century of clinical practice, I have never even heard of a bona fide case of School Phobia which was resolved by any of those methods. In rare cases, the child may decide on his or her own to return to school, but only after weeks or months of absence.

The only approach which has repeatedly proven effective in getting a child suffering from School Phobia back to school quickly is family counseling. In such cases, it is absolutely essential that both father and mother attend the counseling, which often can be completed in under six sessions. The participation of both parents is so critical to the successful treatment of School Phobia that many therapists refuse to treat these cases unless both parents agree to participate from the start.

Some misguided parents try to shield their children, as well as themselves, from what they see as the "stigma" of counseling. They reason that it is better to wait and hope for the problem to pass rather than "subject" their family to the embarrassment of therapy. In trying to protect themselves from this perceived shame, they wind up disgracing themselves much more by the prolonged absence of their child from school.

Each passing day makes it harder and harder for their child to return to school. Material is being taught that the child is missing. Classmates begin to wonder what is wrong and the child's social standing erodes dramatically. Furthermore, as the child gets used to "solving" his or her problem by just not going to school, he or she becomes much less eager to find a real solution.

Parents of children suffering from School Phobia often feel overwhelmed and in crisis. Their children, on the other hand, may appear calm and relaxed, as long as they are not forced to go to school. But make no mistake about it — the child who demonstrates that he or she is beyond the pale of normal childhood functioning (by his or her willfully not going to school) is far more troubled than are his or her parents.

🐚 The Case of Naftoli*

Consider the case of 12-year-old Naftoli. Two months after he began seventh grade he stopped going to school. Bribing and threatening proved useless. The principal was patient and supportive to the parents, assuring them that Naftoli would be allowed back to school whenever they could get him to attend.

After three weeks, the parents were desperate enough to come for counseling. Naftoli refused to join his parents for the session so they had to come alone.

After five sessions with the parents, it became clear to me that they were subtly undermining each other. Their underlying marital problems were interfering with their efforts to get Naftoli back to school. Once that dynamic was identified and addressed, Naftoli returned to school without any further relapses. Although the parents chose not to continue the counseling to fully resolve their marital conflicts, they nevertheless managed to unentangle Naftoli from their disagreements.

Refusing to go to school is a symptom, indicating that something is wrong and must be corrected. At times, it signifies that the child is suffering a medical, social, academic, or emotional problem. Being able to determine the nature of the underlying problem is a daunting challenge for any parent.

Hopefully, the guidelines presented here will enable you to make more informed determinations about the cause of your child's reluctance to attend school, and will enable you to respond in the most helpful manner. We cannot be prepared for every possibility. But the more prepared we are, the easier our job as parents becomes.

---

* Not his real name.

16

Preventing Homesickness at Camp: The *Refuah* Before the *Makkah*

Once, when I was a young child, my parents called an electrician to our home to investigate a strange noise and foul smell emanating from our only air conditioner. After struggling for a half-hour to remove the antique unit from the window, the electrician came out and announced his verdict.

"You need a veterinarian, not an electrician," he announced. He then went on to explain that a bird had managed to build its nest between our air conditioner and the window sill. The mother bird was living there together with three recently hatched baby birds.

Following the instructions we received over the phone from the A.S.P.C.A., we gingerly transported the nest to the edge of our upstairs porch. Peeking from the window, we then breath-

*lessly watched and waited to see if the mother bird would
return to feed her young. Eventually, she did.*

*For three weeks, my family and I witnessed in fascination
and awe the miracle of the mother bird arriving daily to feed
her babies. She did not sleep in the nest, as our porch was too
exposed for her liking. But she did not abandon her brood.
"Posei'ach es yadecha umasbia l'chol chai ratzon, You open
up your hand and provide food for every living creature
according to its desires" (Tehillim 145:16 with Metzudas
David's interpretation).*

*Finally, after the fledglings had matured sufficiently, they
each hopped out of the nest, took a few more warm-up hops
along the porch railing and then flew off, all on the same day.
Neither they nor their mother returned, even for "pachim
ketanim, small jugs." The entire maturational process, from
birth to independence, took approximately four weeks.*

*For humans, the process of maturation which leads to leaving
the nest takes much, much longer. It begins with the first,
brief separations when an infant is left with a babysitter. It
proceeds through the longer separations of going to school
every day. And it culminates in the overnight separations of
summer camp, dormitory living and, eventually, marriage.*

*Each one of these separations challenges the coping skills
of children and their parents. As each hurdle is passed, a child
gains confidence and personality strengths which fortify him
or her to be able to take on the next hurdles when they come.*

*Just as some children grasp and absorb the alphabet more
quickly than others, some children have an easier time coping
with separation from home and parents than do other children. And just as the quick readers are not necessarily
smarter than their slower reading classmates, the quick
accommodators to separation are not necessarily healthier or
better adjusted than their more dependent peers.*

*The role of the parents in all of this is not to criticize or
compare their children with others. Rather, parents need to be
there to sensitively and compassionately assist their children*

in advancing to the next level of separation.

*Those children who never seem ready may need extra help.
And if a child appears to be lagging very far behind in his or
her maturational development, a consultation with an expert
may be warranted. But for the most part, children simply need
patient understanding, encouragement and plain old emotional
support.*

*One of the most difficult separations for some children is
the first four- or eight-week stay at a sleepaway camp. This
represents a quantum leap forward, toward independence, and
it is a leap which is quite challenging for many children. As a
result, these children may suffer symptoms of homesickness
during part or all of that first stay at camp.*

*A little homesickness is natural and is not cause for alarm.
But intense, prolonged homesickness can traumatize a child,
torture the agonizing parents and waste the significant
expense of the camp tuition. Part of the parents' responsibility,
therefore, is to do whatever they can before their children go to
camp to insure that any feelings of homesickness will be kept
to a minimum. And although some homesickness is almost
inevitable, there are still some very concrete steps parents can
take to help prevent major homesickness at sleepaway camp.*

"ELLO, MR. COHEN?" THIS IS RABBI SCHWARTZ" FROM
Camp Kayitz." As we discussed earlier this
week, your son (daughter) just does not seem
ready for camp this year. I have consulted with his (her)
counselor and the division head, and we all agree that...
perhaps you should come up on Sunday and take him
(her) home."

---

* Not their real names.

No one — absolutely no one — would like to be on the receiving end of that phone call. Yet that possibility exists for many parents every year. Like it or not, sleepaway camp has, in many cases, become a fact of Torah life in America today. Many *mosdos hachinuch* even require their *talmidim* to attend a Torah-oriented summer camp to insure that Torah study will continue during the summer. (Few day camps are geared for campers older than 11 or 12.)

For most children who go, camp is the highlight of the year. It is eagerly anticipated, thoroughly enjoyed, and long remembered with much affection. For some, however, the prospect of a trip to camp becomes a nightmare of apprehension and terror, brought on by the thought of separation from home. When that happens, parents are faced with two equally unacceptable choices: leave the child at home and let him or her lose out on all of the educational, social and recreational advantages of camp, or force the child to go to camp and subject him or her to the emotional torture and social disgrace of chronic homesickness and, possibly, receive a call like the one from "Rabbi Schwartz."

Don't all children miss their parents at camp? Of course, *some* homesickness is normal for most children during their first trip to an overnight camp, or at the start of each summer. But there are other children who experience abnormal amounts of distress at camp.

Instead of settling into camp life in a few days, they pine away for their parents, cry often, insist on calling home, and refuse to participate fully in games, learning or activities. They have difficulty falling asleep at night, may become nocturnally enuretic and, in short, cause their bunkmates, the camp staff and administration, as well as their parents, considerable anguish.

Is there anything that can be done to help these children make a better adjustment to camp?

Most problems are more easily solved if the cause and exact nature of the problems are understood. When a child of any age is either homesick or expresses fears of becoming homesick, he is not simply "acting like a baby." Except for those rare cases when a child is willfully rebelling, or "punishing" his parents for "dumping" him or her into a camp for "their convenience," homesickness is not something that a child can control on his or her own. Normally, if the camper could, he or she most surely would keep their emotions and behavior in check. Insulting or shaming the child for such feelings is not only ineffective, it can exacerbate the problem, as well.

🍂 What Homesickness Means

Basically, homesickness means that the child has not yet learned how to trust that his relationships with his parents will remain constant in spite of separation. Since most adults take constancy of relationships for granted, it is often difficult for parents to understand why their child is having so much trouble coping with the temporary separation of camp.

Adults have all had the experience of meeting an old friend after many years of separation. Usually, the two need little time to get reacquainted. They seem to resume the friendship exactly where they left off many years earlier. The reason for this is that both adults carried the relationship within them, unaffected by the separation of time and distance.

Children cannot do that. They have yet to learn, through a time-consuming process, that relationships continue in spite of separation. Infants, for example, burst into tears as soon as their mother leaves the room. This is because, to their immature minds, the mother ceases to exist when she is out of sight. As they mature they learn that if they can hear their mother in the next room, she is still there. After that, they learn to trust that even if they cannot see or hear her in the next room, their mother still exists. Eventually, they can even learn to tolerate mother's leaving by trusting that she will return.

Chazal, of course, understood all of this over 2,000 years ago, when they used the emotional criterion of "not needing his mother" for determining when a boy is obligated (for *chinuch*) to sleep in a *succah*. This stage of emotional development was defined as "waking up and not calling out, 'Mommy, Mommy!' " (See *Succah* 28b and *Tiferes Yisrael* on *Succah* 2:8).

As a result of personality, experiences, or both, some children develop such fear of separation that they cannot go to camp with their peers or even in some extreme cases, cannot go to school.[1]

For children to overcome homesickness, therefore, they must be helped over the developmental hurdle of coping with separation. This is accomplished by their learning to trust the constancy of their relationships with their parents. Sounds good, but how is this done?

If parents take the following steps *before* the summer, they can succeed in helping the vast majority of children who suffer from this annual ordeal. For the child who is most likely to become homesick, here's what parents can do:

❧ Build up to the Major Separation of Camp With Smaller, Trial Runs

Shimmy was 13 when he and his parents decided that he was forfeiting too much learning and fun by staying home every summer. Strongly supported and encouraged by his parents, Shimmy used two out-of-the-neighborhood *bar mitzvahs* to try sleeping away from home over *Shabbos*. Fortified with these successes, he felt less intimidated by a trip to camp.

❧ Build up Frustration-Tolerance at Home

Even at 11, Mimi was so attached and clingy to her parents that she could never simply say, "Good night." She always had to

---

1. See Chapter 15: "I Don't Want To Go To School:" Faking or Phobia? for a full discussion of the latter problem.

pose just one more question, and then one more, to whichever parent came to her room to say, "Good night." This procedure could last 20 minutes or more. The ritualized bedside schmooze never seemed to relax her enough.

To help prepare Mimi for overnight camp, Mimi's parents suggested that she limit after-goodnight questions to one. Each morning, her parents praised her for her restraint the night before. A few weeks of this frustration-tolerance building paid off for Mimi, who was better prepared to cope with the frustration of not being able to speak with her parents every day while she was at camp.

❀ Build Bridges Between Camp Personnel and Family

Hillel, age 12, couldn't wait to play ball at camp, but he fretted about who he would turn to "if he had a problem." He was going to camp with close friends, but he needed "a grownup," as well.

Hillel's father called the camp and was put in touch with the head counselor. During their conversation, they discovered that they had learned in the same yeshivah. The head counselor then told Hillel on the phone, "Any boy whose father attended my yeshivah is practically *mishpachah* to me. If you ever need to talk about anything, be sure to come to me." This precamp contact helped quiet Hillel's nagging fears.

❀ Minimize Fears by Confronting Them Directly, Not Through Denial

Chani's parents believed that if you don't discuss a child's fears, they will dissipate naturally. So when 10-year-old Chani began voicing doubts about camp, they dismissed her feelings and changed the subject. Once she gets to camp, they reasoned, she'll be having so much fun that she'll forget all about being homesick.

During the long drive home from camp, where Chani had spent a grand total of one agonizing, tear-soaked week, her parents silently questioned whether they had really been helpful to their daughter by ignoring her concerns.

Schragie's parents, on the other hand, accepted their 12-year-old son's tendency to get homesick, and they even raised the subject for him. When Schragie denied any apprehensions about his upcoming maiden voyage to camp, they saw this for what it was: massive denial. The second time they brought it up, Schragie's wall of denial began to crack. After the third time, he finally voiced his concerns: *What if he will want to speak with his parents and the camp will not allow phone calls?*

Having identified Schragie's specific fear *before* camp started, his parents contacted the camp administrators and worked out a plan acceptable to all concerned. The first week of camp was not exactly smooth sailing for Schragie, but the remainder of his stay proved to be productive and enjoyable.

❧ Encourage the Use of Concrete Objects to Help Ease the Transition From Home to Camp

When 11-year-old Rifky announced her desire to join her friends at sleepaway camp, her parents dismissed it. They knew how easily she had become homesick in the past, and assumed that her going to camp would be unrealistic, at least for this summer.

Eventually, however, Rifky convinced her parents that she was serious, so they agreed to send her for one trip. Rifky's parents then consulted a specialist whom they trusted. The expert recommended that Rifky bring some special "home reminders" to camp. Together with Rifky, her parents came up with the following concrete objects to send along with her, "just in case she would feel homesick."

• A picture of the family, which she should take out of its envelope only "in emergencies." When looking at the picture, they suggested, she should think of how proud all the members of the family will be on visiting day when they hear that she is happy at camp.

• An article of clothing from each parent, to keep under her pillow. When she feels the piece of clothing, she should remember how much her parents love her, think about her, and how they are looking forward to speaking with her and seeing her on visiting day. (Rifky chose one of her father's ties and one of her mother's *tichels.*)

• A cassette tape, which her parents recorded for her in her presence, with various reassuring thoughts to soother her whenever she might feel most lonely. Making the tape became a fun project, which included cameo appearances by some of her siblings and various home-reminder sound effects.

• Not discussed in advance with Rifky were the little handwritten notes her parents hid in her trunk to be "discovered" upon unpacking her clothes in camp. These eased the pangs of separation on that first, fateful day, when they are often most intense.

To the surprise of both of her parents, Rifky not only stayed through the first trip at camp, but asked to stay for the second trip as well.

Spending three or four weeks at camp is certainly not the only separation from home that could be problematic for children. Teenagers often want to go "out of town," or even out of the country, to learn in yeshivah or seminary. Because of the distance involved, they are often away for months at a time.

If teenagers are prone to feelings of homesickness, their reviewing, together with their parents, the strategies outlined above, and making the necessary adjustments for their older ages, may help them as well.

It can be surprising how well otherwise insecure children

cope with potentially stressful situations, if those predicaments are anticipated with advanced planning and steps designed to minimize the stress are taken. In fact, they may cope so well that their parents may even pick up the phone and hear:

> "Hello, Mr. Cohen? This is Rabbi Schwartz from Camp Kayitz. In spite of what we had discussed before camp, your son (daughter) seems to have adjusted beautifully. I have spoken with the counselor and the division head and we all agree that he (she) is one happy camper!"

PART SIX:
Avoiding Overexposure and Overprotection

17

Children Are What They See:
The Case Against Overexposure

For the first few months after children are born, their diet consists only of liquid nourishment. Although solid foods are healthy and vital for older children and adults, infants cannot chew or even swallow anything other than liquids. As infants mature and develop, solid foods are gradually introduced into their diets, beginning with soft, liquidy foods, such as purée. If infants would be given solid foods too soon, they could, Heaven forbid, choke.

In a similar vein, there are experiences and information from which children need to be protected. While they may be able to tolerate these things much more easily once they are older, exposing them too early — when they are young, impressionable and unprepared — could be damaging.

Hearing or learning about the more sordid aspects of modern society, for example, is not at all beneficial for children.

It can frighten and confuse them, raising questions in their minds which they may feel too embarrassed to ask. Then, left with many unanswered questions, these children may develop elevated levels of anxiety, worry and nervousness.

"But it's all part of life" is not a valid justification for parents to allow their children uncensored access to experiences and information. Parents who do not supervise their children properly are simply not fulfilling their responsibility to shield their children from overexposure.

The Shelah HaKadosh has a beautiful interpretation of the following verse, "Shoftim v'shotrim titen l'cha b'chal sh'arecha, Appoint for you judges and guards at all of your gates" (Devarim 16:18). There are many "gates" to the soul of a man: his ears, eyes, nose and mouth. Make sure, warns the Shelah, that you do not permit anything spiritually harmful to pass through those "gates."

The need to guard our own souls is as great as that of guarding our children's. Nevertheless, adults may feel impervious to what they see and watch. While this attitude is often a distortion of reality, it is incontrovertible that children are very much what they see.

✿

"**Y**OU ARE WHAT YOU EAT" IS THE BATTLE CRY OF THE NUTRItionists. As Jews, we know the truth of that statement — for we understand that the food we consume also has a spiritual impact on us. After all, eating non-kosher food, even unwittingly, causes *timtum halev* — a spiritual callousness that dulls one's sensitivity. In fact, the specifics of dietary laws permit certain domestic fowl, but not birds of prey. The commentators explain that when one consumes a bird that hunts its food, one acquires some of its character traits — especially the undesirable traits. Thus, the Torah enjoins us to protect our souls by eating only kosher food.

Just as we must exercise proper judgment concerning that which enters our mouths, we must be even more discriminatory regarding the images we allow to enter our minds and hearts through our eyes. Indeed, what we see strongly affects how we think and feel. We are the products of what we have seen, both for good and otherwise. If this is so for adults, then it is even more so for children.

Let us take dramatized scenes of violence, for example. Parents might argue that children comprehend the difference between make-believe and reality. But when researchers exposed children of varying ages to violent scenes, even in cartoons, they observed the children acting out the same behavior with dolls, and even with each other, immediately after the viewing.

Dr. Michael B. Rothenberg, a psychiatrist at the University of Washington in Seattle, reviewed 50 research studies on the effects of television. These studies involved over 10,000 children. The evidence clearly indicates that watching violent scenes has an impact on children's emotions. It shows that some children suffer recurrent bad dreams after viewing episodes that adults might consider "entertainment." Other children display symptoms of anxiety or nervousness after having watched a video that included scenes of brutality.

Finally, the character traits which we Jewish parents work so hard to instill in our children — traits like kindness and sensitivity toward others — are easily eroded by viewing acts of cruelty. For example, it is very difficult to convince a child of the importance of not hurting a classmate's feelings after that same child has become desensitized to human suffering as a result of overexposure to scenes of distress and agony.

If we want our children to grow up to be *menschen*, decent human beings, who are empathetic to and respect the rights and feelings of others, then in addition to supervising the foods they eat, we must also try monitoring what they see. Violent images may be momentarily entertaining but, in the long run, are quite antithetical to our moral instruction.

Even still pictures of brutality, like those that appear in newspapers or Holocaust memorials, could do more harm than good to especially sensitive children. The legitimate educational goals that motivate such exposure could easily be met with less corrosive methods. Current events or history classes can impart the same information without having to expose impressionable eyes to such potentially harmful scenes.

One well-meaning yeshivah took an entire elementary-school class to the Holocaust Museum in Washington, D.C. Not all of the children could handle the experience. Two of the students were so distraught by what they saw that they actually vomited — not on the bus, but inside the museum. Do we want our children to be so insensitive to human suffering that they will *not* get sick when they view such pictures? Or do we want our children to retain their Jewish birthright of being *rachmanim*, and then become nauseous when we have them see such scenes? Or, do we want these children to be spared having to make the choice between becoming desensitized and getting traumatized?

Of course, children need to learn about the Holocaust. It is a seminal event in Jewish history, one from which our children should not be shielded. Just as they learn about the the destruction of the Temple and the atrocities which were perpetrated against our people at that time, so too, they need to be informed about more recent manifestations of anti-Semitism.

When we are introducing potentially stressful subjects to our children, however, we must exercise good judgment, using our children's age and developmental levels as guidelines. To bring an entire elementary-school class to the Holocaust Museum in Washington is ignoring the sensitivity and coping skills of 11-year-olds. A classroom discussion with a teacher or *rebbi* would be a much more appropriate venue for educating students of that age about the realities of the Holocaust. And such a discussion could even pave the road for going on such a trip at a later time.

The lessons of the Holocaust need to be learned by children of all ages, just as the words, "*V'he she'amdah lavoseinu*, This is what stood for our forefathers," from the Passover Haggadah need to be explained to all children. But pictures and films of literally *unspeakable* brutality and torture should not be viewed by young children.

It will take deliberate effort on our part to shield our children from harmful images. But if we understand the benefits, it will be no more difficult than supervising the foods they eat.

Remember: Children are what they see.

18

Good Grief:
The Case Against Overprotection

Just as it is harmful to children to be exposed to experiences and information they are not yet mature enough to handle, so too, it is damaging to children to be overprotected. If children are shielded too long from experiences and information that they need, they may be impeded in their psychosocial development. In addition, they may suffer the pain of embarrassment or other more serious injuries.

Suppose you would not allow your 13-year-old to cross the street without an adult escort. He or she would encounter enormous ridicule from peers on a daily basis. In addition, your child would miss out on many opportunities to learn age-appropriate independence. Or, suppose your children's school does not want to frighten the students with the prospect of a fire breaking out in the building. This certainly seems reasonable. But let us presume that this reasoning causes the school never to conduct fire drills. Your children would be in greater danger, because if there were ever to be a fire in the school, they would be unprepared for a safe evacuation from the building.

One final example will suffice. Suppose a parent does not want his or her children to know that so frightening a crime as child molestation even exists. The parent is concerned that such knowledge could arouse too much concern and worry in their otherwise secure children. What that parent is failing to consider, however, is that the lack of knowing what to do and how to handle such a situation could make their children even more vulnerable to attack. If that parent's child is, Heaven forbid, ever victimized, the child would be much less likely to come forward and report the incident, since the parents have not given the youngster any indication that such topics may even be discussed. By not disclosing the incident the child would then be be prevented from receiving the psychological help he or she may need.

No parent should fool himself or herself into believing that telling children that they "may discuss anything with you" is sufficient. Unless parents are somewhat more explicit than that, molested children almost always assume that "anything" still does not include so taboo a subject. In most cases, the perpetrator will threaten the child in order to intimidate him or her into keeping the abuse a "secret," making it even harder for the child to report the abuse to his or her parents.[1] So, unless it is discussed in advance, it is extremely unlikely for children to immediately report abuse to their parents.

This chapter deals with another subject from which adults typically try to shield children: death. While we do not want to unnecessarily frighten our children, to attempt to shelter them from the realities of death, especially when they are confronted by it in their own social circle, would be yet another example of overprotection.

---

1. A case example illustrating this problem was presented in Chapter 15, "I Don't Want to Go to School": Faking or Phobia?

Ben Bag Bag used to say: "Go over (Torah) and go over it (again) because everything (can be found) in it" (Avos 5:22).

THERE ARE NO SITUATIONS IN LIFE THAT FALL BEYOND THE PALE of Torah. From the moment we wake up in the morning until we fall asleep at night, our day's activities are prescribed by the Torah. From the moment of birth until the final rest, our lives are directed by the Torah.

In many cases the guidelines of Torah are explicit and incontrovertible. In other cases, the Torah guidelines are only implicit, and are therefore subject to some speculation.

When someone unfortunately passes on, for example, the entire corpus of *Hilchos Aveilus* guides the bereaved members of the deceased's immediate family. The *Shulchan Aruch* and later halachic authorities clearly spell out what is expected of the mourners at every step, from the time the person passes away, through the funeral, burial and the week of *shivah*, to the end of *sheloshim*, and even the year of mourning.

The extended family and friends of the mourners, however, receive comparatively little in the way of direction from the *Shulchan Aruch*. They are instructed in the proper manner in which to offer comfort and consolation (*Yoreh De'ah* 376) but nothing more. And certainly the laws of *nichum aveilim* need to be properly understood to be properly fulfilled.[2]

Indeed, extended family and friends use *nichum aveilim* to help themselves cope with their own feelings of grief and mourning. In some unusual situations, when children are involved, additional guidelines may be needed.

---

2. See "The Psychodynamics of Grief and Mourning: A Layman's Guide to Making a *Shivah* Visit," *The Jewish Observer*, Jan. '85, pp. 18-21.

Consider the following actual cases:

- A 9-year-old boy became sick over the weekend. The specialist to whom he was brought on Monday misdiagnosed the illness. Two days later, the boy passed away. His parents and siblings, of course, sat *shivah*.

  But what about the boy's classmates? They all were agitated, wound up, and unable to learn. The *rebbi* of the class sought guidance from the *menahel*. He received the following advice: "Whatever you do, don't discuss the death with the class. They are young children and will forget about it in a day or two." By the end of the week, the class was even more uncontrollable than ever.

- The counselor of a bunk of 8-year-old boys was killed in an automobile accident during the summer. That Sunday was visiting day at the camp. One of the boys in that bunk related the incident to his parents. Then he pleaded, "Don't let anyone know I mentioned this to you. We were told that we may not talk about this with our parents. Please don't try to discuss it with me."

- Over a weekend, a kindergarten teacher was killed in an accidental fire in her home. On Monday, all of the staff and administrators walked around with long faces. All that was said to the children about the incident, however, was that their teacher "would not be in school today." When questioned about the way the situation was handled, the director of the pre-school program explained, "These girls are only 4- and 5-year-olds. They don't really understand these things. Most of them do not know about the tragedy. Those who do are probably not thinking about it now. What purpose would be served by bringing it up and upsetting them?"

These are not isolated exceptions, nor are they examples drawn from irreligious schools and camps. In all three cases, the institutions concerned were mainstream Torah-based camps and schools. Where do these attitudes and assumptions come from? They come from some very basic misconceptions about the intellectual and emotional development of children. And they belie the principles set down by *Chazal* and *Poskim.*

Below are several common, widespread myths about children's attitudes toward death and bereavement.

"Children don't really understand death, so they don't really think about it."

Yes, it is true that children, especially young children, have a difficult time grasping the concept of death. But that difficulty does not cause them to think less about it. In fact, it causes them to think even more about it, as they struggle to understand what it all means. If you give a young child who was touched by death the slightest opportunity, he or she will riddle you with an avalanche of questions, all indicating how very much the subject is on his or her mind.

"Children forget about unpleasant things very quickly. Look how soon after hearing such news a child returns to play. That proves how quickly children forget."

No, not at all. Children will turn to play very quickly after hearing upsetting news, but not because they have forgotten it. Play can often serve the same purpose to a child that a heart-to-heart conversation serves to an adult. Play can soothe and comfort a child who has just been traumatized by stressful news.

Perhaps some of the best indications that children do not forget so quickly are the behavioral changes that are evident following the *petirah* of some significant personality in their lives. Some children become aggressive, hyperactive, anxious and inattentive; others become withdrawn, sullen and moody. They may also exhibit any combination of these symptoms. Whatever their behavioral change, adults should be alerted to the difficulties these children are having in coping with the sad news. The fact that these changes can last for days and even weeks indicates that the children have certainly not forgotten the tragedy.

"If you bring up the subject, the children will get more upset. The best thing for children is not to talk about it."

Nothing could be further from the truth! Our sages instruct us not to distract mourners from their grief. On the contrary, we are encouraged to help them face the reality of their loss. Children also must be allowed, and encouraged, to face and come to terms with the reality of their loss, just like the adults. It is the non-Jewish world that emphasizes denial of death through rituals and practices that treat the deceased as if he or she were still alive.

"But you never hear children talking among themselves or with adults about the death. Doesn't that indicate that they don't want to think about it; that it would be too upsetting for them to talk about?"

No, all it indicates is that they have picked up the nonverbal message from the adults around them that *the adults* are too uncomfortable to talk about it. As disconcerting as the whole subject is for us adults, it is even more uncomfortable for us to try to discuss death with children. For that reason, perhaps, many otherwise intelligent, knowledgeable and sensitive adults look for excuses and rationalizations to justify their avoidance of the issue. Children generally take their cues from adults, especially when it comes to unfamiliar matters. So when the adults remain silent about the passing of a loved one, the children follow the example and suppress their own thoughts, questions and feelings.

The silence of the adults, however, is misleading. The adults are only silent on this subject around children. Whenever they get together with other adults soon after the death of someone close, these same people will talk of little else. In doing so, they will reach out for support and indulge themselves in the very outlet that they deny the children. Grief is a natural human emotion, one which is perfectly appropriate for children as it is for adults. When grief is suppressed it can be harmful. When it is expressed and shared, it can be good and beneficial grief.

When death touches the lives of children who do not become *aveilim*, the adults around them need to follow the same guidelines for dealing with death that *Chazal*, in their infinite wisdom, laid out for us in the *Shulchan Aruch*.

1. **Do not deny the death.** Any attempt to do so is misleading and counterproductive. Just as *aveilim* attend the funeral and burial, events which concretize the reality of a death, so too no effort should be made to "shield" children from the truth. Children do not have to be exposed to all the gory details, but the basic facts are necessary for them.

2. **Give them an opportunity to talk about the death, the niftar and their feelings.** *Aveilim* are afforded ample opportunity to commiserate through the *shivah* visits of their friends, relatives and neighbors. Children need similar opportunities to raise their questions, quiet their fears and express their feelings. As mentioned earlier, children take their cues from adults. If discussion is not initiated by adults, it may not take place at all — certainly not in the supportive, constructive atmosphere in which it should be conducted. Therefore, adults need to let children know, by setting the proper example, that it is perfectly acceptable to talk about the death and the *niftar*. Generally, once the subject is raised by adults, children jump at the chance to unburden themselves.

3. **Help the children validate their feelings.** When adults who are sitting *shivah* express sadness, loss or pain, those who

come to comfort are admonished not to tell the mourner, "What can you do? You can't change things, anyway" (*Yoreh De'ah* 376:2). While this ruling is meant to prevent one from sounding as though he or she is criticizing Hashem's actions, it also serves to permit the mourners to give vent to their feelings of loss.

Similarly, adults must help children to accept their own feelings. This is done by hearing the children out and then letting them know that they are not alone, that others feel the same way. In addition, children have many questions about death that may frighten and upset them. These questions need to be answered with sympathy, honesty and respect for their intelligence. Efforts to give false reassurance by feeding into their tendency for magical thinking will only backfire.

We must make note of one extremely common example of such misguided efforts at comfort. We know that we will be reunited with all our departed loved ones when the dead are resurrected. Most children assume that this will coincide with the advent of *Mashiach*. As adults, we are emotionally well prepared for the prospect that the awaited reunion may be long in coming. But when children are told that "*Mashiach* could come tomorrow," and he doesn't arrive, they suffer more disappointment than adults can imagine. And this disappointment is compounded daily, forcing the children to wonder why this reunion is being postponed — in some cases, even blaming themselves for the delay; in other cases, forfeiting belief in one of the fundamental principles of Judaism.

4. **Finally, after questions have been raised and feelings shared, help the children to concretize their feelings through actions.** The mourner is given concrete actions to perform, such as *kriah, shivah, Kaddish* and so on. Children, too, need to be able to express their feelings through concrete actions.

One of the best opportunities to channel children's feelings into action is to prepare them for, and accompany them on, a *shivah* visit. If that is not appropriate, they can write letters to the loved one's family. Another option would be to plan and execute a suitable memorial, such as a *tzedakah* campaign, special learning program, or *chessed* project in memory of the deceased. All of this need not be planned on a grand scale, but rather on a practical level, realistic for the number of children involved and for their age level. The important point here is not how much is done but rather that the children be given an opportunity to channel their feelings into actions.[3]

So as not to be accused of ending with a cliff-hanger, let us return to the three case examples presented earlier. How did they work out and what was the result in each case?

Regarding the class of the 9-year-old boy who passed away, the *rebbi* tried to follow his *menahel's* advice. After a week of getting absolutely nowhere with his class, he became totally exasperated. Finally, he button-holed me at a *melaveh malkah* and asked for suggestions. Basically, he received the same guidelines presented above. He was quite skeptical, to say the least, that a frank discussion of the death would calm the class down, but he felt he had nothing to lose.

The next day, the *rebbi* entered his class and told the boys not to take out their *Mishnayos*. He said he'd like to talk about Yochanan[*] (their departed friend). That opened the floodgates. Some boys shared wild rumors about how he had died. Others had questions about their own health and mortality. But the one issue that touched the *rebbi* most was the almost unanimous feeling of guilt shared by the class. Yochanan was not the most popular boy in the class, and each boy could recall at least one instance in which he had not been as friendly, thoughtful or kind toward Yochanan as he should have been. Now these incidents were hounding the class to the point where they could not concentrate on learning. The *rebbi* then helped his class put these very minor incidents into proper perspective. After an hour and a half, when they finally did take out their *Mishnayos*, the *rebbi* was amazed at how well the class learned for the rest of the day.

---

3. See *Sdei Margalis* on *Tanna Dvei Eliyahu, Parshas Terumah, Shemos* 25:2.
* Not his real name

What about the boy whose counselor was killed in a car accident during the summer? In that case, the parents had a difficult time accepting the camp policy of not discussing the matter with their son. Nevertheless, they felt it was important to support the authority of the camp administration. To resolve their dilemma, they consulted the therapist who was offering them short-term guidance regarding a behavioral problem of one of their other children.

The therapist expressed considerable shock when he heard the camp's approach. He then went on to outline some of the major points stressed in this chapter. The parents felt enormously reassured because their own instincts had told them that something was not right about the camp's policy. The therapist encouraged the parents to first discuss the entire matter with the camp administration. After all, their son may have misunderstood or distorted the camp position. But if their son had, in fact, reported it accurately, he felt that the parents should encourage the camp administration to contact a therapist.

While the parents followed through, the camp administration did not. The parents, however, did discuss the episode with their son. At first, he was quite anxious about violating the camp's imposed code of silence. When he arrived home, however, he was visibly relieved to be able to freely talk about the episode with his parents.

Finally, what happened with the nursery-school class whose teacher was killed over the weekend? In spite of the widespread discussion of the incident in the corridors amongst the staff and faculty, the director of the program was convinced that the children had been successfully shielded from the tragic news. She was so convinced, in fact, that she suggested to a therapist (who served as a part-time consultant to the pre-school program) that the two of them sit in on the class, unannounced, to observe.

The girls were busy playing with blocks, dolls and old clothes when the director and consultant entered the kindergarten. The teacher of the class knew both visitors well and invited them to join in the circle that was being formed for story time. The director and the consultant smiled to the children and quietly sat down in the circle while the teacher went to the bookshelf to select a story.

Before the teacher came back to the circle one little girl apparently read the minds of the adults and blurted out, "Morah Esther* died."

Another girl added, "She's in *Shamayim* now."

A third girl across the room piped up, "But we will all see her when *Mashiach* comes."

The director immediately left the room, feeling somewhat humiliated by the spontaneous disproof of her argument. During an informal meeting later that day, she was helped to recognize the kindergarten children's needs to express their own grief at the death of their beloved teacher. To her credit, she acknowledged her error and explored with the consultant appropriate ways to lead the class in a discussion of the loss and how to include them in the memorial plans the school was already making.

Hopefully, the guidelines presented here will never be needed for practical application. Nevertheless, by reviewing them now, *before* they are needed, parents, *mechanchim* and camp administrators will be properly prepared if, Heaven forbid, a tragedy should strike and a death touches the lives of young children. Like the fire extinguisher on the wall, we hope never to need it; but it's nice to know it's there, just in case.

---

* Not her real name

PART SEVEN:
Understanding Adolescents

19

What Is Adolescent Turmoil?

When their oldest child becomes a teenager, parents often feel unprepared for all the changes which creep up on them without warning. In addition to the accelerated growth spurts, they see dramatic, and often unwelcome, changes in attitude and behavior in their young adolescent.

Parents are often at a loss to understand what has happened to their formerly cooperative, respectful and predictable child. And they are desperate to understand why adolescence is such a problematic stage of development for so many children.

Sometimes parents read or hear about the term, "adolescent turmoil". The term is often cited as an explanation for much that confuses and confounds the parents of teenagers. This chapter answers the question some parents are too afraid to ask: What is "adolescent turmoil"?

T HE LATE TEENAGE YEARS ARE OFTEN REFERRED TO AS ADOLES-
cence. Adolescence literally means that stage of development between childhood and maturity.

Adolescence seems to be an especially emotionally stressful
period. As an age group, for example, adolescents have a disproportionately high rate of psychiatric hospitalizations. In fact, if any
form of mental illness will develop during a person's lifetime, it is
most likely to emerge during retirement, old age, or adolescence.

Why is adolescence such a period of turmoil and stress and
why do adolescents present so many behavior problems for their
parents?

Looking at the life cycle developmentally, each stage in life
can be characterized by the primary task which must be mastered
at that stage. The developmental task of infancy, for example, is
for the infant to learn to establish a close, secure and trusting
relationship with his or her mother. The primary task of adolescence, however, is for the adolescent to succeed in separating
himself or herself from his parents enough to establish his own
independence.

Lest all teenage readers parade to my office to decorate it —
and their parents march behind them to burn it down — I should
clarify what I mean by independence.

Children will always need their parents "till 120," and they
should keep contact with their parents, no matter how old the
children get. Nevertheless, older children should not depend on
their parents to satisfy the same needs as they did when the children were younger. What parents provide for a child of 10 need
not always be continued for the same child five years later, and so
on. In short, independence is to some extent synonymous with
growing up. It means "separation without amputation."[1]

---

1. I am grateful to my colleague, Hannah Parnes, C.S.W., for permission to use this phrase
which she coined.

All of this may sound rather simplistic, especially for parents who have not yet dealt with an adolescent. Anyone who has knows that this is a very difficult stage. But if the adolescents and their parents share the same goal, namely, for the adolescent to achieve greater independence, then what makes it so difficult?

The fact is that both adolescents and their parents are ambivalent; they have mixed feelings about the adolescent's developing maturity. All are concerned about the possible unreadiness of the adolescent. They are all unsure of his judgment, reasoning and experience. All fear the adolescent's failure and are apprehensive about the unknowns of the future. Some of these fears are justified. Others are not.

More specifically, the adolescent and his or her parents don't always see the adolescent's development of independence as something positive. The adolescent, for example, enjoys the luxury of parental support — financial and otherwise — and may be unwilling to give any of it up. The parents, on the other hand, feel more secure and comfortable, with the higher levels of control they were able to exercise when the adolescent was younger.

In short, no one seems to be prepared to easily secede the dependency and control inherent in the parent/child relationship.

So if that is the case, how does an adolescent manage to let go of the rail and learn to swim, so to speak?

There are two major factors which facilitate the growth process and help most adolescents develop to maturity.

The first factor is the growth in importance of peer relationships. Never before adolescence — and never again after — will friends be so important. The friendships made during adolescence, for example, are usually the ones that survive intact, seemingly unaffected by later separations of many miles or even years. When the adolescent succeeds in establishing close friendships, it helps ease the loss of emotional dependency on his parents and eventually makes financial dependency an embarrassment.

The second factor is that some conflict between adolescents

and their parents is normal. At times it is actually helpful. And I must once again clarify that I advocate no disrespect of parents by children of any age. However, conflict between family members can take many forms, the worst of which, of course, is disrespect. Other forms of conflict include maintaining and expressing different opinions, or the adolescent's very painful realization that parents, too, are not always perfect and can make mistakes.

With the support of strong friendships and the impetus of some conflict with his or her parents, the adolescent is helped to complete his or her natural developmental task and grow to mature adulthood.

Is there anything that parents can do to minimize the crisis of adolescence for their children?

Yes, most definitely! Parents should sit down with one another and ask themselves the following four questions.

1. *Is there anything we are doing which makes dependency too attractive for our adolescent children?*

2. *Is there anything we are doing which makes* premature *independence a necessity for our adolescent children?*

3. *Are we opposing our adolescent's move toward independence because of* our *needs or our* child's *needs?*

4. *When our child gives us the mixed message of wanting both dependency and independence, are we more responsive to the former or the latter?*

I mentioned above that the adolescent "usually" succeeds in achieving mature independence. Unfortunately, that is not always so. And the reasons for this failure are manifold.

At times, the adolescent is unsuccessful because he fails to establish close, meaningful friendships. This causes the young man or woman to remain socially isolated and withdrawn. In other cases, the conflict with the parents is so intense that it preoccupies the entire family.

In these instances, professional counseling can often succeed in making the transition proceed more smoothly. Although these families may often feel helpless, they *can* be helped, and the adolescent can be assisted in moving through the natural life cycle and ultimately go on from adolescence to a happy and full maturity.

🐚 The Case of Pinchas*

One example comes to mind, immediately, not so much because the case was unusual, but because of the unique circumstances of the referral.

One of my first private referrals came from Rabbi Boruch Green,* the principal of the Radziviller Yeshivah.* I was flattered by his vote of confidence in my clinical skills. But when I learned that he was referring his teenage nephew, I became quite apprehensive about succeeding enough to maintain the positive image I had in Rabbi Green's eyes.

The nephew had a chronic stuttering problem. This caused the young man considerable shame, resulting in extreme shyness. I quickly discovered that stuttering is hardly amenable to individual psychotherapy. After six wholly unsuccessful sessions, the young man withdrew from treatment. His uncle, I concluded, would never again refer anyone to me.

I was wrong. Five months later, Rabbi Green called with another referral. I was quite surprised. But I was truly astounded when I learned that Rabbi Green was referring his 14-year-old son, Pinchas.

For some unexplained reason, Pinchas was found to have, on more than one occasion, slipped out of yeshivah to go

---

* Not the real names.

home in the middle of the day. While some boys Pinchas' age occasionally do things like that, Rabbi Green acknowledged, this was totally uncharacteristic of Pinchas, who had always been an outstanding student.

Rabbi Green insisted that I meet Pinchas at their home, as Pinchas was too embarrassed to come to my office. Unencumbered by the pressures of a busy practice, I complied.

Pinchas and I met in his bedroom. He felt extremely guilty about having been caught doing something that any rational person would realize would inevitably be discovered. After all, how could the principal's son repeatedly "sneak" out of yeshivah, come home for a few hours, and *not* expect to be caught?

It did not take long for the focus of our conversation to shift to the relationship between Pinchas and his father. Pinchas idealized his father, a prominent member of the community. He saw his father to be a distant, larger-than-life personality. And Pinchas felt himself to be a dismal failure in trying to please his father.

Pinchas could not bring himself to express any of these feelings directly to his father. Instead, he tried symbolically and literally to avoid him, eventually calling attention to himself by his foolish and inappropriate behavior.

Although Pinchas had never discussed any of this with his father, he did agree to meet together with his father and myself the following week — in my office.

The following week, a somewhat stiff, uncomfortable Rabbi Green came in with his reticent, anxious son.

"So, please tell me," Rabbi Green began, taking charge of the session from the outset. "What do you think is wrong with my son? What is your diagnosis?"

"He is suffering from a very common malady," I replied in a somber tone. "It is called 'adolescence.'"

I then went on to explain — as clearly and simply as I could — my analysis of Pinchas' feelings of anxiety and how they were connected to his relationship with his father. Rabbi Green apparently misunderstood what I was trying to convey.

"But Pinchas and I have always been very close," Rabbi Green protested. "How could he be afraid of me?"

"He is not afraid that you will get angry with him," I replied. "He is afraid he will disappoint you, that he will not live up to your expectations for him."

Rabbi Green jerked his head around to face Pinchas directly. "Is that true?!"

Pinchas broke eye contact with his father and looked down at the floor. Then he nodded silently in agreement.

Rabbi Green looked as if he had been hit by a truck. "I had no idea — ," his voice trailed off.

Pinchas burst into uncontrollable sobbing. Rabbi Green shed tears, silently. Then he leaned over to embrace Pinchas. Father and son remained locked in each others' arms for two of the longest minutes of my professional career. I took out a tissue to wipe my own moistened eyes. The emotional discovery which had taken place was intense for us all.

Pinchas never did play hooky again. He resumed his formerly successful learning in the Radziviller Yeshivah. In a follow-up phone call six months later, Rabbi Green assured me that his son was progressing in his studies, keeping up with his friends and, most important of all, maintaining the openness and honesty which began in my office. Seven years later, I met Rabbi Green on the street. He beamed proudly, informing me that Pinchas was engaged and planning to continue his learning in the Radziviller *kollel*.

Over 20 years ago, with what fishermen call "beginner's luck," I had been able to help Pinchas and his father break up the logjam with one another. It took far less time than such work normally takes. Although the length of treatment was unusually short, this case provides a window of just how mired and despondent a child can become when caught in a very typical adolescent conflict. (That conflict will be elaborated upon more fully in the next chapter.)

This case also illustrates how successful an adolescent can become when he is released from his conflict and is enabled to continue on to the next stage in life. Finally, this case also highlights the constructive role professional help can play in the life of a family coping with an adolescent in turmoil.

20

The Casualties of Success: How Successful People Sometimes Fail Their Teenage Children

"*Marbeh n'chosim marbeh da'agah,* The more one increases his acquisitions the more he increases his worries" (*Pirkei Avos* 2:7).

Rabbeinu Yonah comments on this mishnah, *"[A person] should not think that the honor of his wealth and the extent of his holdings will cause him to spend his days and years pleasantly. [Rather] they will cause him to worry about them throughout the entire year."*

One trouble which often tops the list of the many which burden successful people is disappointment with their teenage children. People who are the envy of the community, who have "everything going for them" and who are successful in so many areas of their lives often find themselves failing as parents with their adolescent children.

When successful people blunder and falter, we are aston-
ished, and they are deeply shocked and disappointed in them-
selves. And when such people fail at parenting, the obvious
casualties are their children. Those parents are tortured with
the questions of how and why they did not succeed. Their rela-
tives and friends are equally baffled by this anomaly. This
chapter will attempt to shed some light on this enigma.

⌒⌒

SUCCESS CAN BE DEFINED AS HIGH ACHIEVEMENT IN THOSE areas for which one earns significant status, prestige and recognition.

Regardless of the area of endeavor, all successful people share one or more of the following character traits.

• **Goal oriented.** Some people never seem to know what they want. Successful people, on the other hand, know exactly what they want and they are routinely busy striving to reach their goals.

• **Time efficient.** Some people are always looking for fresh ways to "kill time." Successful people, however, never waste a minute because they value what can be accomplished even in small amounts of time.

• **Conscientious and persistent.** Successful people seem to never give up, no matter how long it takes to get "there." They consistently attain their goals, not so much as a result of good fortune, but due to their unwillingness to accept failure.

• **Detail oriented.** Throughout the ages, great men have been distinguished by their attention to *pachim k'tanim*, the small details that would easily have been overlooked or neglected by others.

• **Future focused.** People who cannot resist the urge for immediate gratification achieve very little in life. Successful

---

1. See *Bayis Ne'eman b'Yisrael: Practical Steps to Success in Marriage* (New York: Feldheim, 1988) Chapter 10, for a fuller discussion of this point.

people, on the other hand, accomplish exceptional feats by virtue of their long-range vision.[1]

Everyone would agree, for example, that all Torah luminaries possess the *middos* listed above. But is is not these traits alone that produce greatness. It is also the proper balance of these attributes which results in unusual lifetime achievements.

There are many individuals who possess enough of these qualities to achieve a modicum of success at work, but they have not reached the proper balance to succeed at parenting.

The Children's Problems

Tzar gidul banim, the pangs of childrearing, are universal (*Shabbos* 89b). But, when successful people fail to raise successful children, the torment of the parents is unusually severe. And with alarming frequency today, some of the teenaged children of successful people are suffering from certain common problems at home and in yeshivah.

Here are some of them:

• **Academic failure.** "I just *know* he can do better work" is a refrain echoed by *rebbei'im*, teachers and parents alike. And then psychological testing confirms what everyone knows already. This child is performing far below his ability. Why is he failing?

• **Acting-out behavior.** In yeshivah, at home and/or at camp, this child is disobedient. There may be a disregard for authority. At times, the child may be openly defiant and disrespectful. Rules are broken; peace and harmony are shattered; and the parents' hopes and dreams are dashed. Why is this child so unruly when all of the other children in the family are so well behaved?

• **Depression and withdrawal.** The child keeps to himself and stays at home. Activities that would interest other children that are his or her age do not appeal to this child. If an adult felt this way, we would call him depressed. Why is this child so withdrawn?

At times, the answer to all of these questions is the same. If the parents are highly successful, it just may be that the same personality qualities that enabled the parents to achieve so much outside are the very traits that have interfered with their parenting at home. Three case examples will illustrate the dynamics of this process.

(The identifying information in the following cases has been sufficiently disguised to the point where the individuals involved should not even be able to recognize themselves.)

❧ Yehudah*

Yehudah's father is a senior partner a large accounting firm with over 50 employees. In spite of the demands of his accounting practice, Yehudah's father keeps a three-hour daily *seder* of learning in a local *kollel*. Part of his *seder* is devoted to learning with a *chavrusah* and part is devoted to completing a *sefer* on *halachah*.

Yehudah's mother teaches at a local preschool, but not because the family needs the additional income.

Both of Yehudah's parents are looked up to by all members of the community as models of Torah and *chessed*. Their home is open to *Shabbos* guests and yeshivah parlor meetings. And their list of friends includes the "Who's Who" as well as the lonely and overlooked members of the community. What problems could Yehudah possibly have with parents like these?

Let us look at Yehudah, however. First, Yehudah has been missing his high school *minyan* more often than he attends it. Second, Yehudah's parents recently discovered that he has secretly applied for no less than three credit cards. Finally, Yehudah has become uncooperative, gruff and uncommunicative with his parents. In addition, as one of the oldest children, he has taken to terrorizing some of his younger siblings. Yehudah's parents hear no

---

* Not his real name

reassurance from his *rebbi*. They don't know how he's learning, when he's learning, or even, if he's learning at all!

Extensive consultations with Yehudah's parents revealed a long history of heated confrontations between Yehudah and his father, and occasionally his mother. His parents initially attempted to correct Yehudah's behavior by being firm and disapproving. When that failed, they tried to simply ignore his misbehavior and treat him cordially. When that failed, they sought a *Rav* to "talk some sense into him." And when that failed — they just broke down and cried.

🌺 Chezky*

Misbehavior was never a complaint of Chezky's *rebbei'im*. If anything, Chezky's behavior was often described as "too good." His academic performance was always above average. What troubled Chezky's parents, however, was his moodiness and social withdrawal.

Chezky's father is a high-profile, high-powered owner of a major travel agency, who is respected not only for his business acumen but also for his integrity and honesty. It is well known, for example, that he would walk away from a six-figure deal without the slightest hesitation if his *Rav* directed him to do so. Chezky's mother does not work outside of the home. But she keeps a large, spotless home humming smoothly, as she devotedly cares for Chezky and his four younger siblings.

By the time Chezky entered 10th grade, he seemed to have no friends at all. He hardly ventured out of his room, except to go to yeshivah and *shul*. Although the phone rang incessantly for Chezky's popular younger brother Menachem, no one ever called for Chezky.

Chezky's parents, especially his father, wanted to have a close relationship with Chezky, but did not know how to proceed in developing such a relationship. Whenever just Chezky and his

---

* Not his real name

father walked to *shul* together, there were often long, uncomfortable silences. Chezky's father remembered how distant he had been from his own father and wanted to change all that, especially with his oldest son. Nevertheless, he painfully and helplessly watched as his family history repeated itself.

In 11th grade, Chezky became even more withdrawn and depressed. Some men in *shul* commented to Chezky's father that they never saw the boy smile. That was when Chezky's parents' concern turned to worry and they arranged for a consultation with a mental health professional.

❧ Aaron[*]

At times, the casualties of misguided — albeit otherwise successful — parents can even be found in the homes of *klei kodesh*. Here, too, the qualities which produce success in the rabbinate or *chinuch* do not always guarantee success in parenting, as illustrated by the following case history.

Aaron's father holds three positions, each of which would be considered full time by anyone else. He is a *maggid shiur* at a prestigious *mesivta*. His teaching is so highly regarded that some parents send their sons to that *mesivta* just so their sons will have him for one year.

In addition, Aaron's father is the *Rav* of a large, well-respected congregation. His responsibilities there include delivering regular *shiurim*, and speaking on *Shabbos* and *Yom Tov*. Finally, as if all of the above responsibilities were not enough, Aaron's father serves as the rabbinical adviser for a major Jewish communal organization.

Aaron's father has earned the respect of colleagues, co-workers, subordinates and the community for the outstanding fashion in which he fulfills his many responsibilities.

Aaron's mother is a talented "balabusta" and *Rebbetzin*, above and beyond the management of her busy, bustling home, she is a

---

* Not his real name

frequent public speaker, active in *chessed* organizations — you get the picture.

With role models like these, how could anything go wrong?

Despite the examples set by his parents, Aaron performed quite poorly in mesivta. He often seemed distracted, and he had no close friends. What troubled his parents most was that he seemed to be increasingly unhappy. Yet both of his parents are known as sensitive and compassionate *baalei middos*, who were always bringing joy to others.

A full battery of psychological tests revealed that although Aaron had above-average intelligence, he suffered from serious academic delays, unmet emotional needs, a fear of his father and an inability to express feelings.

Extensive consultation with the parents revealed that they had extremely high expectations of their children, that they did not provide much emotional nurturing and that most expressions of approval were limited to academic performance.

❧ What Went Wrong?

Considering that they come from such exemplary homes, we would expect at least average, if not above average, behavior and academic performance from Yehudah, Chezky and Aaron. What went wrong?

Many, people have managed to acquire the character traits necessary to succeed in careers outside of the home. But those same character traits, if not modified, can cause these people to fail in their careers at home, as parents.

For example, if one is goal directed, time efficient and persistent *to an extreme*, one can become rigid, demanding and stubborn. When that happens, the high expectations one imposes upon oneself become unrealistic, unreachable goals for his or her children. And when children feel that they can never satisfy their parents, they stop trying, act out, or both.

Furthermore, if someone is overly detail oriented, he could lose his perspective and miss the big picture. When that occurs, a parent will treat every minor infraction as if it were a major catastrophe. This, in turn, serves only to discourage the child.

Finally, too much efficiency can lead to emotional distance. And when parents create a cold, emotionally sterile atmosphere at home, it triggers hurt and angry feelings in the children.

As Rav Wolbe puts it; "In order to make it through the stage of 'fourteen years old' peacefully, an adolescent must be bonded to his parents with a warm, loving relationship."[2]

❧ What We Can Do

Is there hope for Yehudah, Chezky and Aaron? Is it already too late? What can be done to help their parents raise successful children? And what can you do to help your children succeed?

Yes, there is hope. If parents accept that *they* must make some changes, improvement is possible. By taking some of the following steps, parents who are successful in their out-of-home careers can succeed at home, as well.

• **Give some unconditional approval.** There is perhaps no greater motivation for children than the prospect of earning their parents' praise. Parents try to bring out the best in their children by linking approval to behavior or academic performance. But if **all** approval is conditional, or if the parents' expectations are unrealistic, then the children will rebel, give up, or do both. So while it's a good idea to give any child some unconditional approbation, it is absolutely vital for a Yehudah, Chezky or Aaron.

• **Limit criticism.** Children need to be corrected, otherwise they will never learn. But parents who are always finding fault with

---

2 My own translation of *Zeriah Ubinyan Bechinuch* (Hebrew) by Harav Shlomo Wolbe (*Yerushalayim:* Feldheim Publishers, 1995), p. 16.

their children will soon discover that no one is paying attention anymore. The parents' lectures may be on the mark; but if their children are not listening, nothing is accomplished. As *Chazal* have taught, "*s'mol docheh v'yamin m'kareiv*, criticize with the weaker hand and praise with the stronger one" (*Sotah* 47a).

• **Spend private time with each child.** Relationships cannot be imposed and enforced like a dress code. Even parent-child relationships must be nurtured over time. While animals instinctively bond with their parents, humans must deliberately devote time to each of their children in order to build the closeness which is so vital to healthy psychosocial development. And that time must be focused on the child — not on the chore, task or homework that is the agenda of the parent.

• **Admit failure and defeat.** Some parents mistakenly believe that it is good *chinuch* for their children to think parents are perfect and never make mistakes. These parents make every effort to hide their imperfections from their children.

Yehudah, Chezky and Aaron each felt alienated and estranged from their parents, in part, because they saw their parents as vastly superior and unreachable. Once their parents began to share with them some of their own frustrations, errors and even embarrassments, the parents appeared more human, and approachable.

❧ Follow-up

What ever happened to Yehudah, Chezky and Aaron? Their parents swallowed hard and accepted the prescription outlined above. It took quite some time, but all three families were able to reverse their destructive patterns and save their children.

Aaron is now learning well, solidly established in the upper half of his class at a most demanding yeshivah.

Yehudah, now married and learning in an out-of-town kollel, is the pride and joy of his in-laws, much to his parents' surprise. His relationship with his parents has improved dramatically and Yehudah and his parents now regularly exchange phone calls and faxes, and there is more fondness and affection than they ever dreamed possible.

Chezky is still somewhat socially withdrawn, but not nearly as unhappy as he used to be. He is beginning to come out of his shell, though he still has a long way to go. The closer relationship he has recently developed with his father, however, has unmistakably raised his self-esteem — and his parents' hopes.

These three sets of parents are now more successful at home. All successful parents should see how they can learn from these three families. Then we can hope to see fewer casualties of success.

21

Getting Down About
Teenagers Not Getting Up

The developmental stage of adolescence is notorious for fostering conflicts between parents and children. These disagreements include, but are in no way limited to, hair styles and haircuts, clothing expenditures and clothing styles, study habits and study partners, eating habits, choice of friends and choice of language, money management and time management.

Adolescents — can and often do — argue with their parents about anything or everything. To a great extent, how parents cope with these confrontations determines whether their child's adolescence will be a catastrophic disaster or simply a period of turbulence.

Parents cannot be fully prepared for every eventual dispute; indeed, the potential arenas of discord are infinite. But parents can master basic principles which can apply to just about any point of contention between them and their testy adolescents.

Since there are so many times throughout the day when bickering between parents and teenagers is touched off, it often feels as if the arguments start the first thing in the morning and last until late at night. In fact, one of the most common points of contention is what time the adolescent child should get up in the morning. It is for this reason that this chapter focuses on the all-too-common phenomenon of parents getting down about their teenage children not getting up on time.

☙❧

SINCE THE DAWN OF OUR PEOPLE, THE IDEAL SERVICE OF *HASHEM* has always been performed as early in the day as possible. The verse, "*Vayashkeim Avraham baboker*, And Abraham woke up early in the morning" (*Bereishis* 22:3), is not merely a narrative detail but rather a clarion call for all future generations.

Perhaps no one more than David *Hamelech* has emphasized the premium placed on early rising. After all, David's daily Divine Service began before dawn — "*A'irah shachar*," I shall awaken the dawn, "*chatzos laylah akum*," At midnight I get up, and "*kidamti baneshef*," I got up before dawn (*Tehillim* 108:3, 119:62, 119:147).

Finally, as if to remove any vestige of doubt regarding the importance of getting up early, the *Shulchan Aruch* begins with the following words of introduction:

> One should strengthen himself like a lion to rise up in the morning to serve his Creator. [He should get up so early that it would appear] that he is waking up the dawn (*Orach Chaim* 1:1).

Although not all of us achieve that exalted level of serving *Hashem*, all agree that the ideal daily schedule for a Jew should begin before dawn.

Parents don't always expect their children to rise before dawn. But they do expect their children to get up in time for *minyan*, for the school bus or for the car pool to yeshivah. When children oversleep or can't get out of bed in the morning, parents often experience painful disappointment which is indescribable.

"What do you mean, 'they oversleep'?" some might ask. "Just go in there and wake them up!"

Unfortunately, it is not always that easy. Listen to what one parent recently told me.

> "He asked us to make sure that he was up because the *Mashgiach* had told him that if he misses *minyan* one more time they would expel him from the yeshivah. So we knew he wanted to get up — or, at least, that's what we thought. At first, I banged on the door until he answered. A few minutes later I returned and repeated the same procedure. Finally, I came into his room and pulled off the blanket. Two minutes later I came back and he was under the blanket again, sound asleep.
>
> "At that point I was really feeling angry. I had to get to work and I was going to be late because he wasn't getting up. I knew that if I left the house, my wife would never be able to get him up by herself. I felt so desperate that I just didn't know what to do. It was too early for me to call you so I... I... I picked up his *negel vasser* and dumped it on his head!
>
> "That certainly woke him up... But even that didn't get him out of bed. He just sat up straight, mumbled at me and went back to sleep! I felt totally helpless."

"These must be kids from dysfunctional families," you might say. "After all, what boy from a *normal* home would act that way?"

Although the scenario described above was an extreme example, the pattern of frustrated parents nagging their adolescent children out of bed is repeated every morning in many fine homes, where the parents are concerned, educated, and whose other children all get up on time.

When Yoeli* gets up late and misses *minyan*, his parents are not only concerned about the poor start to his day, they are also looking down the road and shuddering at what they see ahead.

"If this is how he is acting now," one mother said, "where will it lead? He could stop going to *minyan* altogether, *chas v'shalom*. He could get kicked out of yeshivah. Then what would we do? I'm afraid he could end up like some of those 'dropouts' we hear so much about. Frankly, I'm terrified!"

Parents of such children are hounded by painful questions. *"Why is this happening to us? What did we do wrong?"*

As is common, parents often blame themselves for the misbehavior of their children. Every child, however, is born with unique personality and character predispositions for which the parents can be blamed only genetically. Or, as I often tell parents, "You may not have contributed to the problem; but you can surely contribute to the solution."

Of course, sometimes what provokes an adolescent to rebel beyond the bounds of normal misbehavior are the strains in the parent-child relationship. At such times, a most powerful weapon the adolescent can wield in the battle with his parents is not getting up in the morning.

Simply by missing the bus, the *minyan* or morning *seder* in yeshivah, a child can disrupt the lives of both parents beyond belief. Parents are then hurled into a dismal world of anxiety and hopelessness.

In despair and feeling totally exasperated, parents of chronic late-risers will try almost anything to correct the problem. One oft-tried approach is to ignore the behavior completely, adopting a "business as usual" attitude.

While this approach does have merit — for starters, it reduces the level of conflict, confrontation and conflagration — it can

---

* Not his real name

often lead the offending child to feel that his or her parents don't care about him or her. Months or years later he may tell his parents, "When you stopped trying to wake me up, I felt you gave up on me. It was then that I really felt alone and abandoned. I thought that I just didn't matter to you any more."

Other parents try to "get someone to speak with him." This often involves arranging for concerned or interested relatives, educators, rabbis, or therapists to "have a talk" with the oversleeper. These talks often take on the character of a private *mussar shmuess.*

This approach also has some benefit. First, it focuses the attention of the parents away from the child. "Who should we get? How should we approach that person? When can we arrange for them to meet?" etc. Secondly, it gives the parents something to *do* so they don't feel so helpless. Arranging for such "meetings" generally expends considerable time, effort and, in some cases, even money.

In the final analysis, even after such meetings are conducted, the problem is rarely solved. There is often some temporary improvement. But in a few days or weeks, the situation usually reverts to exactly where it had been. Only now, the parents feel even more frustrated.

The more desperate parents attempt the "stuck key approach."

Anyone who is having a difficult time opening a lock soon feels frustrated. A rational approach to such situations is to check and see if you are using the correct key. Some people, however, stubbornly refuse to consider whether or not they have the right key. They simply apply more and more force until they break the lock, the key, their finger, or all three.

The "stuck key approach" to oversleeping adolescents is to act in a way which will increase the level of conflict. Parents who use this approach will take the same steps that have heretofore proven futile, but now will try them even harder.

This escalation often includes threats and raised voices. These only serve to highlight the parents' mounting feelings of frustration and despair.

❀ What Can Be Done

While all of the approaches outlined above may at times be useful with younger children, they will prove quite ineffective in dealing with an adolescent's chronic, consistent and confounding inability to get up. Once a child has reached the age of 16, 17, or 18, different methods of dealing with this problem are indicated. (The following suggestions, by the way, may be found to be helpful in other situations where parents of adolescents feel enough frustration to want to bang their heads against a wall.)

Declare defeat. Just as declaring bankruptcy can ease the financial pressure of someone in debt, acknowledging defeat can reduce the parent-child struggle immediately. How is this done?

The parents need to admit, first to themselves and then to their child, that they are not able to physically force an adolescent child up and out of bed in the morning.

This admission achieves several objectives. It gives the child a sense of power, which may be just what he or she was looking for in the first place. In these cases, this sense of empowerment may be all that is needed to get the child back into a more productive daily schedule. Once the child has won the war, there is no longer any purpose in his or her fighting any further.

Another benefit of declaring defeat is that it helps the parents get off the treadmill of searching for the "right" approach to make their sleepyhead more eager to rise and shine. *Declaring one's inability to accomplish a task is never as humiliating as demonstrating that inability.* Feeling less frustrated, the parents often become less angry and resentful. This, in turn, helps to further reduce the parent-child conflict.

Address the adult within the child. Adolescents, by definition, are part adult and part child. When they act immaturely and irresponsibly, they are acting like children. This usually prompts the parents to treat them like children. But nothing incites an adolescent to rebel more than being treated like a child.

The parents seem to be faced with an irresolvable dilemma:

"First he says we should trust him, that he really wants to get up on time. But when we leave it to him, he sleeps until noon. Then, when we try to discuss the matter with him, he complains that we are demeaning him. What are we supposed to do?"

Since you can't treat him like an adult and a child at the same time, I would suggest that you address the adult within the child. Explain the new policy as follows: "Since you are 18 now, you really are old enough to take care of when you go to bed and when you get up. We will not be trying to do this for you anymore. From now on, you're in charge. If you need a new alarm clock, just let us know."

Don't ignore the behavior. Sounds like a contradiction to what was suggested above? Not really. I'm not saying to involve yourself in waking up your adolescent. Nor am I advocating ignoring the behavior *without* giving any explanation, because that would be viewed by the adolescent as wholesale abandonment. Just ignoring him or her means you just don't care; that you've given up.

On the other hand, explaining, *in advance*, that you are going to adopt a new policy regarding his or her getting up in the morning will send the message that you do care. You are telling your child that you are not waking him or her up because you expect him or her to assume that responsibility, and if not, to suffer the consequences.

But what if it means he gets kicked out of yeshivah, stops *davening* altogether, or worse? These are frightening prospects, for sure. But consider the alternative. Stubbornly continuing the tug-of-war will only make things worse.

Isolate the problem. Yes, not getting up on time *is* a terrible tragedy in any Torah home. But it may not be as bad as what you fear it might lead to. In addition, the fear that this behavior may lead to worse does not mean that it should be treated *as if* this were already the worst-case scenario. A toothache can lead to gangrene, but no one calls an ambulance for a toothache. To treat moderate misbehavior with the concern normally reserved for more serious offenses will only confuse the child.

Let us analyze the following: If parents were to treat missing one day of yeshivah as though their child dropped out of school altogether — since that is where a day's absence could potentially lead — then the parents will act with the alarm reserved for such an extreme possibility. But if the parents do react in that way, the child may think the following: "I've just missed a day of yeshivah. My parents are treating me as if I've dropped out completely. So I might as well not go back, since I'm already suffering the most severe reaction anyway."

In short, if parents react to smaller problems with an intensity appropriate for major disasters, they may unwittingly bring about the realization of their own prophecies of doom.

～☙ ❧～

No one can assure parents how their children will turn out. That uncertainty is part of every parent's *tzaar gidul banim* — the agony of childrearing. But if it will reassure even one parent, let me report that in any case where parents have followed the guidelines outlined above — and stuck to them as a team [1] — they were rewarded with *nachas* beyond their wildest dreams.

On occasion, some of that *nachas* is even shared with me. When I get such a call it goes something like this:

"Dr. Wikler, we thought you'd like to know that we just got off the phone with Yoeli's *Rosh Hayeshivah*, and he told us that this *z'man*, Yoeli has been learning up a storm in the *beis midrash*. He's at the top of his *shiur*. He's well liked by the other boys, and — I still can't believe it — he's *on time* for *minyan* every morning.

---

1. See Rav Samson Raphael Hirsch's commentary on *Devarim* 21:18 for insight into the importance of parental unity and the consequences of its absence.

22

Parenting a Troubled Adolescent in a Torah Home: Where Did We Go Wrong? What Can We Do Now?

While virtually every child finds that adolescence is a period of turbulence and turmoil, some teenagers seem to become more troubled than their peers. These children tend to act in ways that go beyond what is considered normal, even for an adolescent.

Some people maintain that there are more troubled teens today than there were in previous generations. Others contend that the numbers, certainly as a percentage, are the same, but that we are simply more aware of and ready to acknowledge the problem. Still others assert that while as a statistic, the amount of teens who are in crisis has not risen very much, the level of misconduct has increased dramatically.

There is no disagreement, however, that the parents of "adolescents at risk" are embattled and under siege in their own homes. They are lost, bewildered and overwhelmed. They are distraught, disoriented and distressed.

Trying to raise these troubled adolescents becomes an even greater struggle when parents attempt to maintain the standards of a Torah home. These parents often find themselves asking, "Where did we go wrong and what can we do now?" Hopefully, this chapter will help provide some much-needed answers.

⟳⟲

ADOLESCENCE — THAT DEVELOPMENTAL STAGE OF LIFE BRIDGING childhood and adulthood — is a critical turning point in a person's growth and development. In previous generations, young people were considered adults well before their 20th birthday. In modern Western society, adolescence is thought to correspond roughly with the teenage years — or beyond, according to some authorities. Whatever the exact age, adolescence represents a transitional stage of development. As such, this period normally entails the uncertainty, anxieties and conflicts that are associated with transitions of any kind. And while some transitions are smooth and peaceful, adolescence is generally a tumultuous transition period.

The reason behind the turbulence of adolescence is that it is the shaky start of an unpredictable voyage. It is the journey of a youngster departing from the secure moorings of childhood to cruise the uncharted waters of adulthood. And since no one goes through adolescence twice (*Baruch Hashem*), no one ever has any advance practice in making this transition!

As adolescents try to adjust to the shift from childhood dependence to mature independence, they struggle to understand their changing responsibilities, opportunities, limitations and freedoms. The many changes taking place all around the adolescents — in their relationships with friends and relatives, and even within their own bodies — inevitably generate considerable turmoil for them. During this period of instability, adolescents instinctively reach out to their friends for support. This explains the extraordinary — almost obsessive — importance of peer relationships in the life of an adolescent.

In response to the many changes taking place, all of the old parental expectations, guidelines and structures for the adolescent have to be altered or replaced, just as his or her clothing needs to be changed to accommodate the adolescent's growth. Indeed, adolescence is as much a period of transition for parents as it is for the adolescents themselves.

🌿 Adolescent Rebellion

At times, and with alarming frequency, this pattern of adolescent turmoil also includes elements of rebellion which can literally rock the foundation of any home. The rebellion can range from milder cases of disrespect or lack of cooperation to verbal abuse and antisocial behavior.

In secular society, only the most severe cases of adolescent rebellion are cause for concern. Milder manifestations may not be welcome, but they are nevertheless accepted. Parents may even shrug their shoulders and say, "What can you expect? (S)he's a teenager!"

While all parents of troubled adolescents find their task difficult, Torah families deal with unique conditions which can combine to produce tension, conflict and excruciating heartache in even the best of homes. Acts of rebellion considered tame in the secular world can cause grief and anguish of the most extreme proportions in a Torah home. Reuven slackening off in his general *mitzvah* observance or Rivkah adopting a less modest mode of dress is enough to precipitate a major crisis in each of their homes.

While adolescent girls can become as rebellious and defiant as adolescent boys, guidance counselors and therapists who work with troubled youths agree that the preponderance of acting-out adolescents are boys. This is as true in the Torah community as it is in society at large. The etiology of this disproportion is open to speculation. But one thing is eminently clear: Our system of yeshivah education for boys is in no way a factor contributing to this problem. If it were, then the proportion of young men acting-out in the Torah community would be disproportionately larger than that of the larger society. And it is not.

In a Torah home, acts of rebellion can trigger a wide range of parental reactions. The parents may feel enraged, hurt, frustrated, tormented, depressed, ashamed, hopeless, worried, frightened, or all of the above. They feel anger toward their adolescent for disappointing them. They are preoccupied with trying to figure out a way to effect a change in the adolescent's behavior. They are apprehensive about what other acts of rebellion may follow and where all of this will lead — for this child and for their other children. And they often feel stigmatized in the community for having a child who does not look and act like a proper yeshivah or Bais Yaakov student.

Of course, *Chazal* understood these intense emotional reactions thousands of years ago and they appreciated the severity of the situation: "Rabbi Yochanan said in the name of Rabbi Shimon Bar Yochai, 'A degenerate child in one's home is worse than the war of Gog and Magog'" (*Berachos* 7b).

In most families with a rebellious child, the other children are model yeshivah students. They, too, are shocked at the behavior of their sibling. They, too, may feel anger, especially for the heartache being caused to their parents. And they may feel so ashamed that they discourage their own friends from visiting for fear of being embarrassed by the nonconforming brother or sister.

To understand more fully how such problems develop, we must go back to the very first signs of trouble. To illustrate this process, let us examine the case history of one acting-out adolescent. Let's call him David Schwartz.*

---

* Not his real name.

David was born three years after his older sister, Rochel. When he was a small child, there was little sibling rivalry between them. A younger sister and brother followed three and four years later, respectively. In preschool, David appeared to be bright in some ways, but otherwise quite average.

Third grade: The English teacher suspected that David had a reading problem and recommended an educational evaluation. The Schwartzes had David tested, and the consultant noted some mild learning deficits, but recommended no further testing or remediation. Retesting was advised in two to three years.

Fourth grade: David had a bad experience with his *rebbi*, who had a propensity for harshly punishing his students for even mild offenses. This *rebbi* was not rehired the following year. While Mr. Schwartz openly blames this *rebbi* for "ruining" David, Mrs. Schwartz points out that none of the other boys in this class turned out like David did.

Fifth grade: This seemed to be a watershed year for David. Both his *rebbi* and English teacher complained that David was not completing his homework and they both felt he could be doing better than his just-passing grades. No testing was recommended by either the *rebbi* of the English teacher.

Sixth grade: David's academic decline accelerated. He nearly failed two subjects, but a tutor was engaged and seemed to save the day. Mrs. Schwartz thought David should get counseling, but Mr. Schwartz felt it would be a waste of money. Over the course of the year, the principal complained, on separate occasions, of disrespect to teachers, possession of firecrackers, and even smoking (the latter never substantiated).

After each report, David's parents would try to discuss the matter with him. David would either deny the incident or accuse the yeshivah of exaggerating. Mr. Schwartz would lose his temper more often than his wife, but neither one got through to David.

At this point Mr. Schwartz agreed with his wife that it was time to seek outside help. A local family service agency recommended counseling, initially for the entire Schwartz family and then just for David and his parents. The sessions turned into shouting matches, sometimes between Mr. and Mrs. Schwartz, sometimes between them and David. After three months the Schwartzes saw no improvement. So when the therapist announced she was leaving the agency, the Schwartzes decided to leave as well.

Seventh grade: David began socializing with less observant boys, and becoming totally uncooperative at home. At times he was even provocative with his brother and sisters. More professional help was called for, and a psychiatrist who specialized in treating adolescents prescribed medication. Though David refused to take the medication, he did continue to meet with the psychiatrist on and off through most of the year. The Schwartzes received little guidance from the psyciatrist, but at least they felt they were "doing something" about the problem.

Toward the end of the seventh grade, David's principal called in the Schwartzes to tell them that, "unless David gets a haircut this week, he will be suspended." The principal implied that the Schwartzes were shirking their parental responsibility. The Schwartzes, for their part, did not inform the school of David's psychiatric treatments for fear that it would be held against him in some way. David finally did get a haircut and was spared suspension.

Halfway through the summer, however, David was sent home from camp for setting fires. David said that he was "just playing with matches."

Eighth grade: David was beginning to socialize with less observant girls. His clothing reflected his new attitudes and once again the Schwartzes were called in to the principal: David was adversely influencing other boys and was therefore being expelled.

Where could they take David in the middle of the year? The principal was sympathetic but unrelenting.

The Schwartzes pulled out all the stops, reaching out to prominent Rabbis and pivotal philanthropists. Finally, the principal agreed to keep David, but only on probation.

Shortly before graduation, David cursed his *rebbi* in front of the class. For this he was expelled, immediately — though he was allowed to graduate. But it had long been clear there was no way David would be allowed to continue into the yeshivah's ninth grade.

Two new yeshivos for high school: David lasted only three months in the first high school that he attended. He completed ninth grade at a second *mesivta*, out of town, and the Schwartzes were hopeful.

Early that summer, David was thrown out of camp for driving without a license. He "hung around" for the rest of the summer, keeping erratic hours and irritating the entire family.

Tenth grade: David came home on his own after one month. He refused further counseling and spent the day listening to the radio, sleeping, or just "hanging out."

David eventually returned to the *mesivta* but never received credit for the tenth grade as a result of too many incompletes.

The following year: David attended a yeshivah for "troubled teens" in *Eretz Yisrael.* This move proved to be equally unproductive, as David frustrated all of the *rebbei'im* and *yungeleit* who tried to work with him.

David returned to the States a year later and lived at home for several months. He began working at an electronics store and eventually moved out of his parents' home. By this time he no longer wore a *yarmulke, tzitzis* or *tefillin,* and his parents suspected that he was using drugs.

A Parents' Support Group

Several years ago, while working with another couple whose predicament was similar to that of the Schwartzes, I realized that, more than my advice and counsel, they needed the support and encouragement of their peers — other parents of acting-out, troublesome teenagers. They needed a support group where they could hear from other parents that they were not alone, crazy, or completely at fault. Such groups do exist and many are run under the aegis of a national self-help organization. But all of these groups include mostly non-Jewish parents, and this couple needed a group for *Orthodox* parents. Since I could not find such a group, I decided to organize one. My colleagues greeted the idea with skepticism: "You'll never get Orthodox parents to meet with you in a group setting. They'll be too embarrassed."

Many parents *were* too ashamed; there were many more telephone inquiries than there were attendees. But a parents' support group was formed in February 1984, meeting weekly for 90-minute sessions. The group, which ran for almost two years, had a fluid membership. A total of eight couples, including the Schwartzes, participated in the group, although not all of them came to each meeting. The group was terminated when the active members felt they no longer needed help.

The group meetings served a twofold purpose. First, they provided encouragement and peer support to the members. When one parent told another, "I know *exactly* how you felt!" the sense of empathy and sharing was almost palpable. The second purpose was to provide an opportunity for group problem-solving. Each week, members raised issues and recounted incidents, and the entire group responded with constructive and creative feedback.

🐾 Where Did We Go Wrong?

Certainly, each family was unique. In fact, all that some members had in common was their Orthodoxy and the fact that they had a troublesome teenager who did not respond to individual or family psychotherapy. But during the life of the group, one question kept resurfacing like a trained dolphin leaping through hoops: "Where did we go wrong?"

Parents must not blame themselves fully for the emotional or behavioral disturbances of their children. Genetic endowment plays a major role in determining a person's character and personality. Of course, environment also plays a significant role. But while parents need not blame themselves for causing their child's difficulties, it is true that they still may have contributed to the exacerbation of their child's problem.

Retrospective analysis of what could have or might have happened is highly speculative. However, it is often the only diagnostic tool available. So while no firm conclusions were ever reached, the group was able to identify a number of predisposing factors that *seemed* to have contributed to their children's problems. In my work with individual adolescents and their parents — both before and since the parents' support group — I have found the following factors present in most cases. What follows, then, are the lessons learned not only in the group, but also reinforced by my clinical experience with scores of other Orthodox families with troubled adolescents.

Parental disharmony: Raising any adolescent is an enormous challenge. Even when both parents work together as a team, the parenting road is full of potholes. But if the mother and the father do not see eye to eye, then a manipulative adolescent can have a veritable field day playing one parent off against the other.

We can all recognize the devastating influence that severe marital conflict has on any child, regardless of age. When parents are openly hostile toward one another, everyone suffers. What I am referring to here, however, is not to the blatant, aggressive form of marital discord, but to a more subtle form of disagreement, where one parent adopts a more lenient position towards the child while the other parent is more strict. (See Rabbi Samson

Raphael Hirsch's *Commentary* on *Devarim* 21:19, which is most relevant to this subject.)

Of course, no two parents can agree on all child-rearing issues. But in troubled families, there is often a pattern of one parent pushing for more freedom for the adolescent while the other parent advocates greater restriction. Frequently such couples consult with Rabbis or mental health professionals and ask which parent's approach is correct. Invariably the "answer" — that it may be irrelevant *how* the parents respond, but what is important is that they respond *in tandem* — disappoints them.

Undiagnosed learning disabilities: As with David Schwartz, many of these acting-out adolescents had some history of academic failure or underachievement in the early elementary grades. In some cases, the learning disability was misdiagnosed, in others, it was detected too late. Sometimes it was overlooked altogether. While it is impossible to assess exactly how large a role learning disabilities play in later behavioral problems, many of these children would certainly have benefited from early evaluation, remediation and, in some cases, special education. There is no guarantee that this intervention would have prevented the characterological degeneration that developed later, but it might have at least minimized it.

Parental rigidity: All of the parents I dealt with seemed to find it especially difficult to differentiate between rigidity and consistency. It is important for parents to set clear, firm behavioral expectations and guidelines for their children. That is consistency. The parental values remain constant and the consequences remain stable.

On the other hand, there are times when good judgment dictates that it is preferable to ignore a minor infraction of the rules rather than make an "issue" of the matter. This is flexibility. Every successful general knows that to win a war, one must be selective about which battles to engage. If you fight every battle, you will lose the war.

In many cases, one or both parents would dig in their heels on relatively minor issues. They might even become enraged, demonstrating their helplessness and frustration. Such loss of control generally provokes reciprocal hostility, widening the communication gap between parents and child, and providing the adolescent with justification to his claim (to himself and others) that his parents "really *are* crazy."

In short, parents must endeavor to avoid confrontations and power struggles with their children.

Harav Shlomo Wolbe emphasises the far-reaching consequences of adopting a rigid and harsh parenting style when children are growing. "If parents treat a 2-, 3-, or 4-year-old child with harshness, if they are rigid, if they hit him and demand more than he is capable of — they destroy the warmth of the parent-child relationship ... The hitting and the rigidity and harshness penetrate the subconscious of the child without his being aware of it. The matter remains hidden in his soul. Then, during adolescence, the matter comes out and is revealed. The parents see that they have lost their connection with their child. For the parents it is a terrible anguish. For the child it is terribly destructive."[1]

Overlooking options: Often, when recounting an explosive episode, one of the parents would say, "I just didn't know what else to do!" They saw their options as limited to either giving their children complete free rein or clamping down like a steel vise, overlooking possibilities of negotiation.

Negotiating is never easy, especially when dealing with a manipulative, deceitful adolescent who has already proven him- or herself to be untrustworthy. Nevertheless, by sitting down at the bargaining table and drawing up a behavioral "contract," parents stand the greatest chance of reaching a working compromise with their children. This approach enhances the adolescent's

---

1. My own translation of *Zeriah Ubinyan Bechinuch* (Hebrew) by Harav Shlomo Wolbe (*Yerushalayim:* Feldheim Publishers, 1995), p. 7.

sense of autonomy, self-esteem and responsibility, while insuring that vital lines of communication remain open.

Parental overinvolvement: By the time serious behavioral problems were manifested, these parents' lives understandably focused almost exclusively on the problematic child. But well before the situation became so serious, one or both parents were generally overinvolved with one or more of the children. One of the "homework" exercises that the group gave such couples was to require the couple to spend one hour a week *alone* — just the two of them. That may sound easy, but to some it became an enormous challenge. One couple returned each week and sheepishly reported that they had been "too busy" to complete their assignment. Then one week this couple proudly announced that they had gone out for a long walk together — and the entire group burst into applause. Interestingly enough, there were noteworthy improvements in their son's behavior that very week.

❧ Is There Hope?

When parents find that their child fits the description of David Schwartz, is there any hope?

It is never too late. But parents should not expect magical solutions that will transform their long-haired son into a yeshivah *bachur* or their miniskirted daughter into a *Bais Yaakov* girl overnight.

The support group described here no longer exists, but others do, and additional groups can be formed. In this way, if parents can overcome their fears of embarrassment, they will be able to get the support and guidance they so desperately need.

In addition, parents can — and must — seek guidance, *as a couple*, from qualified *Rabbanim* and experts in the mental health field. These counselors will help them cope with the myriad of challenges presented by troublesome adolescents. Even if the child refuses to attend individual or family sessions, the parents still have much to gain for themselves.

Finally, parents can read and reread material — like that presented here — which can enable them to learn from the mistakes of others. Unfortunately, there are no quick and easy solutions to long-term, complex problems. Rabbi Yisrael Salanter once said that the hardest thing in the world to change is a character trait. If this is so even when one wants to correct *himself*, how much more does it apply to the near-impossible task of trying to change someone *else*, especially when that person is a troubled adolescent who only sees flaws in others!

Neither therapists nor *Rabbanim* get much feedback on the long-term outcomes of the earlier crises that were brought to their attention. Nevertheless, several years ago I was treated to a rare follow-up. While attending a wedding reception, I met Mr. and Mrs. Schwartz. They told me that David had recently married a Bais Yaakov graduate with her own history of rebellion. He was working at a *glatt* kosher take-out food store, and whenever they saw him, his head was covered. The Schwartzes respected David's independence and privacy, so they did not ask him questions about his *Yiddishkeit*. But they became cautiously optimistic when David came home a month before his wedding and picked up his *tefillin*.

Yes, there is hope.

PART EIGHT:

Preparing Children for Successful Marriages

23

Preparation for Marriage: Prevention of Divorce*

"Rabbi Yehudah says, 'Whoever does not teach his son a trade teaches him to steal.' Is this to be taken literally? Rather, 'It is as if he teaches him to steal'" (Kiddushin 29a).

Rashi comments on this Gemara, *"Since [the son] will not have a trade and will have no bread [to eat]. He will [be forced] to go to the crossroad and rob people."*

The implication here is that when parents do not adequately equip their children to succeed in life, they are responsible for the children's failures. If this is true regarding the earning of a livelihood, it is even more so regarding the attainment of success in marriage.

---

* An earlier version of this chapter was originally published as an article in *The Jewish Observer*, Jan. 1979: It was later included in my book, *Bayis Ne'eman b'Yisrael: Practical Steps to Success in Marriage* (New York: Feldheim Publishers, 1988), and is reprinted here with the permission of the publishers.

All parents want their children to be happily married. This is, perhaps, a parent's greatest hope for his or her child. Little else provides as much deep nachas and contentment as does seeing one's children settled into satisfying, secure and stable marriages. And nothing causes parents as much grief and heartache as when their child's marriage ends in divorce.

In order to prevent the tragedy of divorce, parents must assume their responsibilities to adequately equip their children for marriage. The chapters which follow suggest some steps that parents can take now to help prepare their children for future marriage.

⌒◌⌒

"Daniel, if you don't *chazer* the *Gemara* more often, they will never accept you in the *mesivta!*"

"You'd better study your *Chumash*, Esty, if you're serious about attending Seminary next year!"

THESE ARE FAMILIAR SOUNDS IN MANY A TORAH HOME. PREPARATION for all levels of Torah study is taken seriously by most of today's parents. These parents are not professional educators. Rather they are *shomrei mitzvos*, following the teachings of our Sages (*Kiddushin* 29a) that preparing a child (and providing) for Torah study is a major parental responsibility.

The *Gemara* also includes preparation for more of life's necessities, such as having a trade and being able to swim, in this list of parental responsibilities. Finding the proper *shidduch*, the *Gemara* explains, is another top priority.

Unfortunately, the advance preparation for marriage often stops there. Certainly *finding* the proper *shidduch* for a child *is* extremely important, but do parents look to the finding of a *shidduch* as the entirety of their assignment, or rather as part of a more complex chapter in parental responsibility?

Today, marriage (and parenthood) are taken too much for

granted. At age 19, 20 — or 22, 23 — a seminary graduate and a yeshivah *bachur* are suddenly considered "ready for marriage," without any further preparation. Yet being a proper spouse and parent are probably the greatest challenges they will ever face. Why should immature members of our community be permitted to flounder in the sea of family life without adequate swimming lessons?

No, our *bubbies* and *zaydies* never had preparation for marriage beyond what they saw at home. But, then again, their generation also did not witness the epidemic of divorces plaguing the Torah community today, and so it was clear that they required no additional pointers.

Needless to say, many complex factors contribute to the tragic breakdowns of today's young families, but certainly, with proper preparation, at least some of those dissolutions could have been prevented. A brief case history will illustrate one type of marital breakdown which perhaps could have been prevented.

❧ The Case of Rena*

Rena was always a good student and her parents heard only praises from her teachers. Although quiet, she kept up with a small circle of close friends all during her elementary-school years.

Shortly after beginning high school, however, Rena seemed to become even quieter than before. Her contacts with friends decreased and the occasional smile was seldom seen on her face.

Rena's parents attributed her seriousness to the increased academic demands of high school. "Surely by next year," they reasoned, "Rena will outgrow this."

By her senior year, Rena had no friends, went out of the house only for errands and school, and spent most of her time in her room.

---

* Not her real name.

Her parents received positive reports of Rena's academic progress, and they continued to assume that she would "outgrow" her withdrawn nature. Student teaching in seminary, they concluded, would help to "bring her out."

Two years later, the picture remained the same. By now, many of Rena's classmates were becoming engaged. Her parents speculated that she was envious of the other girls, yearning for her own *chassan*. They inquired about *shidduchim* and after several meetings with Levi, a well-recommended *talmid* at a high-caliber yeshivah, they encouraged Rena to accept his marriage proposal.

Before the end of her first year of marriage, Rena became so upset with marital problems that she wanted to leave Levi and move back to her parents' home. Both sets of parents encouraged the couple to consult a Rav, who eventually referred them to me for professional help.

Levi refused to meet with me and preferred to speak with another Rav. Two years later, after many frustrated efforts to resolve the marital conflicts, Rena and Levi were divorced. Levi remained in the couple's apartment and Rena returned to her parents' home — with her baby.

Rena's parents knew of the first Rav's earlier efforts to refer Rena and Levi for professional help, so they encouraged her to meet with me to help her recover from the blow of the divorce.

I never did meet with Levi. From Rena's reports of his behavior, however, it was clear that he also brought his own *"peckalah"* of emotional difficulties into the marriage.

In time, with therapy, Rena unraveled the mysteries of her own feelings. It seems that Rena suffered from chronic low self-esteem — she never really felt very good about herself. In addition, she was prone to periodic bouts of mild to moderate depression. Finally, she had a markedly distrustful side to her personality which made it difficult for her to trust others and to establish warm, close relationships.

Rena's mother, a Holocaust survivor, did not raise any of her four children with much warmth. That was simply not her style.

Rena's American-born father was somewhat autocratic and critical. While Rena's siblings did not appear to be as affected, she was unable to overcome the impact of her parents' cold, critical treatment. As a result of her upbringing, therefore, Rena learned only to distrust and avoid intimacy, a sure-fire recipe for failure in marriage.

The crucial aspect of this case was the relationship between Rena and her parents. Although they were deeply concerned parents, they felt more comfortable consulting Rena's teachers and a *Rav* than consulting Rena herself. It was never easy for them to sit down and actually talk with any of their children. Rena, however, was the hardest to talk with, because she was the most withdrawn and reticent. As a result, she was the first to be overlooked by her parents.

No one can say just what would have happened if Rena's parents had made greater efforts to really get to know her. Of course, it is quite possible that their initiatives might have been rebuffed by Rena. In other words, just because her parents would have tried to learn from Rena what was bothering her does not mean that she would have told them. Nevertheless, greater direct involvement by Rena's parents could have resulted, at the very least, in seeking professional help while she was still in high school. Had this happened, it is very possible that her trip to the *chupah* would have been only "one way."

Case illustrations can be as dangerous as they are helpful. Defensive, frightened parents can read Rena's story and respond smugly, "Oh, that doesn't apply to us!"

Rena's story, however, is unfortunately all too common. Many contemporary parents raise their children without ever really getting to know them.

All of this may sound to some people like a modern, secular point of view. "Teach a youngster in accordance with his ways" (*Mishlei* 22:6), however, would seem to imply that parents are required by the Torah to examine the unique individuality of each child's feelings, attitudes, abilities and aspirations (see *Metzudas David* ibid.).

Preparation for marriage, like preparation for *any* of life's goals, involves parental teaching, modeling, guiding, advising and listening. This preparation process, which must be tailor-made to fit each parent and child, should be based on a solid foundation of parental understanding of one's child's individuality and specific needs. (Some specific topics which are worthy of being addressed are outlined in the next chapter.)

❦ The Role of Mechanchim

Parents should not shoulder the entire responsibility alone. Teachers, *Rabbanim*, and *rebbei'im* — the parental surrogates for *talmud Torah* — also need to focus attention on the unique emotional and personality needs of — and differences between — their *talmidim* and *talmidos*.

Furthermore, marriage-preparation classes and study groups are needed within the Torah atmosphere of the yeshivah. Often, the only training a *chassan* and *kallah* receive are the accelerated *"chassan"* and *"kallah"* classes which deal only with the laws of *taharas hamishpachah* (family purity). This is certainly necessary, but not sufficient.

Indeed, several Torah institutions have taken the initiative of providing their students with a broader-based preparation for marriage. Hopefully, others will follow.

The Be'er Yaakov Yeshivah, in Israel, offered a series of *vaadim*, or small group conferences, with then *Mashgiach Ruchani*, Harav Shlomo Wolbe, on topics of marital life. In these *vaadim*, Harav Wolbe discussed such topics as: the emotional needs of a wife and the husband's responsibility to meet them; the qualitative differences between the close relationship of a *bachur* and his *chavrusah* and the husband-wife relationship; the meaning to a wife of the appearance of the home; the emotional and spiritual differentiation between man and woman, and how this can lead to harmonious complementarity, or *chas v'shalom* to frustrating conflict.

Harav Wolbe printed a booklet of these discussions which, due to the specific legacy of his late father-in-law, Rabbi Avrohom Grodzensky, is not available to the public.

Harav Wolbe also wrote a second booklet, in consultation with Rebbetzin Jacobson of Jerusalem, designed for young women. This booklet, together with a foreword written by Rabbi Yehuda Meisels, has been published by the Beth Jacob Sara Schenirer High School and Teachers Seminary in Brooklyn and is available to the public.

In the second booklet, Harav Wolbe discusses such topics as: the impact of life in a yeshivah dormitory on a *bachur*, and the many changes involved in his adjustment to married life; the importance of patience and tolerance from *both chassan* and *kallah* during the first year of marriage; the necessity of avoiding the all-too-common hazard of sharing private, husband-wife matters with others — friends *or relatives.*

A number of girls' schools in the New York City area now sponsor marriage-oriented discussion groups for 12th grade students. In some cases, the discussions are led by a senior member of the faculty. In other cases, the leader is a married mental health professional who adheres to the same Torah values held by the school. These discussions provide the girls with an opportunity to share their expectations for and apprehensions about courtship and marriage. They also help to clarify many of the students' misconceptions.

Boys' yeshivos have also introduced similar programs for their students. Like the girls' groups, the sessions for boys are conducted by senior members of the yeshivah faculty, who have extensive experience in guiding young people into successful marriages.

Unlike the programs for girls, however, the ones for boys are not offered to high-school seniors but rather to post-high-school, or *beis medrash* level, students. Another difference is that the girls' programs are provided before any of the girls have become engaged. Typically, the boys' groups are designed only for young men who are already engaged to be married. Finally, most of the boys' programs are less of an open-ended forum and are presented more as lectures, or *shmuessen*, with limited discussion.

Ultimately, these sessions help young people to gain a clearer understanding of marriage, in general, and themselves, in particular, all from a Torah perspective and in a Torah environment.

Twenty years ago, such learning opportunities were the exception, rather than the rule. Today, these preparation classes are viewed as essential components of our educational system which are needed to stem the rising tide of divorce.

Twenty years ago, when I published my first article in *The Jewish Observer* calling attention to the need for marriage preparation classes in our community, my suggestion was not received with unanimous approval. It is especially gratifying for me, therefore, to see how many yeshivos and seminaries now take such classes for granted.

In the case of Rena, cited above, her parents were certainly not "responsible" for her divorce. Divorce has many casual factors, only some of which can be avoided. The emotional problems that Levi brought to the marriage, for example, were clearly beyond the control of Rena's parents. Nevertheless, had her parents prepared Rena more thoroughly for marriage, that divorce *might* have been prevented.

It is highly doubtful, however, whether marriage-oriented discussion groups would have helped Rena. If such a group had been available to her, she might have chosen not to attend. Even if she did attend, she likely would have remained passive and uninvolved. Her emotional problems at home were too deeply rooted. There are many other cases, however, where a yeshivah or seminary *can* play a vital role in preparing young people for marriage and thereby prevent divorce, in spite of problems originating in the family.

💐 The Case of Asher*

Asher comes from what could be described as a "middle-of-the-road Orthodox" family. Although his father did not have an extensive yeshivah background, Asher's parents did not object to his decision to continue his full-time yeshivah studies after high school. While they did question him about his future vocational plans and prospects, they never pressured him to leave the yeshivah.

At 26, Asher was not the oldest *bachur* in the yeshivah, but all of his close friends were already married. Even though his parents did not pressure him to get married, Asher still felt overwhelmed by the subtle social pressure of his peers.

Asher had always been a somewhat tense young man. This was due, in part, to the marital conflict between his parents, to which he had been witness. Asher adapted to his unpleasant family environment by ignoring it to the best of his ability. When he was unable to ignore it, he planned elaborate avoidance maneuvers. Asher learned to use a similar approach in dealing with all of his anxieties. They never went away, nor did his parents' marital conflict disappear; but at least he was able to live with them.

When Asher's *chavrusah* (study partner), two years his junior, became engaged, Asher panicked. He had often felt self-conscious, but now he felt even more so. He was tormented by his single status and felt compelled to get married.

Asher's apprehensions were not unusual, but his way of dealing with them had some very unfortunate consequences.

What were Asher's worries? First of all, he was afraid that he would make "the wrong choice" and thereby condemn himself to repeat his parents' turmoil. In addition, since many of his parents' arguments focused on financial matters, Asher feared poverty.

---

* Not his real name.

Having no firm source of income, Asher hesitated to take on the financial responsibility of marriage. Finally, Asher knew that he had in the past coped with unpleasant feelings by ignoring them and that he had handled anxiety-provoking situations by strategically planning to avoid them. He understood that these tactics could not realistically work in marriage.

Even while out on a date, Asher was plagued with these thoughts and was painfully aware of how inadequate his old adaptations were to this new situation.

"How absurd!" he thinks to himself. "Here I am, going out and at the same time I'm hoping that nothing really comes of it!"

Characteristically, he did not discuss his fears with any friends although he was most eager to do so. But even Asher could no longer suppress his fears of marriage by the time he turned 26.

He consulted the *Mashgiach* of his yeshivah. He was so self-conscious, however, that he could not be completely open and failed to present his problem in its fullest proportions. He posed the problem in vague financial terms, and as a result, received an inadequate response. How could the *Mashgiach* know what was really troubling Asher?

Asher finally did become engaged to Chaya,* a seminary graduate who was now working as a secretary. When thinking of his vocational plans, he tried, unsuccessfully, to satisfy himself with vague generalities and abstract prospects. Every time he thought about it, he became more and more anxious. In addition, even the slightest, normal disagreement with Chaya aggravated his fears of repeating his parents' ordeal. Furthermore, the multitude of new situations with Chaya, his future in-laws, the wedding plans, and so on, challenged his avoidance strategies. As his uncertainties snowballed, he had difficulty learning, became depressed, feared it was noticeable and tried desperately to hide this, too.

Asher's marriage to Chaya lasted for an agonizing seven months.

---

* Not her real name.

Although Chaya certainly could have been much more supportive to Asher, it was his apprehensions and anxieties which had clearly planted the seeds for this divorce. The most frequent causes for Asher's worry were questions about financial responsibilities in marriage, coping with the future, the inevitable strains in the husband-wife relationship, and avoiding the pitfalls of his parents' marriage. Many young men and women share similar, even identical concerns. Some of them defuse the time bomb of these concerns with hours of "heart to heart" talks with friends, relatives and *Rabbanim*. A large number of young men and women, however, try — as did Asher — to cope with these *valid* questions by ignoring or suppressing them. In spite of such efforts, these questions often resurface later, in much more frightening and unmanageable dimensions.

Asher was convinced that, had he shared his fears openly, his *Mashgiach* would have ridiculed him. That is most doubtful. Nevertheless, if a marriage-oriented discussion group or *vaad* had been available to him, it is likely that Asher would have attended. Even if he would not have "opened up" there, hearing the similar concerns — and solutions — of others might have had a positive, cathartic effect in calming his tensions.

Shortly after his divorce, Asher sought career guidance from a vocational guidance service. The perceptive counselor referred Asher to me for individual therapy. The treatment, in part, addressed issues of concern which could have been effectively handled in a premarital discussion group. Had this been the case, it is quite possible that Asher and Chaya's divorce might have been prevented.

There are no easy answers for difficult questions. Even if parents and *mechanchim* make the effort to get to know their children and students more intimately and work to provide opportunities for marital life education, divorce will not be entirely eliminated from the Torah community. As mentioned earlier, each case of divorce within the community is caused by a unique set of many factors, only some of which may be avoidable. Nevertheless, if even *one* divorce is prevented, this work will be well worth the effort.

In addition to the "*kol chassan v'kol kallah,*" then, perhaps we will be hearing sounds which will lead to more sustained *simchah* and *sasson*, such as:

> "You know, Temmy, there is more to becoming a *kallah* than just selecting a diamond ring ..."

> "Avrumie, there is more to becoming a *chassan* than simply deciding who should be the witnesses under the *chupah* ..."

24

An Outline for
Premarital Guidance*

Even if children attend premarital education classes or lectures, they still need to receive premarital guidance at home, from their parents.

In some homes, it will be the mother who will advise her children about marriage. In other families, the father will provide the necessary counsel. Ideally, children should receive instruction on this most critical aspect of life from both parents.

Some parents may flounder and balk at the prospect of preparing their children for marriage. They may wonder where

---

* An earlier version of this chapter was originally published as an article in *The Jewish Observer*, May-June 1983. It was later included in my book, *Bayis Ne'eman b'Yisrael: Practical Steps to Success in Marriage* (New York: Feldheim Publishers, 1988), and is reprinted here with permission of the publishers.

Please note: While most of the discussion in this and the following chapters is applicable to all premarital situations, the focus and the particulars are based on the common practice of a *shadchan* proposing a match and for the young man and young woman to then "date" several times to establish their compatibility. In many communities, however, the standard practice is for parents to play a much greater role and for the young people to meet much less. It is not my intention to express a preference for either system.

to begin, what subjects should be covered, and how to go about offering all of this advice.

This chapter is offered as a syllabus for those informal talks between parents and children. It may also be used as a guide for discussion between mechanchim *and their* talmidim *or* talmidos. *It should not be used as a text but rather as an outline of topics which can be addressed in whatever order and manner feels comfortable to all concerned.*

Ideally, these talks should take the form of a conversation *rather than a lecture. The parents must be as willing to ask and listen as they are to instruct and inform. They should try to begin at the point of "readiness" the young people are at; and they should determine that starting point by first eliciting their child's questions, and then proceeding to their agenda as parents.*

Finally, parents need not have all of the answers to the young people's questions. They can table some for further reflection, defer others to more experienced authorities and answer still others with a straightforward, "That's a good question. I really don't know."

This chapter represents an outline of workshops I conducted for a group of rabbinical counselors and mashgichim *associated with various yeshivos in Eretz Yisrael, who conduct marriage preparation classes and discussion groups. These workshops took place over 15 years ago for three consecutive summers.*

THE ACTUAL FORMAT FOR GUIDANCE IS CERTAINLY NOT AS IMPORtant as the content, but as the format varies, so does the impact of such sessions. For parents, it should be on the individual parent-child level. For *mechanchim*, it should ideally take place in the context of the one-to-one mentor/*talmid* relationship. Young people sometimes have some very individualized needs and problems, which cannot — and should not — be discussed in a group setting. If this is not possible however, other arenas for guidance can be used, such as public lectures or more private *vaadim, shmuessen* or discussion groups. Finally, when direct contact with a mentor is unavailable in any form, one can resort to reading material in the form of books, pamphlets and articles.

The following outline deals with my suggestions for the content of guidance programs for both young men and women, regardless of the format. While the case illustrations presented here highlight either the role of young men or young women, each of the illustrations can be equally applied to both.

What Marriage Is Not

Many young people have a thoroughly distorted view of marriage, and their expectations are totally unrealistic. When people marry with these misconceptions, they will probably face deep disappointment or, worse, marital conflict and discord.

Some of these misconceptions may strike those who are happily married as unusual or unbelievable. To many single people, however, they may sound all too familiar.

Misconception #1: "Marriage is a solution for loneliness, depression and feelings of inferiority."

Certainly, marriage provides companionship, encouragement and feelings of being important to someone else. It was clearly in the design of Creation for people to have certain needs fulfilled through marriage, as the Torah states: "It is not good for man to be alone" (*Bereishis* 2:18). A single person with many friends, for example, still experiences a void which can be filled only through marriage. This is normal and appropriate. Nevertheless, marriage cannot provide a cure for deep-seated emotional problems or social handicaps. If someone is beset with so many emotional difficulties that he or she has failed to make friends, then the complex challenges of married life will probably only add another failure to the long list of earlier ones.

Should depressed or lonely people not get married? Of course they should. But they should not expect marriage to solve their social problems. These young people should seek out the guidance and advice of their *Rabbanim*, mentors or anyone else equipped to help them overcome these hurdles *before* talking on the challenges of marriage.

One respected *ben Torah*, who is now happily married to his second wife, confided to me:

> When I was 18 years old, I and all of my friends in yeshivah honestly believed that whatever problems we had would somehow disappear after we would stand under the *chupah*. To tell you the truth, if I had not been such a hothead and hadn't run off and insisted on a *get*, after only two weeks, my first marriage might have been saved.

This young man was not a client of mine, nor did he ever receive any form of mental health service. He was simply sharing his personal experience with me in the hope that I pass it on and help others avoid the mistakes he made.

Misconception #2: "Marriage is a solution for immaturity and irresponsibility."

Anyone who has enjoyed the relative independence of being single can certainly find the increased responsibilities of marriage a maturing experience. Suddenly, money, time and other resources need to be budgeted more carefully. Another person's needs and desires must be taken into account in a new and more intense fashion than ever before.

These realities of married life do help young people mature as they grow into new responsibilities and adjust to them. But marriage itself can never create maturity, *ex nihilo*. It is not an elixir which imbues a person with a sense of responsibility where none existed before.

Take, for example, the common area of going to bed and getting up on time. Single people are notorious for keeping late hours — probably a time-honored custom for many generations.[1] The demands of married life often force people into a more practical and responsible schedule. Instead of going to bed at 1:30 a.m. and getting up at 8 a.m. or later, a young married person may retire at 11:30 p.m. and arise before 7 a.m.

If, on the other hand, someone's daily routine is so severely impaired that he or she has no schedule whatsoever, marriage *per se* will not be the answer. Someone who retires anytime between 9 p.m. and 4 a.m. or who can *never* get up in time to attend morning *minyan* is at serious risk. To this person, marriage can mean even greater trouble.

Unfortunately, not only young people mistakenly assume that marriage will solve chronic problems of immaturity or irresponsibility. Parents may also share this misconception.

Consider Sarah,* an attractive 21-year-old girl from a deeply religious family. Sarah does not work or attend any educational programs. She lost her last three jobs due to tardiness, low productivity and absenteeism. According to Sarah's mother, however:

> Sarah is such a lovely girl. She is so considerate sweet, and *frum*. All she needs now is to find the right *shidduch*. I'm sure that once she has her own home, she will straighten out.

The sad fact is that if Sarah does not "straighten out" *before* she gets married, the prospects for her marriage will be quite bleak. She will inevitably approach her household responsibilities in the same indifferent, immature and haphazard fashion in which she approached her responsibilities at home, school and work. Since obviously her parents cannot offer Sarah proper guidance, they should direct her to someone else who can. As long as Sarah's parents expect marriage to have a therapeutic impact on their

---

1. See Chapter 21, "Getting Down About Teenagers Not Getting Up," for a full discussion of this topic.
* Not her real name.

daughter, she stands a good chance of adding to the already unacceptable statistics of divorce.

As my *chavrusah* in our yeshivah days summed it up (we were both single at the time):

> I'm fully aware that getting married will probably not solve any of my problems. But I'm just getting to the point in life that I'm tired of my old problems and I'm ready for new ones!

❧ What Marriage Is

Marriage is a *nisayon* — not in the sense of being an "ordeal" but as a "test." As one of life's greatest opportunities, marriage is a test as to how well we will take advantage of what it offers.

The opportunities, of course, are not unlimited. One's choice of spouse is certainly a factor in what can be achieved. Generally, though, those who approach marriage as an opportunity invest more into it than those who view marriage as a solution.

Marriage can also be understood as a partnership in which both spouses must try to contribute 90 percent in order to enjoy an equal share of the benefits. To paraphrase a former United States President, "Ask not what your spouse can do for you but rather ask what you can do for your spouse!"

❧ Guidelines for Dating and Courtship

Even those singles who delude themselves into thinking that they "know all about marriage" are aware that they need guidance in the area of dating. A complacent, self-assured young man, for example, will suddenly come alive and listen most attentively if his *rebbi* discusses how to select a proper mate.

The three questions raised most often regarding dating are: *When to start? What to look for?* and *How long to date the same person before deciding about marriage?* Single young men and women discuss all three questions extensively, most often among themselves. Nevertheless, they are receptive to input on these issues from *rebbei'im* and teachers — even more so at times than they are from their own parents.

1. When to start dating?

Most young people tend to be well attuned to their own internal timetable, and are the best judges of when they are "ready." Others do need some assistance.

But can someone feel "not ready" when in fact he or she may not only be "ready" but "overdue"? In other words, can someone be overly cautious about waiting? The answer is a resounding "YES!" If so, how can those in doubt accurately assess their own readiness for marriage?

Questions of this nature are too individualized to be handled in groups or through published guidelines, and can only be adequately addressed in one-to-one discussions. The group session, however, can still be very effective by introducing young people to *Rabbanim* to whom they can turn for private conferences on this and other subjects.

Once the decision to begin dating has been made, the next question is often raised:

2. What to look for?

The general requirements of a potential marriage partner can be discussed very effectively in the group context. Much has been written on this subject by Torah giants of previous generations. Parents and anyone who runs a guidance class or discussion group would benefit greatly from reviewing some of this material.

Perhaps the most succinct, general guideline was offered by the Talmud's classical summary of the traits of the Jews: *baishanim, rachmanim, v'gomlei chassadim,* modesty, compassion, and generous kindness (*Yevamos* 79a). In-depth discussions on the meaning of these three qualities can provide an excellent starting point for discussing other important factors:

• First and foremost, prospective spouses need to share common values and priorities; what is important to one should be important to the other. While this may seem too obvious to mention, the area of values and priorities can become extremely problematic when the young men and young women are not fully honest with themselves, or each other.

Consider, for example, a young person whose friends are all adopting a *kollel*-life after marriage, where the wife works to support the husband's full-time learning. This young man or woman may not know what such a life entails, nor truly aspire to that life. Not wanting to stick out from the crowd, however, he or she expresses a desire for a *kollel*-type mate. Such deception — of self and prospective partner — can have destructive consequences.

• What role should appearance and attractiveness play in selecting a mate? Most young people assume that their teachers and *Rabbanim* would advise them not to consider appearance. They even feel they are cheating in some way by looking for an attractive mate. Most *Rabbanim*, however, would probably advise that attractiveness *is* important but that it must be kept in perspective. No one should ever agree to marry someone they find unattractive. At the same time, however, no one should look only for "good looks."

> Consider Yisroel.* All of his friends and relatives knew he wanted two things: looks and money. He went out with almost 50 girls until he got married. Everyone thought he got what he wanted — as did Yisroel — when he married a very attractive girl from one of the wealthiest Orthodox families in the area. After three years, Yisroel learned the

---

* Not his real name.

hard way that there is more to marriage than beauty and money. Now divorced, he is looking for a mate who may possess neither beauty nor money, but with whom he will be able to get along.

• How much importance should be placed on the relationship factor — that is, personalities and how the two get along with each other?

With some exceptions, most yeshivah students and seminary graduates tend to pay too little attention to the relationship factor, and tend to have little background for making such assessments. Yet the need to evaluate this factor cannot be overemphasized, as a painfully clear clinical observation makes obvious. In all of my experience working with divorced individuals, I never met one person who could not recall seeing in the ex-spouse — before marriage — the very same traits that later led to divorce! Before marriage, these people either denied, ignored or overlooked the problems. Of course, many insignificant differences should be overlooked, and others become critical only later. But if *all* relationship problems are overlooked, serious marital conflict can develop.

The question of what to look for in a spouse is an extremely critical one which must be addressed at great length. It has only been touched on here in outline form. The next chapter, therefore, will expand on this topic in much greater detail.

Once a single person has a better idea as to what to look for, the next question often surfaces:

3. How long to date?
(and the corollary question:)
How do I know he (or she) is the ONE?

People wonder: Does something inside tell me that this person is for me? Do I start seeing stars or hear bells ringing? How can I tell?

One experienced seminary teacher advises students: Do you find the company of this young man pleasant? Does he possess those character traits and goals in life that you admire? Does he have any habits or attitudes that make you uneasy? If the answers to the first two questions are positive and the answer to the last is negative, he advises going ahead. He reminds them that Rabbi Samson Raphael Hirsch points out that first the Torah tells us, "Yitzchak brought (Rivkah) into the tent of his mother Sarah and took her ... as his wife," and only *after that*, "and he loved her" (*Bereishis* 24:67). In a Torah society, true love comes with marriage. When overwhelming infatuation sets in too early, caution is in order.

In spite of all the advice young people inevitably receive, no timetables can be given. Telling single people how long they should date each other before "deciding" can be destructive, because each person's needs are different.

Some single people tend to be more nervous and anxious than others when meeting prospective mates, and they may need to see the same person more than their friends would before making a decision. When these people are pressured to make up their minds after seeing someone as many times "as everyone else," serious consequences can result.

At the very least, young people who are already quite tense can be made more uneasy. At worst, this pressure can contribute to an incorrect decision. How many good matches never happened only because someone insisted, "If you can't decide by the _____th date, then it's probably not for you!" Even some unhappy marriages — and some divorces — could have been avoided if someone had not coaxed, "If you've already gone out on _____ dates, then you must really be meant for each other!"

Another group of young people run the risk of postponing a decision almost indefinitely, and they need encouragement to make up their minds. In fact, the longer they see the same prospective mate, the harder it becomes for them to finally decide. These young people probably spend a year looking for "the right yeshivah," or a month looking for "the right dress." They have found it difficult to make decisions in the past, and the decision about marriage is no exception. To be sure, marriage is a serious matter that demands careful consideration, but even "careful consideration" has limits. Some young single people even become *old* single people because they carried "careful consideration" too far.

How do single people know to which group they belong? How do their parents and friends know? If someone says, "I think I need to see him (or her) some more before I know for sure," how can you tell if (s)he should be encouraged to take his/her time or to make up his/her mind?

An individual consultation with a *Rav, rebbi,* or other mentor will be necessary to answer these questions. Many details of personality, personal and family history, the age of both partners, and the specific nature of the apprehensions should be examined in a private, confidential consultation.[2]

If individual consultations are necessary to resolve such doubts, is there any point in including the issue in group guidance settings? Simply, yes. It can be helpful for a number of reasons: First of all, the process of resolution can certainly begin with group discussions. In addition, participants may identify the group leader as someone to turn to for individual consultation. At the very least, participants may be discouraged from trying to force themselves into anyone else's timetable. They may even come away with a greater sensitivity to their own individual needs regarding the time factor in dating and courtship.

❧ Shanah Rishonah: The First Year of Marriage

No guidance program would be complete without a thorough discussion of what to look out for during the first year of mar-

---

2. Additional helpful guidelines for assessment can be found in *Bayis Ne'eman b'Yisrael: Practical Steps to Success in Marriage* (New York: Feldheim Publishers, 1988) Chapter Five: "Engagement Anxiety: How Do I Know for Sure?" pp. 61-76.

riage. Even if it takes a lifetime to learn all about marriage, there are some very basic trouble spots in the first year that can be avoided if anticipated, in line with the maxim — "Who is wise? He who anticipates the future" (*Tamid* 32a). While premarital guidance cannot prevent all marital problems, it can help minimize them, and possibly stem the rising tide of divorce among young *frum* couples.

While there are at least as many different problems that confront a young couple as there are young couples, three of the problems which seem to crop up most often can usually be traced back to *shanah rishonah*.

The term *shanah rishonah*, of course, should not be taken literally. The problems outlined here may be overcome by some couples after two months of marriage, while others may struggle with these issues for two or three years. The point is that these problems generally surface during the initial adjustment phase of marriage, which typically lasts one year.

1. Impatience and Stubbornness

Some young married men and women have a very short-sighted timetable for change, growth and adjustment. These people believe that if their spouse does not make immediate concessions to their way of thinking, they lose all hopes of negotiating the issue in the future, as though marriage were a political struggle, with wins and losses.

Most often, both partners acknowledge that the issue is intrinsically insignificant. It only becomes "an issue" because one or both spouses believe that their entire future is at stake.

Devorah* and Heschie* were married three months before Pesach. As *Yom Tov* approached, they began discussing

---

* Not their real names.

their holiday plans. Heschie assumed that they would spend *Yom Tov* with his parents, who were scheduled to move out of town right after Pesach. Devorah insisted that traditionally the first *Yom Tov* "belongs" to the wife's parents. Heschie agreed, but since his parents would thereafter be living out of town, he suggested that perhaps Devorah should "give in." Devorah saw a principle that was much larger than the question at hand. She felt that unless she stood firm on this issue her husband would "walk all over her" in the future.

Heschie and Devorah are still married and are not even considering divorce. The resentment generated by their initial intransigence, however, still surfaces today, almost five years later.

Protection Through Silence

The advice of *Chazal* is full of injunctions to remain silent, and some even interpret the trait *baishanus* as referring to modest reticence. In contrast, a prevailing contemporary attitude — albeit one which is most antithetical to Torah — can be summarized by the hackneyed cliche, "Express yourself!" We certainly do not believe that every thought and emotion must be shared openly with the entire world, or even with one's spouse. To the contrary, a person must practice restraint and refinement, and strive to internalize that external mien. In secular society, people try to achieve just the opposite by "letting it all hang out."

Nevertheless, there are certain situations in which excessive silence can be destructive. Silence, like any other ideal, must be kept in perspective. In an unreasonable effort to emulate his impression of Torah giants, a young married person may weaken the entire foundation of his or her married life.

Take Raizy* and Aryeh.* When they first got married, some of Raizy's habits disturbed Aryeh. While he could accept most of these habits, one really annoyed him. It was nothing unusual, but Aryeh's reaction created a major rift that still exists today.

Often when Aryeh would be leaving the apartment, Raizy would remember something she wanted to tell him. Even if he was rushing out the door, late for *minyan*, a *shiur* or just an appointment, Raizy would insist that Aryeh wait briefly until she told him what she had just remembered.

Every time this occurred, Aryeh reminded himself of Talmudic injunctions to remain silent, and with great self-control he suppressed his impulse to criticize Raizy.

Aryeh felt very noble about his self-sacrifice. After all, he was avoiding conflict and was sparing his wife the displeasure of being criticized. "If I point this out to Raizy," he reasoned, "it could lead to an argument."

In a way, Aryeh's reasoning was valid. He certainly should try to overlook his wife's human imperfections. And unnecessary criticism and possible conflict should always be avoided.

Nevertheless, Aryeh made two errors. First, he assumed that Raizy would be hurt if she knew that one of her habits offended him. In truth, she wanted nothing more than to please Aryeh. Had she been told openly, she probably would have immediately changed her behavior.

Aryeh's second mistake was much more serious. He thought that he would eventually get used to this habit and come to accept it. He was wrong. As time went on, it bothered him more and more, until he started wondering why Raizy didn't realize *on her own* that he was annoyed by her habit. At that point, the die was cast. His annoyance quickly grew into resentment. And the harder he tried to control this resentment, the angrier Aryeh became.

---

* Not their real names.

Finally, after seven months, Aryeh exploded. His burst of temper was set off by a small, irrelevant incident, but he raised his voice and used foul language quite unbefitting a *ben Torah*.

The outburst did clear the air somewhat, but Aryeh felt so guilty about it that he was more determined than ever to keep quiet. Raizy, of course, was shocked and hurt. She felt that she had failed to please her husband and worried about their future.

For the next 11 years, Aryeh and Raizy's marriage was strained with occasional violent outbursts. Finally, they sat down with a counselor and began to unravel their tangled feelings. When they were through, they realized how Aryeh's overly zealous efforts "to look away" from his wife's faults had led to a disastrous chain of events, which, fortunately, was finally resolved.

Certainly Aryeh's misguided effort to remain silent was not the sole cause of his marital problems. Complex marital and family problems seldom stem from one simple source. Nevertheless, if Aryeh had realized that his efforts to remain silent could do more harm than good, and if he could have found a proper way to express his feelings, much of his and Raizy's unhappiness could have been prevented.

3. Passing the Tests

By far, the most pervasive and most serious problem encountered in the first year of marriage is that of "testing."

Everyone comes to marriage with a long shopping list of expectations, hopes and dreams. That is as it should be, for these expectations provide the incentives that help single people take the plunge into marriage.

While these lists are highly personalized, there is one item at the top of many people's lists, whether or not they are aware of it: to be loved and cared for by their spouse.

No, there is nothing wrong or unusual about that expectation. Some people, however, also come to marriage with a large suitcase full of self-doubt, insecurity and low self-esteem. Even though they desperately want to be loved and cared for, deep inside they believe that they are so unworthy and inadequate that no one could ever really love or care for them.

One could assume that their spouses do care for them, or they would not have married them. Yet in spite of an expression of caring from their spouses, these people feel the need "to test" them.

This may sound farfetched, but, then again, have you ever heard someone say, "If (s)he really cared about me, (s)he would _____!" Such a statement and all its variations indicate that one spouse is testing the other; that the person feels that the care and concern of their spouse can be measured only by the criterion of doing "this" or "not doing that."

Sometimes these criteria are valid. No one would take issue with: "If he really cared about me, he wouldn't insult me like that in front of my friends!" By contrast, consider this criterion: "If she really cared about me, she wouldn't have put so much mustard on this sandwich!" No, not too many men would make such a statement. But many young married men and women have similar *thoughts* about their spouses, and such thoughts drive a wedge between husband and wife, leading to irreconcilable differences.

Single people should know, before they get married, that inappropriate questions of "Does (s)he really care about me?" — whether expressed vocally or just in thought — can lead to severe marital conflict. At times, such testing can even lead to divorce. If single people are alerted to the danger of testing, especially during the first year of marriage, they stand a better chance of steering clear of this most dangerous obstacle to success in marriage.

🍂 A Look to the Future

As noted previously, fortunately, fewer questions are being raised today about whether or not marriage preparation is necessary. And many yeshivos and seminaries are organizing such programs for their students.

But even if your son or daughter attends one of these classes, you still need to discuss all of these same topics with him or her. Parents simply cannot assign the full responsibility for preparing their children for marriage to their *mechanchim*.

The topics outlined above are ones which some parents may not feel comfortable discussing with their children. The consequences of not doing so, however, are so great that parents can not afford to ignore their responsibility in this matter.

The future success or failure of our children's marriages absolutely depends on our accepting this responsibility.

25

Teaching Children
What to Look for in a Spouse

The decision of whom to marry is perhaps the one decision in life that has the greatest impact on one's future. Choosing the right partner will benefit your child "until one hundred and twenty." Making a mistake can, chas v'shalom, *cause untold hardship and heartache for years to come.*

Children should not make this monumental decision by themselves. They need, and should have, their parents' assistance, input and support.

One of the best ways that parents can help their children with this decision is by teaching them what to look for in choosing a spouse and explaining to them what is important and what is not. In addition, parents need to guide their children as to how to evaluate their feelings about the people they are dating.

*Parents also need to be clear — to themselves and their
child — about their own role in the marriage decision-making
process. To leave it all up to the child is abandonment.
To completely take charge is to infantalize the child by overly
interfering, and to make a decision the parents alone are
usually not qualified to make. Just what role should the
parents play in their child's choice of a mate? How much
involvement is enough and how much is too much?*

These and other shidduchim *related questions will be
addressed in this chapter.*

∽♢∾

❧ What to Look for in a *Shidduch*

PEOPLE NEED TO LOOK FOR MANY THINGS IN A *SHIDDUCH.* AS
noted, the essentials to consider are compatibility, shared
values, and similarity in basic *hashkafos.* I think it is important, too, to look for someone who not only respects *halachah* per
se, but also makes it a practice to consult *rabbanim* and Torah
authorities in personal matters. The mavericks who think they
know best about everything — whether young men or young
ladies — generally pose a clear and present danger to themselves
and to a potential spouse. Keep in mind that those who are so independent that they feel they don't need to consult anyone will not
be open to influence in the unfortunate event that a major conflict
should arise.

We have noted that the three cornerstones of Jewish character
— modesty, mercifulness, the doing of kind deeds — are vital.
Being "modest" does not necessarily mean that a person has to be
shy, but rather that he or she has a sense of propriety. *Tznius* is
not only a mode of dress; it is an attitude and a life style. A *rach-
man* is one who has a certain level of sensitivity that would make
it difficult for him or her to be the source of another person's pain.
And a *gomel chessed* is important to look for, because if people

don't have *chessed* built into their lives, they may be selfish and self-centered — not good candidates for marriage.

As far as other attributes, most single people bring to the *shidduch* process a long laundry list of qualities they are looking for in a mate. I have found that young people sometimes encounter difficulty in making the decision to marry when they don't know how to differentiate between the priorities on their list and the extras. It would be helpful if single people thought in terms of these two categories — what is essential and what is not so important — when considering their requirements in a *shidduch.*

In addition to the above considerations, there are three factors that people often overlook or misunderstand when seeking a *shidduch.*

1. Appearance

The most controversial is "looks." I'm *not* saying that appearance is the most important factor in a *shidduch.* I want to stress that at the outset. What I *am* saying is that it is not unimportant, either.

A *rosh yeshivah* in Yerushalayim told the following story to a *talmid,* who shared it with me. This *rosh yeshivah* has a large family, and his first three children were girls. When his oldest daughter came of age, she got engaged to the very first boy to whom she was introduced. The second daughter started dating and also became engaged to the first boy she met. So, the *rosh yeshivah* assumed it would go smoothly and quickly with the third daughter, as well. But after the third daughter went out with 17 young men, she still could not find one she was interested in marrying. When she turned down the seventeenth one her father started to get worried.

So, as we all should do whenever we have a question or a problem, the *rosh yeshivah* consulted his own *rosh yeshivah* — R' Elazar Menacham Shach, Rosh Hayeshiva of Poneviezh in Bnei

Brak. After he told Rav Shach about the "problem with his daughter," Rav Shach said, "Poneviezh is a big yeshivah. Maybe there's someone here who is appropriate for your daughter. Let me think about it. Please come back in a couple of days." The *rosh yeshivah* came back two days later, and Rav Shach said, "I have gone through all the young men in the *beis midrash,* and I have one who I think would be a good match for your daughter."

The *rosh yeshivah* was delighted. "Thank you very much. Can you give me some details, just something I can tell my *rebbetzin* and daughter about the fellow?"

Rav Shach said, "He happens to be one of our best learners. He also happens to have a good character; and in addition, he's a good-looking fellow."

When he heard that, the *rosh yeshivah* said, "I'm very glad to hear that Rav Shach thinks the boy learns well and has good *middos,* but why would the *Rosh Yeshivah* mention that the boy is good-looking? My daughter went to the finest Bais Yaakov in the country. She's a *baalas middos.* She's not interested in things like that. She has much loftier ideals."

Rav Shach turned to the *rosh yeshivah* and said, "If that's what you think, then you don't know your own daughter!" The *rosh yeshivah* went home and told his family about the *shidduch.* His daughter went out with the young man, and, not only are they happily married, but they now have many children of their own.

🐚 The Case of Leah[*]

I'd like to cite another example closer to home — a case from my practice, about a young lady whom we'll call "Leah." Leah had dated a few young men before she met her *chassan.* She was introduced to this young man, whom she found pleasant, and they met several times. The whole relationship seemed to

---

[*] Not her real name.

develop very quickly, and before she was ready, he proposed to her. She couldn't think of any reason not to agree to marry him. Besides, everyone was pushing her to accept the young man's proposal. He seemed fine enough and so they became engaged.

After the engagement Leah began to have second thoughts and doubts. Something about the young man's appearance troubled her. She thought it would go away, but the next day it bothered her even more. After a week she got very nervous and worried. She thought she had made a terrible mistake. But what should she do about it now? To whom could she tell this? To say that you don't like the way your *chassan* looks is not the type of thing you can talk about to your friends!

Finally, she felt she had to unburden herself. Leah sat down for a heart-to-heart talk with her older sister. She said she was afraid to go ahead with the marriage and was thinking of breaking off the engagement.

Her sister said, "He's such a fine young man. The whole family is crazy about him. What's the matter with you? What's the problem?"

Leah replied, "Well, to tell you the truth, there's something about his appearance that bothers me very much."

The older sister retorted, "That's all you're worried about? The way he looks? That's not what marriage is about!"

Leah cried, "Well, I know. But I can't get it out of my mind. It's making me very uncomfortable."

The older sister turned to Leah and said, "Listen, I'm already married for three years, and I have a little experience that you don't. He's a fine young man. You're going to upset the whole family if you break off the engagement. I think you should go through with it."

"But how can I live my whole life with someone if I don't like the way he looks?" Leah pleaded.

Her sister answered, "I guarantee you that after you get married it just won't be a problem; it's just that you're nervous now.

You'll see, after the wedding, you'll think totally differently about this. Trust me."

Leah trusted her sister, and with trembling hands and a pounding heart she went down to the *chuppah*. And guess what? The day after the wedding she didn't feel any differently. Now her husband's looks bothered her even more, because now she was married to him. She thought that maybe she would feel better after the *sheva berachos*. But after *sheva berachos* she felt even worse. A few weeks later she felt she had to share her feelings with other relatives, who were very upset. "How can you do this? You married him; you have to work it out. You'll see that you'll feel differently about it."

Leah responded, "My sister promised me that I would feel differently about it, but I don't." At this point, the family sent her to me to "talk sense" into her. But, even a therapist cannot make a person feel differently about the way someone else looks.

Soon, Leah's marriage became unbearable. If the potential spouse's looks (or anything) bothers someone enough to cause them to experience serious doubts, then they are making a mistake if they get engaged. They'll make an even bigger mistake if they get married and then have to get divorced.

The point of this case history is that while appearance may not be the most important aspect in a *shidduch*, it is not an insignificant matter, either. Because Leah's sister gave her very bad advice, she went ahead with a marriage that should never have been.

2. In-Laws

Many people think, "I just have to evaluate the individual; I'm marrying the girl, or I'm marrying the boy; I'm not marrying the parents."

When I got married I also felt that way, and I made a terrible mistake. Had I known when I was going out what I know now, I would never have considered this an insignificant factor in *shid-*

duchim. Had I realized then how much my in-laws would enhance my life, how much joy my father-in-law, a"h, and my mother-in-law have given me over the years, I never would have taken this factor lightly ... although I still would have married my wife.

My own wonderful experience is in stark contrast, however, to many of the cases I deal with. In-laws can also disrupt a marriage, in a variety of ways. And the personalities of the parents of a proposed spouse are certainly worth taking into consideration.

3. Clones

One thing that people sometimes look for but shouldn't is a clone of themselves: someone with the same tastes, the same interests, the same personality, and the same attitudes. Certainly you have to share values, and you have to share *hashkafos,* but you don't have to share the same tastes in music or food. You are not looking for a Siamese twin.

A few years ago, a *mashgiach* in Eretz Yisrael, who has made it a practice to give a series of talks on *shidduchim* to the single young men in his yeshivah, asked me to listen to his tapes and give him some feedback. He made this point about clones that I hadn't heard anyone mention before. The *mashgiach* explained to me why he included it.

When he was single, he thought to himself, "How do I know what to look for in a *shidduch?* After all, I'm a young man, a *bachur.*" Although many *bachurim* think they know everything, this future *mashgiach* had no such illusions and he approached his *rosh yeshivah* for guidance. The *rosh yeshivah* gave him a very long talk about what to look for. To emphasize this point about clones, the *rosh yeshivah* made the following self-disclosure:

"Before I was engaged to my wife," the *rosh yeshiva* said, "I hadn't met her family. Once we became engaged and I got to know them, I realized that one of my *kallah's* sisters would have made a better *shidduch* for me than my *kallah.* I thought I had made a terrible mistake. My *kallah* was the talkative type, a social butterfly. She had a good background and wonderful *middos*, but when I met her sister and saw that she was the intellectual type, a deep thinker like I was, I thought to myself: I should have gotten engaged to my future sister-in-law, not my *kallah*! But by then it was too late."

The *rosh yeshivah* continued, "I've been married for 35 years, and I realize now that marrying my wife was the best thing I ever did. Had I married my sister-in-law, who is a deep thinker and a very profound person, every day in my home would have been *Tishah b'Av*! I am a serious person; I have always had my head in learning. If my wife were that way too, what kind of atmosphere would that have been in which to raise children? But, because I married my wife, who is a very opposite personality — she is always having people over, talking on the phone — my children grew up in a normal environment. It was the best thing I ever did."

I think that this illustration shows not necessarily that opposites attract, but that one must evaluate whether someone is *compatible* even if he or she is not necessarily *identical*.

❧ The Dating Process

In our society, that evaluation occurs through the process of dating. Some young people make the mistake of thinking that the goal of a date is to decide whether or not to marry the other person. It is not. It is also not the goal of a date to impress the other person or get him or her to like you. Those who go out with those goals in mind add stress to an already stressful situation. The goals on a date should be to relax, have a pleasant evening, and try to get to know the other person. The date will be much more successful if the young people go out with this attitude and then analyze their feelings when they get home.

After a first date, the question comes up whether or not to

go out again. There should not be any rules about the number of times someone must go out. As with the entire *shidduch* process, the only hard and fast rule is to be aware of — and try as much as possible to address — individual needs. Young people do not have to follow "rules" other people impose — including those recommended by Meir Wikler!

Certainly there are times when someone knows very definitely that a second date would be counterproductive and misleading (and you never want to be misleading in the dating process). On the other hand, some people have a tendency to impulsively reject *shidduchim*. For *them*, it might be good advice to go out twice before making a decision to terminate the relationship.

Gut feelings — how your child feels with the other person — are very important. But every person has to know him or herself — and parents must know their child. People who are generally shy when meeting people for the first time shouldn't discount a proposed match just because they feel uncomfortable on the first date. On the other hand, if people who are generally relaxed and easygoing feel awkward or uncomfortable on the first date, this could be more significant. It is also important for your child to differentiate between feelings generated by the dating experience and feelings triggered by the person he or she is with.

Of course, further along in the dating process, your child should not hesitate to bring up the full range of future plans, serious issues, aspirations, values, and goals. He or she should not think that any of these subjects is too personal to discuss. If your child is considering marriage, he or she must be able to bring up *any* subject as a way of getting to know the other person better.

❧ The Role of Parents

A few years ago, I was invited to make a presentation at the grand rounds of the NYU Medical Center in Manhattan. I was speaking about my clinical work in the Orthodox community.

During the question-and-answer session which followed, a non-Jewish therapist said she was working with a young, depressed chassidic woman with very severe marital problems. The therapist wanted to know my opinion as to whether the marital problems resulted from the fact that this woman got married through "an arranged marriage." Of course she meant a *shidduch*.

I told the therapist, "Let's assume, for argument's sake, that arranged marriages cause marital problems, because that's your hypothesis. In order to test this hypothesis, we have to find a group of people *without* arranged marriages and see what kind of results they have. In America today, it is not hard to find such a group. The non-Jewish and even the non-observant Jewish world is meeting and marrying through casual social contact."

I continued, "Now let us look at the success rate of that other group. The statistics for marriages in the larger society indicate that over 50% of marriages end in divorce. (That doesn't mean that the other 50% are happy.) No one will deny that in the Orthodox community the rate of divorce is much, much lower. So, obviously, this woman's marital difficulties are not due to the fact that it was an arranged marriage."

The audience liked that answer, and that's where I left off. But in the back of my mind I had another answer. Arranged marriages, translated as *shidduchim*, do not contribute to marital problems — *as long as* the parents are doing their job properly.

One crucial aspect of that job is the CIA-type investigatory activity that parents have to undertake. Background checking is very important, because the young people themselves are not always able to identify the most important considerations in a *shidduch*. In addition, young people are often motivated only by their emotions.

Once, a family came to see me after their daughter had already started seeing a boy whom she liked. When they checked him out further — after the two had met — the parents didn't think he was appropriate. The daughter said, rightly, "You shouldn't have let me go out with him until you had *completed* your investigation!"

Parents sometimes wonder whom to ask. There are two categories of people you should consult. There are those with whom you have a personal relationship — you can trust their honesty, even though they may not know the family that well. Then there are those whom you don't know but who know the boy or girl or the family very well — rabbis, *rebbeim*, teachers, or principals, for example. Talking to the young person's friends is ideal, if you can find out who they are.

When soliciting information, I think it is most useful to ask for examples of a particular characteristic. People tend to talk in generalities: "She's a wonderful girl!" "He's a real *baal middos*!" If you request specific episodes or illustrations of just how so-and-so is a *baal middos*, they have to back up their statement. Then you will find out if they really know, or if they are simply telling you what they think you want to hear.

When inquiring about a *shidduch*, parents should look for those personality characteristics and *middos* which they feel would be important and meaningful for their child, and not just those which will enhance their own social position. What your child needs will not necessarily be the characteristics and qualities that are currently the most popular or high status. In this regard, it is critical to know your child, know what's important, and keep the right priorities in mind.

I heard the following true story from Mr. Moshe Yanofsky, principal of Machon Bais Yaakov in Boro Park, who gave me permission to repeat it. It is an example of how parents can sometimes harm rather than help.

Not too long ago, a young man came into yeshivah on a Sunday morning to learn with his *chavrusa*. His face was so sour and he seemed so distracted that his *chavrusa* asked him, "What's the matter? Your head isn't into learning today. What's going on?"

The *bachur* turned to his *chavrusah* and said, "Last night I thought I was getting engaged. I met a wonderful girl, and we were so excited about each other. Then her parents came to visit my parents and now the *shidduch* is off."

"The *shidduch* is off? You like her? She liked you? Her parents liked you? What happened?"

"I don't even know myself. My parents got so upset they don't even want to discuss it with me. Now I don't know what's going to be with this wonderful *shidduch*."

The *chavrusah* said, "This is terrible. You can't let this go." The two of them decided this was an emergency situation and marched into the *rosh yeshivah's* office to discuss the matter. When the *rosh yeshivah* heard the whole story, he said, "You have to get someone to talk to your parents, but it has to be someone who has experience and knows how to deal with these situations."

The *chavrusah* knew the Yanofsky family and suggested that Mr. Yanofsky get involved. That very evening, the would-be *chassan* pleaded with Mr. Yanofsky to speak to his parents. Mr. Yanofsky said he would see what he could do.

Mr. Yanofsky went over to the young man's house and asked the parents what happened.

"What happened? We don't want anything to do with such a family! We're lucky we got out in time!" the would-be-*chassan's* father fumed.

Mr. Yanofsky, noting how upset the father was, asked, "Yes, but what is it about those people?"

"It's their values! They're so extravagant! They have no concept of what it means not to throw money away on trivialities."

"Well, of course, that is an important factor," Mr. Yanofsky agreed, and then asked for an example of their extravagance.

The father gave this example: "We were discussing the wedding, and considering various halls. We wanted to make it in such-and-such a hall. And do you know they wanted to make it in that other hall!"

Mr. Yanofsky replied, "Well, I know this hall, and I know that hall. They seem to be comparable halls. What's the difference?"

"The other hall charges *a dollar* more per person!"

Mr. Yanofsky said, "How many people were you going to invite to the wedding?"

"We were planning to invite 125 couples."

Mr. Yanofsky excused himself for a moment, wrote out a check for $250, handed it to the father, and said, "I'll pay the difference. Let the match go through."

The *shidduch* went ahead, and the couple got married and are still very happy today. (By the way, the father never cashed the check.)

The point of this story is that parents invariably play a vital role in the *shidduchim* of their children. But sometimes, by losing perspective, they do harm.

What should young people do if their family is playing a destructive role in their *shidduchim*? Do the same thing this young man did: Ask a rav or a *rosh yeshivah* to get involved. First, the young man or woman may be wrong. And even if they are right, this is not a matter they can handle on their own.

Both parents and young people often feel apprehensive about the *shidduch* process. But the fact is that anxiety is built in because you can never really know someone fully before you are married to that person. Therefore, I think it is important for you, as the parent, first to do the basic research, speaking to people who know the candidate well. After that, you should allow your child to go out and meet the prospective mate face to face to see how they feel when the two of them interact. Third, it is critical that you not ignore any major area that's troubling your child about the other person (helping put into perspective, of course, what is a priority and what is secondary among your child's requirements). Fourth, if your child has major doubts, he or she should consult with a third party — one who is not emotionally or materially involved — before getting engaged.

Finally, if the research comes back positive and the face to face meetings are satisfactory, if your child feels comfortable with the other person and no major problem arises, then I believe there is an element of *bitachon*, faith and trust in *Hashem*, that is required. You should accept that even though the young people don't know each other inside out, you can rely on the Divine providence of their having met. Trust that it is He Who has guided your child to his or her *bashert*, intended mate.

26

Coping with Rejection
in *Shidduchim* and Dating

Rabbi Nochum Cohen, head of the Sadigerer institutions in Yerushalayim, often quotes his mentor, Reb Elya Roth, a spiritual giant of the previous generation, on the subject of rejection in the area of shidduchim.

"Whenever a shidduch *was being proposed to us for one of our children and the answer came back that the other side was not interested, I was always full of joy, and I would say a special prayer to Hashem.*

"I would say, 'Thank you, Hashem, for protecting us as You always do. You realized for some reason that this shidduch *was not good for us, that it was not in our best interest to proceed. And not only did You make sure that we would not stumble into a situation which was not in our best interest. You also made it come from the other side. Now no one can have any complaints against us! Your kindness knows no bounds!' "*

Reb Elya would then tell his disciple, "Nochumke, do you realize how lucky you are that they said they are not interested in your child?!"

Most of us are not on Reb Elya's level of pure trust in Hashem. For the rest of us, parents and children alike, rejection in shidduchim *is a bitter pill to swallow. It upsets our equilibrium, it undermines our self-esteem — and it can even throw us into depression.*

This section on preparing children for dating would not be complete, therefore, without including some advice on the often overlooked but critical subject of coping with rejection.

L ET US TAKE A LOOK AT THE *SHIDDUCH* PROCESS: A MATCH IS suggested. Both sides give the matter ample consideration and then agree that the young man and woman should meet. The meeting goes well and both parties decide to meet again. After a few more dates, marriage is proposed and accepted. *Mazel Tov!* Congratulations!

That is the ideal scenario. It happens like that sometimes. But the vast majority of *shidduchim* that are suggested do not end this way. More often than not, after the first date, one side does not want to continue. What should the "rejected" party do then? What are the guidelines? Marriage manuals seldom address these questions. Yet these are very important issues.

❧ Thanking the Matchmaker

The first consideration must always be expressing appreciation. Regardless of the reasons for rejecting any *shidduch*, both parties must not overlook their obligations of gratitude to whoever took the time and made the effort to suggest the *shidduch*.

Although this may sound elementary to some, it is so often neglected that it must be mentioned.

> One of my *rebbeim* told me about a *shidduch* he tried to arrange for a young man, over twenty years ago. After one meeting, the young man did not feel that a second date would be worthwhile. A few weeks later the bachur met this *rebbi*, who asked, him what happened. The young man replied, "Oh, *Rebbi*, she's not for me at all!"
>
> In a gentle tone the *rebbi* taught that bachur a valuable lesson: "When I suggested that *shidduch*, I did not mean to guarantee that she would be the right one for you. I only meant that she *might* be for you. I'm sorry if there was some misunderstanding."
>
> The young man immediately apologized for his rudeness, as well as his failure to get back sooner with an explanation of his intentions.

Single people often fail to understand and fully appreciate all the time and effort that go into proposing *shidduchim*. That is why they often neglect their obligation to express proper gratitude.

> Word was out that the Sanzer *Rebbe* was looking for a *shidduch* for his daughter, and *shadchanim*, matchmakers, from far and wide trooped to the *Rebbe's* door. One *shadchan* presented the *Rebbe* with all of the relevant details about a particular young man. When the *shadchan* was finished, the *Rebbe* indicated that he was not interested, and handed the *shadchan* some money.
>
> "What is this for?" asked the bewildered *shadchan*.
>
> "That is the matchmaking fee," the *Rebbe* answered.
>
> "But I am not entitled to this money," the *shadchan* protested. "The *Rebbe* did not even agree to meet the young man."
>
> "That is true," the *Rebbe* replied. "But just as we

believe that every match is decided in Heaven, we also believe that it is predetermined just *how many* proposals we must listen to until we hear the right one. Your suggestion brought us one closer. For that you are entitled to the matchmaking fee."

Even if you do not feel any appreciation towards the *shadchan*, it is nevertheless to your advantage to thank him or her. Frankly, failure to do so does not look good on your resume. Moreover, you may have to wait a long time before that same *shadchan* thinks of you and your single child again.

🍃 Being Clear

In addition to expressing gratitude, your child has an obligation to let the other person know if he or she wishes to continue or not as soon as possible. Be clear. If the answer is "No," don't say "Maybe." If you are not sure, then by all means say so. But do not leave the other side hanging any longer than is necessary. Your child need not decide whether or not he or she wants to marry this person; only whether or not your child is interested enough to meet again.

Sometimes, in the interests of "not hurting" the other side, the rejector will hedge, hesitate, or evade the *shadchan*. When this is done, the rejected person is never spared, but often gets hurt even more.

A young man I know dated a young lady three times. After the second meeting, they decided to bypass the *shadchan* and communicate directly. When he called her for a fourth date, she told him she was busy. They had a pleasant chat and then he said he'd keep in touch. Not one to take things personally, he continued this procedure for *five weeks*.

When she told him she was busy for the sixth week in a row, he decided to take a more direct approach and asked, "Tell me, are you really busy or is this your way of telling me you're not interested in going out again?"

"Well, uh, to tell you the truth," she practically whispered, "you're right. I'm not really interested."

"Did you just decide now, or did you feel that way six weeks ago?" he asked.

"I felt that way after our last date."

"Then why didn't you just let me know when I asked you out the following week?"

"I didn't want to hurt your feelings."

Guess what? ... His feelings were just as hurt.

Had the *shadchan* still been involved, this misunderstanding could have easily been avoided. But this example illustrates the importance of letting the other side know as soon as possible of a decision not to continue.[1]

❧ Coping with Rejection

Rejection is an issue that must be dealt with whether there has been one date, a longer relationship, or even no dates at all: in any situation where you and your child felt that the *shidduch* was right for him or her — but the other party did not feel the same way. What do you say to yourself? What do you say to your child that can ease the pain of the rejection?

If you're like most people, you probably say something along the lines of, "Well, I guess it just wasn't *bashert* for us." Of course, you would be absolutely correct in that analysis. But if sharing that evaluation with a rejected suitor ever lifted his or her spirits,

---

1. Generally, the *shadchan* acts as a go-between, conveying the decisions from one side to the other. When doing so, however, the *shadchan* must avoid sharing your reasons if that would, in any way, constitute *rechilus*. (See *Guard Your Tongue*, by Rabbi Zelig Pliskin (1975), p. 180 #14.) Later, however, the *shadchan* might be able to use your comments (only without attribution) as a basis for coaching the other person, while not inflicting the pain of embarrassment.

then you would be eligible for entry into the *Guinness Book of World Records*. ("First person to lift spirits by saying, 'Well, I guess it wasn't *bashert...*'")

So what *can* you say to yourself or to a child who has just been turned down by what seemed to be the "ideal match"?

The first thing you need to do is acknowledge the disappointment. *It does hurt.* Ask anyone who has been rejected and they will tell you. It can be a crushing blow to the self-esteem of the most confident person. By acknowledging the validity of the feelings, whether your own or your child's, you are starting the process of healing the emotional wound.

The next thing you can do is try to put the disappointment into proper perspective. No, it wasn't *bashert*. But how can you get this message across in a helpful way? I like to use the following metaphor.

We all remember the tragedy of the Challenger, the space shuttle that exploded in midair, seconds after take-off, killing everyone on board. One of the passengers was not even an astronaut. She was a public school teacher who was supposed to give the first elementary school lesson from space.

This teacher was selected from approximately 10,000 applicants — all of whom had to request, complete and submit an extensive written application. It is safe to assume that all of the 9,999 applicants who were rejected — especially those who had also been interviewed — must have felt varying degrees of disappointment.

Then, in one brief flash, all 9,999 rejected applicants must have gasped in unspeakable gratitude when they learned of the disaster. Suddenly, instead of seeing their rejection as the missed opportunity of a lifetime, they realized that it had been nothing less than *lifesaving...* The Challenger rejects were able to see the great blessing of their being denied inclusion on that ill-fated flight.

Even if we *never* see exactly how we benefit from a rejection (whether in *shidduchim*, yeshivah, seminary, or job applications, or any other disappointment), we must endeavor to accept it as though it were as beneficial to us as the rejection letters received by the 9,999 applicants for the Challenger mission. As Rabbi Akiva was wont to say, "*Kol d'avid Rachmana l'tav avid* — everything that *Hashem* does is for good" (*Berachos* 60b).

In the final analysis, we can really find strength to cope with rejection in *shidduchim* by remembering Who is responsible for making all *shidduchim*.

Our sages have observed, "Pairing people is as difficult as splitting the Reed Sea" (*Sota* 2a). Many have pondered: how can any task be referred to as "difficult" for *Hashem*?

The *sefer Simchah Bim'ono* offers the following explanation: Matchmaking is no more difficult for *Hashem* than any other daily miracle He performs. The difficulty in *shidduchim* arises when people delude themselves into thinking that *they* are in charge of the process. That is why *Chazal* emphasize that, "Pairing *people* is as difficult ..." When people think that the process of *shidduchim* is really up to them, then it truly becomes as difficult as splitting the Reed Sea.

I recently had a private discussion with a well-known Torah personality. He is respected throughout the world as an inspiring orator, sagacious advisor, and expert in matters of marital harmony. He made the following self-disclosure:

"When my first child was ready for *shidduchim*, I thought that it would go easily for me. I felt that my years of experience with so many couples would enable me to find the perfect *shidduch* for my daughter. And when she got married, I was convinced that I had, indeed, selected the best son-in-law in the world. Two agonizing, torturous years later, when she finally received her *get*, I understood how foolish I had been.

"Do you know, Meir'l, how good *shidduchim* are made? Only through prayer. If you and I were successful with our own *shidduchim*, it was not because we were smarter than anyone else. It is because of the tears shed by our grandmothers and grandfathers when they said *Tehillim* so that we would find the proper mate. I learned the hard way. The only way to find good *shidduchim* for our children is to pour out our hearts with *Tehillim*."

May *Hashem* hear and answer all of our *tefillos* for good *shidduchim* for our children, and may He ease the pain of our disappointment when we are rejected by *shidduchim* that we mistakenly thought would be good for us.

PART NINE:
Confronting
Divorce
and Remarriage

27

Two 'Ex's' and a 'Why?':
Parenting Children After Divorce

"Whenever a man divorces his first wife, even the
mizbei'ach, *the Altar in the Holy Temple, sheds tears for*
him." (*Gittin* 90a)

Divorce unleashes a flood of tears, and not only from the
Altar. Regardless of which spouse initiated the dissolution of the
marriage, both husband and wife suffer greatly throughout the
process. Their respective friends and relatives may also shed
tears for the home that is being broken apart. There is no doubt,
however, that the ones who weep most are the children.

Children whose parents are separating cry for many rea-
sons. They grieve and mourn for the loss of their intact family
and all that it has come to mean to them: togetherness around
the Shabbos *and* Yom Tov *table, joint summer vacations,*
shared chol hamoed *outings, stress-free family* simchas *and,*
perhaps most importantly, that cozy sense of security which
comes from going to bed knowing that both parents are sleep-
ing right down the hall.

Children are also saddened by the negative attention they now receive. They have become "children of divorce." They are now identified by their peers and other adults as different. They feel themselves to be the objects of ridicule, teasing or pity. And they wish with all their might that they could just be like everyone else again.

In addition, children whose sense of security has been shaken feel uncertain and apprehensive about the future. They worry about the health and welfare of their custodial parent. They are distressed about whether or not they will be able to maintain a close, ongoing relationship with their noncustodial parent. And they fret over the prospects of either or both parents remarrying and how that will affect them.

Furthermore, children whose parents are divorcing are often racked with guilt. Research has shown that the younger the child at the time of the divorce, the greater the chances are that the child will blame him or herself for the divorce.[1] These children reason to themselves that if they had been better behaved, their parents never would have taken such a drastic step. As a result, they experience intense feelings of remorse and regret which can lead to depression and, in some cases, even suicidal thoughts.

Finally, children sometimes shed tears because of the insensitive and destructive manner in which their parents handle the divorce. In fact, children can suffer much more from the way in which their parents go about getting divorced than they do from the separation itself.

If and when you do need to become someone's "ex," you can spare your children enormous heartache if you avoid the common errors outlined in this chapter, which can serve as a first aid kit for parenting children after divorce.

---

1. Wallerstein, Judith and Kelly, Judith, *Surviving the Breakup* (New York: Basic Books, Inc., 1980).

AS HAS BEEN OPENLY ACKNOWLEDGED, "EVEN IN TORAH OBSER-vant circles, marital problems are increasing — a fact illustrated by the growing incidence of divorce in Orthodox families."[1]

To be sure, we must do what we can to prevent divorces when they threaten, but we must also be prepared to face the consequences of divorce if it does occur.

When a couple finalizes their decision to divorce, whether by mutual consent or as a result of an adversarial process (a Rabbinic court or otherwise), the die has been cast for the marriage to be dissolved, but the two principals are by no means finished with one another. The bill of divorce must be written and executed, and joint property must be divided. This process may take weeks, months, or even years to complete, depending largely upon the willingness of both sides to cooperate and compromise. If a spirit of hostility prevails, however, the process of finalizing these arrangements can drag on indefinitely.

In addition to the *get* and property settlements, questions of child custody and visitation must also be addressed. Again, the attitudes of the two sides will determine whether these questions will be resolved smoothly and amicably, or whether they will trigger friction and heartache.

Social scientists have, perhaps, spent more time studying divorce and its aftermath than any other social phenomenon. From all the research, a consensus emerges: the ones who suffer most from divorce are the children.

This chapter will not even attempt to categorize the full range of psychological and emotional consequences experienced by children when their parents divorce. But one point cannot be emphasized enough: The emotional fall-out of divorce for children is intensely magnified when the conflict and acrimony of the unsuccessful marriage enter into the custody and visitation arrangements.

---

1. "Books On Marriage," in *The Jewish Observer*, June 1989, p. 33.

❧ Destructive Behavior

These parents obviously do not get along with each other, but they often do not realize, or ignore the reality, that they destroy the lives of their children by using custody and visitation as the new battleground for their hostilities. *Why* can parents not agree, at the very least, to act in a way that is in their children's best interests?

The following pages will focus on the destructive behavior referred to — based on the author's clinical experience in treating children of divorce and conducting child custody evaluations for *batei din* and family court. Tragically, these are situations which have become prevalent *even* in the Torah community. Since mothers and fathers are equally to blame for these violations of common sense, decency, and civility, the neuter term "parent" will be used.

By-passing Torah law: One parent may try to circumvent the process of a *din Torah* by initiating a legal action in a secular court in the belief that (s)he will receive a better arrangement. Unless such action is approved by a halachic authority, this parent could be violating the severe prohibition against bringing a fellow Jew before a secular court.

Fanning the adversarial flames: When the venue has been determined for resolving the custody and visitation issues, one parent may try to fan the adversarial flames by hiring the toughest, most aggressive advocate, whether it be a *to'ein*, representative to a *din Torah*, or a lawyer in court. Either way, the intent is, clearly, to *demolish* the other side, rather than to mediate or arbitrate a mutually acceptable agreement. *Rabbanim*, as well as divorce-mediators, can generally resolve differences peacefully. But when one parent hires a "top gun," then only fireworks, anguish and astronomical legal fees can follow.

False accusations: Driven by the most noble motivations, a parent may feel (s)he "deserves" custody of the children, so (s)he assumes an imagined halachic mandate to deliberately distort or falsify the facts. Thus, during the *din Torah*, or in court, one parent may fabricate stories of substance abuse, compulsive gambling, immorality, criminal behavior, mental illness or even child abuse.

Once abuse has been alleged, the court or *beis din* may have no other means of verifying the accusation other than to question the child. The child understands only too well that his or her testimony will hurt one or even both parents, and by testifying he or she runs the risk of rejection and alienation from at least one parent — the last thing any child of divorce needs. Children who undergo such a traumatic ordeal often develop symptoms of anxiety, depression, or both, which can remain long after the visitation and custodial issues have been settled.

Frustrating the schedule: Once custody and visitation have been determined, some parents thwart, undermine and disregard both the spirit and the letter of the agreements, again to the detriment of the children.

Daily and weekly routines are more easily maintained when visitation schedules are honored faithfully. More importantly, children can learn to adjust to the predictable visits of the non-custodial parent.

But when the schedule is not honored, routines are upset, children are disappointed, and instability has been injected into the lives of young people who have already suffered lengthy periods of crisis. For example, one parent may arrive late to pick up the children or not show up at all. Another parent will not have the children ready to be picked up at the appointed time. One parent may leave the children at a location other than that agreed upon, or will make sure to be out of town. Another parent will arrive at the wrong time or day of the week and insist on seeing the children. Some parents have even gone to a child's school to see their child, even though such visits were not agreed to in advance. This last tactic in particular causes the children to be so disrupted that it is virtually impossible for them to learn properly, and so disturbs the yeshivah personnel, that the visit can adversely affect the class, or even the entire school.

Using the children as spies: Some parents maintain an unhealthy curiosity about the private affairs of their ex-spouses. They want to know everything their ex-spouses do, with whom they speak, and how they occupy their time. So whenever the child returns from visitation with the other parent, they pump him or her for information, sometimes in a round-about fashion, at other times more directly.

Either way, the children understand why these questions are being asked, and they literally *hate* being placed in this no-win position. As a result, they feel so much stress that they can develop physical ailments such as sleeplessness, enuresis, headaches, irritable bowel syndrome, nausea and even ulcers.

Utilizing children as allies: Some children, especially older teenagers, may simply refuse to report to one parent about the other. But there are still other ways for parents to embroil their children into the parental conflict, despite all of the children's efforts to remain neutral.

Most unfortunately, some parents use their children as sounding boards for their pent-up resentments and frustrations. The children become captive audiences with nowhere to hide. These parents will find every opportunity to disparage their "ex's" in front of their children. Once again, this is always done *"l'sheim Shamayim*, for the sake of Heaven," to warn the children as to "what kind of person the other parent really is."

These parents often violate the prohibitions against gossip-mongery — talebearing, slandering, and lying, all within the same conversation. They will quote their ex-spouses out of context, bring up incidents from years past, and reveal — and distort — whatever they can to discredit their ex-spouses in the eyes of their children. Their stated motive is "to set the record straight." Their real objective is to hurt their ex-spouses and retaliate for all past and current injustices, actual and perceived. Their ultimate achievement, however unintended it may be, is to inflict psychological damage on their children. And this harm can require years of psychotherapy to undo.

This last point begs for elaboration. Almost as much as they require air and water, children need to feel loved and accepted by *both* parents. Even when a child is orphaned, (s)he can derive enormous comfort from the memory of having been loved and accepted by the now-deceased parent. When parents divorce, a child normally feels that the parents' love and acceptance has been challenged, and the child will typically reach out for and demand more reassurances of love and acceptance from both parents.

When one parent disparages the other in front of the child, that parent is in effect telling the youngster: *If you love me and want me to love you, you must repudiate your other parent.* This message need not be stated, but it is always implied. It is as if that parent were asking: *Whose side are you on?*

Eventually, virtually all children placed in such a double bind do choose one parent over the other. But after having done so, they are usually left with residual feelings of guilt that can result in social isolation, shyness, poor concentration in school, fearfulness, disrespectful and disruptive behavior, poor appetite, depression, and even, Heaven forbid, suicidal thoughts.

True, even married couples, unfortunately, can and do disparage one another in front of — or to — the children. This is unhealthy for the same reasons. But an intact family structure offers many opportunities to somewhat ameliorate the destructive impact of that criticism. For example, the parent who may at times disparage the other will, at other times, be supportive and express appreciation or kindness to their spouse. Such opportunities do not exist for families of divorce.

❧ Financial Questions

Finally, the divorcing couple must also resolve financial questions, such as the distribution of assets and the determination of alimony and child-support payments. Unfortunately, these questions can also serve as a handy battleground for old conflicts. Once again, the target is always the ex-spouse, but the ones who are hurt the most are the children. Once again, both fathers and mothers are equally at fault. And once again, we must ask how parents can have so little compassion for their own children!

For example, a father may refuse, "forget," or simply delay making his agreed-upon support or tuition payments. He may even acknowledge his obligations but claim that his business has suffered a set-back. If his claims are valid, it is possible that he is not expected to provide that which he does not have. But if his claims are distorted, his vindictive stinginess may succeed in causing not only his ex-wife to suffer, but may also cause his children to be denied a new outfit for *Yom Tov*, a trip to summer camp, or even an occasional ice cream cone. The children will certainly survive, but if they were accustomed to a higher standard of living, this unnecessary material deprivation will serve only to heap upon them additional shame and disappointment, on top of that which already exists as a result of the divorce itself.

A mother may also try to "punish" her ex-husband, by repeatedly dragging him into court to renegotiate the alimony and child-support agreement. She might claim that the prior agreement was inadequate for her and the children's needs, or that her husband is now earning considerably more money than he did at the time they signed the agreement. If the claims are valid, she may have every right to renegotiate. But if not, she will hurt her children much more than she will harm her ex-husband.

The children will especially suffer if their mother's vindictive greed results in their loss of contact with their father. When alimony and child support payments become too burdensome or court hearings too frequent (and costly), many fathers decide that in spite of how much they would like to see their children, it is just not worth the hassle. In effect, they trade in regular visitation for relief from financial flagellation, with the children becoming the greatest losers.[3]

When any couple finds their differences so irreconcilable that they must divorce, the tragedy is so profound that the very Altar sheds tears. But *why* must the tragedy of divorce be compounded by the senseless and inhuman traumatization of the children?

We can only assume that the perpetrators of the injustices outlined here were so emotionally imprisoned by passionate resentment for their ex-spouses that they failed to comprehend the full impact of their behavior. Hopefully, this chapter will open their eyes, and the eyes of others — friends, parents and other relatives — who become partisans in the Wars of the Ex's if they recommend such damaging tactics of reprisal.

In short, the feelings of hostility between divorcing and divorced parents may be justified. Using children as a weapon or as a battleground is totally indefensible, however.

Let us try to eliminate the need for any couple to divorce. But as long as there continue to be new "ex's" in our community, let their treatment of their children no longer provoke us to exclaim, "*Why?!*"

---

3. See, "Visitation and the Noncustodial Father," by Mary Ann P. Koch and Carol R. Lowery, in the *Journal of Divorce*, Winter 1984, pp. 47-65.

28

From Step-Families to Blended Families: Parenting Children After Remarriage

No matter how long something exists, we do not really seem to notice it until it gets a name. Take the "wind-chill factor," for example. Ever since Creation wind has made the temperature feel colder. But not until the term "wind-chill factor" was coined did we realize just how cold we feel during the winter.

The same is true for social phenomena. For centuries, families have been broken by the shattering tragedies of death and divorce. In many cases, the surviving or divorced spouses remarried. It was not until recently, however, that these new families have been called "step-families." The emergence of this new term, then, seems to signal either a new awareness of an old phenomenon, or, perhaps, an increase in the number of such families.

What is a "step-family"? Are there really more such families today? What are the unique challenges which step-families must face? Are there any guidelines or practical measures step-parents can take to help them overcome these obstacles to having a harmonious home? What special dilemmas confront step-children? In what ways can both parents in a step-family help their children cope with these stresses? This chapter will attempt to offer answers to these questions.

༄༅࿐

A STEP-FAMILY CONSISTS OF TWO PARENTS AND THEIR CHILDREN, like any other family. What is unique, however, is that the two parents are not the biological parents of all the children in the family. Some of the children may be the product of the wife's first marriage or the husband's first marriage. There may also be children who are the product of the current union. Or, to put it more simply, the children in a step-family may belong to one of the following three categories: *yours, mine* or *ours*.

In some cases, both parents in the step-family were married before. In other cases, only one parent was previously married. But in either case, when there are children, at least one parent becomes a step-parent to at least one of the children; hence, the term step-family.

Although families are not torn apart by the death of one parent any more often today than in previous generations, we are witnessing an increase in the divorce rate. While the divorce rate in the Torah community is nowhere near the rate of the larger society, everyone will agree it is higher than it has ever been. As a result, there are more parents remarrying than ever before.

❧ Challenges Facing Step-Families

Regardless of the goodwill, excellent character and sterling personalities of the parents, there are some challenges that must be faced by all step-families by virtue of their unique family structure. How well the family clears these hurdles will determine the amount or absence of domestic harmony these families will enjoy.

Grieving the loss: When a step-family is formed, many relationships are actually or symbolically permanently lost or altered. A widow, for example, can speak openly about her late husband until she remarries. From then on, she must weigh the impact of her words on her new husband. Before, she could visit her late husband's grave for prayer or comfort whenever she felt the need. Once she remarries, even occasional visits may be considered improper. Although her first husband may have died years before, once she remarries, she suddenly loses connections that may have been quite meaningful for her.

When a mother wins custody of her children following a divorce, the children do not have to share her with anyone. After she remarries, her children will lose the exclusive claim to her attention which they once enjoyed. Depending on their ages and other factors, they may experience their mother's remarriage as a crushing loss of what they saw as a private relationship, one which now must be shared with an interloper, the stepfather.

Children can, at times, become so depressed at the loss of exclusivity in the relationship with their biological parent that adults around them may become alarmed. The reality is, however, that for the child, old emotional wounds — such as the original loss of the noncustodial parent at the time of the divorce, or of the deceased parent at the time of death — often become reopened by the remarriage.

Building trust: All members of a step-family must acknowledge the need to build trust in their relationships with each other. First and foremost, the husband and wife must learn to trust each other that allegiance to children will not threaten the new marriage. Next, the children must learn to trust that their biological parent still loves them just as much as before. They must also learn that their step-parent will not try to sever the close bond they previously enjoyed with their biological parent.

Passing the tests: Because the new family arrangement engenders so much anxiety and insecurity, family members often try to reassure themselves by testing others in the family unit. While this may go on in any family, the sudden changes brought about by a remarriage often heighten the anxiety levels in step-families, and thus often lead to unconscious testing.

For example, the stepfather may feel insecure about his new wife's loyalty to him and may try to test her by being overly strict toward his step-children. (See *Kesubos* 60a for an example of this attitude of a step-father toward his step-children.) He may even try to discipline them too harshly. If she comes running to their defense, he may interpret that as disloyalty on her part. If she supports him, he will feel reassured that his marriage is solid.

This, of course, puts the wife in a dilemma. If she supports her husband, her children may be unfairly punished. In addition, they will likely feel abandoned by her. But if she defends them, she runs the risk of threatening the foundations of her new marriage.

The children, on the other hand, may also engage in testing behaviors. Otherwise well-behaved children may begin to speak disrespectfully or act rebelliously after a parent remarries. This may represent a test of the loyalty of the biological parent, a test of the tolerance of the step-parent, or both.

Heightened sibling rivalry: Whenever there is more than one child in a family, there will be some competition, jealousy and even conflict between siblings.[1] That is normal and expected. But in step-families, the battle-lines can be more sharply drawn between father's biological children, mother's biological children and/or the children of both parents.

---

1. See Chapter 12: "A Parent's Survival Guide to Sibling Rivalry" for practical suggestions on this subject.

This increased tension may surface, for example, during visitation. Suppose that a divorced man marries a divorced woman with children from her first marriage. He establishes a new home with his new wife and stepchildren, but every other week, he is allowed to have the children from his first marriage come to his new home for *Shabbos.*

His biological children may feel they are entitled to special attention, since they have not seen their father for almost two weeks. His stepchildren may feel that they are entitled to special privileges since this is their home. Neither set of step-siblings may be willing to defer to the other, creating a confrontation that would test the mettle of any parent.

Setting limits: Every family must address the issue of where, when and how to establish rules.[2] Some rules apply to everyone, others are meant only for some (i.e. the men, the children, those who attend school, etc.).

Generally, family rules evolve over time. They are imposed as the need arises. And they may be rescinded or ignored when they become obsolete.

In step-families, however, two or more groups come together in a new family, with each group expecting all of their *old* rules to apply. Since that is clearly impossible, a new set of rules is needed *immediately.* Realizing this need is the easy part. The hard part is getting everyone to agree on the new rules and to let go of the old rules. When custody is shared, for example, this can become a veritable negotiating nightmare.

Becoming a family: Most families simply take it for granted that all members share the common identity of belonging to one family. Does a boy ever question, for example, whether or not to call his mother "Mommy"? Of course not. But in step-families, the

---

2. See Part Three: Establishing Structure and Setting Limits for a thorough discussion of this topic.

issue of what to call the step-parent strikes at the core of the challenge of becoming a single family unit.

When nine-year-old Shaindy's eyes well up with tears and she shouts defiantly, "But you are *not* my '*Tatty*'!" she is reminding everyone how far they are from becoming a family. The difficulty in creating this new sense of togetherness may cause the greatest amount of frustration to the new parents. As they juggle the adjustments of living with each other, the new couple must help their biological and step-children work toward becoming "one family."

Once that eagerly sought-after, shared family identity will have been achieved, everyone will feel more secure, less threatened and more comfortable with the new family arrangement. Instead of feeling like they come from a "broken family," they will feel like they belong to a "blended family."

❧ Becoming a Family

How can step-families overcome all the challenges they face? What can they do to make the transition from step-family to blended family easier?

First, there are some things which all step-families need to know.

• Becoming a family takes time. In the example cited above, Shaindy might be willing to call her stepfather "*Tatty*," "Daddy," or "*Abba*," after she has spent a few months living "in the same family as" — and getting to know — him. But if she is forced to use a title that is uncomfortable for her before she is ready, she may never bridge the gap of resentment generated by her parents' impatience.

Part of Shaindy's resistance to calling her step-father "Tatty," may lie in her feeling disloyal to her biological father if she uses the title that she feels "belongs" to him. Calling her step-father "Daddy" or "*Abba*" may be more palatable for Shaindy, at least until she is more comfortable with her mother's new husband.

• *No matter how well everyone got along before the remarriage, stresses and conflicts can and will emerge once the new family has been officially reconstituted.* It doesn't mean you did anything wrong and it doesn't mean you made a mistake by getting remarried. It just means you are a typical step-family going through the pains of adjustment.

• Because of the dramatic and sudden nature of the changes in everyone's lives, *all rules and limits need to be openly and frequently discussed, stated clearly and concretely, and imposed on a trial or temporary basis only.* The rules also need to be reevaluated and closely monitored for how they affect all concerned.

• *When punishment is needed, the one imposing it must be the biological parent, at least initially.* But, you may ask, will this not undermine the authority of the step-parent? Will it not discourage the child from treating the step-parent like a *real* parent? Will this not delay the process of becoming a family? No, no, and NO!

If the punishment comes from the biological parent only, at least in the beginning, it allows the child to develop a positive relationship with the step-parent. It will also acknowledge the reality that the step-parent *does* lack authority by virtue of his or her strangeness.

If you met someone for the first time, and that person was only critical, it is likely that you would want to have nothing to do with that person. You would certainly be reluctant, at best, to change your behavior based on that person's criticism. But if your best friend finds fault with you, you can usually accept it, regardless of how severe the rebuke may be. Why? Because if you have an *established* relationship with someone, you can tolerate criticism from them.

Step-parenting is no different. Step-parents can and should punish their step-children, but *not right away*. They must allow time for a positive relationship to develop before they can risk imposing sanctions. This may take months, not days or weeks.

• *A family is not a democracy.* Yes, every member of a family must get the message that his or her feelings are important and that these sentiments are taken into consideration. But votes cast by parents must always carry more weight than those cast by children, otherwise the parent-child relationship becomes inverted, like a tail wagging the dog.

🦋 What Step-Families Can Do

In addition to what step-families need to *know*, there are some practical things that step-families can *do* which will help them to successfully meet the challenges they face.

• **Consult other step-families.** You simply cannot imagine how normal your difficulties are until you speak with others who are — or have been — in the same situation. This comparing of notes reduces isolation, generates support and provides many practical solutions.

• **Respect all prior relationships.** Everyone has faults. And that includes people who used to be married to each other. But it is not the job of a step-parent or a biological parent to denigrate the other biological parent.[3]

During custody or visitation, the other parent may act in ways you disapprove of, but you will not score points by criticizing your ex-spouse or your spouse's ex-spouse in front of the children. Such conduct on your part will only send a message to your children that parents are not to be respected. Ultimately, you will pay for that mistake with dividends of *chutzpah* aimed at you.

• **If problems arise, don't delay in seeking help. Help is available.** The structure of a step-family is new to all its members. But step-families themselves are not new. Instead of trying to reinvent the wheel, step-families can benefit from resources of accumulated wisdom, based on the experiences of other step-

---

3. See Chapter 27: "Two 'Ex's' and a 'Why?': Parenting Children After Divorce," for an in-depth anaylsis of the destructive consequences of overlooking this fact.

families. Not to reach out for help when it is needed would be not only foolish but cruel.

The word *bayis* means both "house" and "home." As every homeowner knows, it takes time for a house to feel like a home. After much work and some time, however, most houses do feel like home. The same is true for step-families. In time, adjustments can be made which will enable everyone to feel at home in the new family.

The word *shalom* also has two meanings: "peace" and "complete." So when a step-family — or any family — achieves peace and feels complete, then they have achieved real *shalom bayis*.

WHERE TO GET HELP

• Pamphlets, publications and books on step-families and step-parenting can be obtained from The Stepfamily Foundation, Inc., 333 West End Avenue/ New York, NY 10023/ **(212) 877-3244.**

• To find a good family therapist in private practice who is Orthodox and experienced in working with step-families, call the Yitti Leibel HelpLine **(718) HELP-NOW** for a referral. While the HelpLine is located in New York City, referrals are made to therapists in other major Torah centers throughout North America.

• To find a good family service agency with reduced fees or a sliding scale: in New York City, call the Yitty Leibel HelpLine; out-of-town, ask your local rabbi or your family physician.

Glossary

afikomen ...portion of matzah eaten at the end of the *Pesach seder*

ahavas Yisrael....................love of fellow Jews

aidelkeit........................refinement of characted

aleph beis.........................the Hebrew alphabet

Am Segulah ....The Chosen People

aninus...the initial period of mourning, before burial

Aniyei Ircha.............................the poor people of one's own city

Asseres Hadibros......The Ten Commandments

aveil, pl. *aveilim*.................................mourner

aveilus ....the period of mourning

Avinu, pl. *Avos*..........................lit., "our father," esp. the Patriarchs

avodah zarah.................................idol, idolatry

avodas Hashem ....Divine service

eidim...witnesses

baal (fem. *baalas*) *middos* ..one who has good chacter traits

baal teshuvah ....One who "returns" to religous observance

bachur, pl. *bachurim*.......................young man

Bais Hamikdash ....The Holy Temple

Bais Yaakov ......Orthodox Jewish girls' school

Baruch Hashem ....Thank G-d

bashert..........................predestined, esp. one's predestined mate

beis medrash, pl. *batei medrash* ....synagogue; house of study

bayis...*house*

bechor..firstborn

bentch ....bless

ben Torah...............................student of Torah

berachos ....blessings

Bircas Hamazon....................grace after meals

bitachon ....faith and trust in G-d

bubbies..grandmothers

chassan, pl. *chassanim* ....bridegroom

chasunah ....wedding

chas v'shalom ....Heaven forbid

chavrusah, pl. *chavrusos*.............study partner

Chazal..our sages

chazer ....review

chessed..kindness

Chevrah Shas ....Talmud study group

chiddushim ....novellae

chinuch..education

Chol Hamoed ....the intermediate days of Pesach and Succos, when many forms of work are permitted

chulent...........................a hot stew eaten at the Sabbath day meal

Chumash, pl. *chumashim* ....one of the Five Books of the Torah

chupah.....................................wedding canopy

churban..................................destruction, esp. the destruction of the Temple

da'agah ....worry, concern

daf shiur ....daily Talmud class

daf yomi ....daily Talmud study program

dan l'kaf zechus ....to judge favorably

daven ....pray

derech eretz ....proper behavior

devar Torah, pl. *divrei Torah* ....Torah thought

derashah, pl. *derashos*.............exgesis, sermon

Erev Shabbos ....Friday

Erev Yom Tov..............the day before a holiday

es kumt mir........................"It's mine by right"

esrog..................citron, one of the four species taken on Succos

frum..Orthodox

gabbaim ....synagogue functionaries; rabbi's assistants

Gedolei Torah, gedolim ....Torah giants

goy...non-Jew

gragger..................................Purim noisemaker

hachnasas orchim ....welcoming guests

hadrachah..guidance

Hakadosh Baruch Hu ....The Holy One,
Blessed is He

hakafah (pl. *hakafos*) ......festive circuits made
in the synagogue on *Succos*,
Shemini Atzeres, Simchas Torah

hakaras hatov ....gratitude

Hamelech ....the king

hashgachah ....Divine preordination

hashkafah, pl. *hashkafos*................philosophy,
outlook on life

havdalah ....the ceremony which marks
the end of the Sabbath or a festival

hechsher ....rabbinic approval

Hoshana Rabbah .....the seventh day of *Succos*

Imeinu, pl. *Imahos*..........................our mother,
esp. one of the Matriarchs

Kaddish..............one of the responsive prayers,
esp. one recited by mourners

kallah, pl. *kallos* ....bride

kavanah........................concentration, intent

kavod..honor

kevurah ....burial

kibud av v'aim......................honoring parents

Kiddush ....prayer recited over wine
at the start of the Sabbath and festival meals

kiddush Hashem ..sanctifcation of G-d's Name

kinus ....gathering

kiruv........lit., bringing closer, esp. introducing
Jews to Torah and *mitzvah* observance

Klal Yisrael ....the Jewish people

klei kodesh......................religious functionaries

kollel ....advanced study programs
for married men

kriah..................rending garments in mourning

krias Shema ....the daily recital of *Shema,*
accepting G-d's soveriegnty

lashon hara........................evil speech, slander

levayah ....funeral

licht ....candles, esp. Sabbath candles

limud ....study

l'sheim Shamayim ....for the sake of Heaven

lulav, pl. *lulavim* ....palm branch, one of
the four species taken on *Succos*

Ma'ariv ....the evening prayer

machnis orchim ....one who hosts guests

maggid shiur.....one who gives Torah lectures

mashgiach, pl. *mashgichim* ....rabbinic
supervisor; Dean of Men in a yeshivah

Mashgiach Ruchani....................spiritual guide
of a yeshivah

Mashiach ....the Messiah

mechanech, pl. *mechanchim* ....educator

mefarshim....................................commentators

melaveh malkah..........................festive meal to
usher out the Sabbath

menahel, pl. *menahelim* ....principal

mensch ....lit. "person," someone
who is well mannered

mesiras nefesh ....self-sacrifice

mesivta.............................yeshivah high school

mesorah ....tradition

middah, pl. *middos*.................character traits

minhag ....traditional practice

minyan .quorum of men for communal prayer

mishnah, pl. *mishnayos* ....compilation of
teachings that forms the basis for the Talmud

mishpachah..family

mitzvah, pl. *mitzvos* ....a good deed mandated
by the Torah

m'kareiv.....................to bring someone close;
to forge a close friendship

Morah..teacher

mosdos..institutions

motzi shem ra..slander

mussar ....rebuke; teachings regarding
self-improvement

mussar shmuessen ....talks regarding
self-improvement

nachas ...feeling of satisfaction and fulfillment

Navi ....prophet

nechamah..consolation

neder ....promise

negel vasser...........washing of the hands upon
awakening; the water used for this purpose

neshamah, pl. *neshamos*........................soul

nichum aveilim................consoling mourners

niftar, pl. *niftarim* ....a deceased person

nisayon, pl. nisyonos ....tests

Olam Haba ....the World to Come

pachim k'tanim.....................lit., "small jugs";
trivial matters

peckalah ....small package

perakim ....chapters

pesukim ....verses

petirah...passing on

poseik, pl. poskim ....halachic decisors

pushka...charity box

Rav, pl. Rabbanim ....rabbi

rebbe, pl. rebbeim ....chassidic leader

Rebbetzin...rabbi's wife

rechilus ....talemongering

Rosh Hayeshivah.........................yeshivah dean

retzei ....a special paragraph added into
Grace After Meals on the Sabbath;
a portion of prayer in which we ask for our
prayers to be accepted and for the return of
the services to the Temple

ruchnius ....spirtual matters

s'chach ....the material used for the roof
of a succah

schmooze...chat

seder.......the festive meal on the first nights of
Pesach; a study period

sefer, pl. sefarim ....book

seudah...meal

shadchan, pl. shadchanim............matchmaker

shadchanus ....matchmaker's fee

shalom bayis ....domestic harmony

shanah rishonah..................lit. "the first year,"
the first year of marriage

sheloshim ....lit. "thirty," the 30-day period
of mourning

shemiras Shabbos ....Sabbath observance

sheva berachos...the festive meals attended by
the bride and groom following the wedding

shidduch, pl. shidduchim..................proposed
matrimonial match

shiur, pl. shiurim............................Torah class

shivah ....lit. "seven," the seven-day
period of mourning

shmuess, shmuessen ....lecture

shoresh...root

shuk ....marketplace

shul...synagogue

Shulchan Aruch..........the Code of Jewish Law

simchah ....festive occasion

succah.................................hut used on Succos

Succos...................the festival commemorating
the Jews being sheltered in the wilderness

taharas hamishpachah....................the laws of
family purity

talmid chacham ....Torah scholar

talmid, pl. talmidim..............................student

techias hameisim ......resurrection of the dead

tefillah, pl. tefillos ....prayer

tichel...............................woman's headcovering

tikun hanefesh ....correcting one's soul

timtum halev.....lit. "obstruction of the heart,"
something which prevents
spiritual achievement

Torah shebichsav..................the Written Torah

tov, pl. tovos ....good; goodness; favors

tzaddikim...............................righteous people

tzar gidul banim ..the pain of raising children

tzedakah ....charity

tzitzis...the Torah-mandated fringes on a four-
cornered garment

vaad, pl. vaadim...................communal board,
discussion group

Vaad Hakashrus ...kosher-certification agency

vort, pl. vertlach.................pithy statements or
short Torah thoughts

yarmulke...skullcap

yetzer hara ....the evil inclination

yetzer tov ....the good inclination

Yiddishkeit..Judaism

Yom Tov..festival

zaidie..grandfather

zechus ....merit

zemer, pl. zemiros.....................................song

z'man...semester; time

This volume is part of
THE ARTSCROLL SERIES®
an ongoing project of
translations, commentaries and expositions
on Scripture, Mishnah, Talmud, Halachah,
liturgy, history, the classic Rabbinic writings,
biographies and thought.

For a brochure of current publications
visit your local Hebrew bookseller
or contact the publisher:

Mesorah Publications, ltd

4401 Second Avenue
Brooklyn, New York 11232
(718) 921-9000